LAND OF
VISION
AND
MIRAGE

LAND OF VISION AND MIRAGE

WESTERN AUSTRALIA SINCE 1826

GEOFFREY BOLTON

University of Western Australia Press

First published in 2008 by
University of Western Australia Press
Crawley, Western Australia 6009
www.uwapress.uwa.edu.au

Reprinted July 2008

National Library of Australia
Cataloguing-in-Publication entry:

Bolton, G. C. (Geoffrey Curgenven), 1931– .
    Land of vision and mirage: a history of Western Australia since 1826.

    Bibliography.
    Includes index.
    ISBN 978 0 980296 40 2 (pbk.).
    1. Western Australia—History. I. Title.

994.1

Cover image by Anthony Urbini
Consultant editor Amanda Curtin
Designed by Anna Maley-Fadgyas
Typeset in 11 point Jenson Light by Lasertype
Printed by McPherson's Printing Group

Contents

List of illustrations

Abbreviations

ABC	Australian Broadcasting Commission (now Corporation)
AIF	Australian Imperial Force
ALP	Australian Labor Party
BHP	Broken Hill Proprietary
CALM	Department of Conservation and Land Management
CBH	Co-operative Bulk Handling Limited
CML	Colonial Mutual Life
COR	Commonwealth Oil Refineries
CSR	Colonial Sugar Refining Company
CWA	Country Women's Association
DLP	Democratic Labor Party
IWW	Industrial Workers of the World
RSL	Returned & Services League (originally Returned Soldiers, Sailors and Airmen's Imperial League of Australia)
TAB	Totalisator Agency Board
WADC	Western Australian Development Corporation

Conversions

Australian currency changed from pounds, shillings and pence to dollars and cents in 1966. Because of variations in currency values over time, actual conversions are difficult. At the time of the currency changeover, the following conversions applied:

1 penny (1d)	1 cent
1 shilling (1s)	10 cents
1 pound (£1)	2 dollars

Acknowledgments

I should begin by acknowledging Jenny Gregory, who when Director of University of Western Australia Press suggested that I might attempt a short history of Western Australia. She has had to wait a long time for the result, but I hope it meets her expectations. I have enjoyed the challenge. I am also indebted to the present Director of the Press, Terri-Ann White, and to the members of its staff with whom I have worked, notably Kate McLeod, who saw the final draft through production. I also owe much to the admirable editorial skills of Amanda Curtin. I record my warm appreciation to my valued research assistant Andrew Morant and Birgitte Gabriel, who word-processed the final draft.

Friends and colleagues have patiently discussed aspects of this history with me, and several have read the manuscript in draft, in part or wholly. Such support remains the best form of quality control for which historians can hope, and I have been fortunate. Thank you Wendy Birman, David Black, Brian de Garis, Andrea Gaynor, David Hutchison, Lenore Layman, Jenny Mills, Bobbie Oliver, Heather Radi, Bob Reece, Roger Bolton and Tom Stannage. My greatest debt is as always to my wife Carol.

My grateful thanks to Geraldine Byrne whose friendship has survived several collaborations, and to whom I am particularly indebted for work on the endnotes, index and photographs.

For generous permission to reproduce the illustrations in this book I am especially grateful to the State Library of Western Australia, also to the Holmes à Court collection, Jenny Keenan and Geraldine Byrne.

I greatly appreciate Tony Urbini's permission to use the photograph that forms the basis of the book's cover, a souvenir of a fortunate goldfields encounter.

Finally I thank Murdoch University for constant institutional support and encouragement. And, like all Western Australian historical researchers, I give thanks to the staff of the Battye Library.

Geoffrey Bolton

Introduction

Summer holidaymakers on the beach at Rottnest's Thomson Bay sometimes observe on the eastern horizon the shimmering outlines of high-rise buildings above the mainland. As the outlines change shape and dissolve, they are seen to be mirages, reflecting and exaggerating the profile of Perth's central business district.

These mirages illustrate a major theme in Western Australian history. Beginning with the first Governor, Captain James Stirling, bold entrepreneurs have pushed projects for investment and development on the basis of inadequate research and over-hopeful assessment. Caution has been scorned as inexperienced settlers were urged into the role of pioneers. When disappointment and human hardship followed, the leaders would proclaim undaunted faith in the validity of the enterprise, blaming setbacks on hostile critics, unforeseen bad luck, and insufficient effort on the part of the workers. The myth of dynamic entrepreneurship, both state and private, has survived nevertheless. Doubters are seldom encouraged to question the capacity of an underpopulated Western Australia to sustain the infrastructure or to provide the specialised human talent required for well-planned developmental programs.

The great visions never resulted in total failures but left a residue of modest growth. Perhaps that growth would not have occurred without the first prodigal input of capital and labour summoned up by the leaders, but it was more often the result of canny improvisation and unspectacular hard work by their followers. Western Australia was, after all, one of the many frontiers of Western capitalism during the nineteenth and twentieth centuries, vying with a host of competitors for investment and migrants. Geographically isolated, its economic development could not await the calculations of rational planners. Instead stimulus came from the visionary with limitless faith in the West's resources and too little appreciation for the need for assessment and conservation of those resources.

Isolation has fed a number of Western Australian attitudes and stereotypes. With a coastline too long for realistic defence and a small and unevenly distributed population, Western Australians understandably fear invaders who might move in on them as they moved in on their Aboriginal predecessors. The Americans, Irish Fenians, rabbits, Germans, Japanese, bikie gangs, unauthorised 'boat people', cane toads—how could they be resisted if they came with sufficient force of numbers? More than most Australians, the inhabitants of the West rely on the protection of great and powerful allies, but such dependence breeds its own ambivalence. Nineteenth-century Western Australians valued membership of the British Empire but resented the heavy hand of the British Government. Western Australians voted to join the federated Commonwealth in 1901 but spent the next century girding at the encroachments of federal authority. Sometimes, as with the secession referendum of 1933 or during the perceived threat of Japanese invasion at the height of World War II, they voiced an active mistrust of the Eastern States.

The political and cultural dominance of the Sydney–Canberra–Melbourne axis—the 'Hume Highway hegemony' of Geoffrey Blainey's phrase—has often been tempered in Western Australia by a notable capacity for innovation fostered rather than discouraged by the state's remoteness. Where Brisbane and Adelaide have frequently been drawn into the commercial and cultural orbit of the Hume Highway hegemony, Western Australians, challenged by greater distance from the dominant south-east, have found scope for independent initiative. Sometimes this spirit of initiative has led to commercial excesses, sometimes to a naive provincial boastfulness in matters of culture, but in a society of limited resources, the tally of achievement since colonisation has often been creditable.

Sporadic debate arises, as similar debates arise in Queensland and Tasmania, as to whether Western Australians are developing a provincial character and ethos distinct from that of other Australians. Most measures of such distinctions are superficial, but as Terry Eagleton has observed: 'It would be surprising if people who have shared roughly the same culture and material circumstances over long periods of time did not manifest some psychological traits in common'.[1] Linguists have detected a glossary of 750 distinctively Western Australian words, some borrowed from Aboriginal sources, others English. Words that 'arrived' in Western Australia with early settlement found the jump across the Nullarbor too exhausting to undertake. Examples include the use of 'brook' for a small stream, and the identification of fertile land as being 'in good heart'.[2]

Factors such as class, ethnicity, gender and religion possess the same potential for divisiveness in Western Australia as in any other regions of Western civilisation, but at least until the second half of the twentieth century there persisted among many Western Australians a belief that in their isolated community, disagreements should never be pushed too far, but all should stick together. No doubt this belief was convenient to those who wielded political and economic power in Western Australia, and no doubt troublemakers and dissenters often found it hard to gain a serious hearing, but this clannish sense of fundamentally shared identity of interest seems to have formed an effective social cement. From the 1960s, as the economy grew and diversified and the effects of postwar migration began to make their mark, Western Australian society became more complex and in some respects more adversarial. New strains emerged in the federal compact as Western Australia, like Queensland, took a greater share in earning Australia's export income and in competing for trade and investment in East and South Asia. If there was no longer a unifying consensus about what it meant to be Western Australian, there was still an inherited sense of local identity that strongly influenced responses to social and economic change, and even to the challenge of globalisation.

Once in every generation a single author has attempted to summarise and interpret the history of Western Australia since British occupation and settlement in 1829. In 1897 a visiting American, Warren Bert Kimberly, an early example of the freelance professional in search of a commission, produced an account of nineteenth-century Western Australia that, despite his comparatively short sojourn in the colony, contained many acute insights on which later historians have built.[3] One who built on Kimberly was Dr James Sykes Battye, who published a carefully uncontroversial account in 1924, which also stopped short at the end of the nineteenth century.[4] Strongest on the history of exploration and constitutional change, Battye's history was the standard reference until the arrival of the energising influence of the young Frank Crowley at The University of Western Australia during the 1950s. Crowley summed up the results of a decade's archival research and graduate supervision in *Australia's Western Third*, published in 1960.[5] Believing that the 'prize of history is the understanding of modern times', Crowley devoted more than half his book to the twentieth century, with a much greater emphasis on social and economic history than his predecessors. To this day his comprehensive account retains its value.

Since its publication, however, Western Australian historical writing has advanced enormously. Vigorous research at the state's five universities has been buttressed by the increasing professionalisation of freelance historians and bodies such as the Royal Western Australian Historical Society. All this activity has been unable to do justice to the wealth of archives and primary sources preserved and classified at the J. S. Battye Library of West Australian History and the State Records Office of Western Australia. In 1981 Tom Stannage edited a multi-author anthology that incorporated many of the findings of recent research, but much more has been produced since then.[6] It would be vainglorious for any individual historian to think that he or she could produce a short history that adequately summarised all the new approaches and insights that have been bubbled up among lively-minded historians of Western Australia during the last twenty-five years. All the same, it is time that a short history was produced for the convenience of non-historians and historians alike. This book will have served its purpose if it does no more than stimulate the appearance of other and better short histories.

I

A shabby-genteel society, 1826–1850

On Christmas Day in the morning in 1826, the brig *Amity* anchored in the magnificent harbour of King George Sound on the south coast of Western Australia. Four weeks later a party of soldiers and convicts under Major Edmund Lockyer hoisted the Union Jack at what would become the town of Albany.[1] Thus British sovereignty was claimed over the one-third of Australia that had been known to Europeans longer than any other part of the continent, and was least wanted. Western Australia's coast was probably sighted by the Portuguese in the 1520s and accurately charted by the Dutch between 1616 and 1697. They reported the coast as dangerous, the landscape as barren and the Aborigines as uninterested in trade. Later in the seventeenth century the English traveller William Dampier confirmed these impressions. Consequently, Australia's western third was undisturbed during the eighteenth century, except probably for a few European castaways and the seasonal visits of fishers from Macassar in the Sulawesi region of Indonesia, who came to the north coast in search of bêche-de-mer. In the late eighteenth century, as European interest intensified in the Indian and Pacific oceans, St Allouarn left a claim of French sovereignty at Dirk Hartog Island in 1772 and George Vancouver raised the Union Jack at King George Sound in 1791, but their home governments showed no interest in taking possession.

Nobody sensed Western Australia's potential economic strengths. These included a south-western enclave stretching about 800 kilometres east and north of Cape Leeuwin, with an assured winter rainfall of the Mediterranean pattern; a northern region of almost equally regular summer rainfall, which a later generation would name the Kimberley district; and, concealed within the arid interior, an unimaginable store of minerals. Even after Britain sent Governor Arthur Phillip and the convict fleet to New South Wales in 1788, the 2.5 million square kilometres of Australia west of the meridian 129° east remained in the keeping of the Aboriginal hunter-gatherers who had peopled the continent for at least 40,000 years.

As elsewhere in Australia, Aboriginal occupation was unconsciously preparing the ground for European settlement. The yam patches and clumps of edible plants gathered by Aboriginal women often fore-shadowed the sites of homestead blocks for farms and grazing properties. In the Yamatji country north of modern Geraldton, it seems that native plants were systematically cropped. The carefully fostered skills and techniques accumulated over a thousand generations of hunting would make Aboriginal guides and stockmen a valuable resource for European pastoralists. The tracks they travelled would lead surveyors along the easiest lines of cross-country access. Thus a major highway leading east from Perth across the Darling Scarp was originally known as 'King Dick's road' after the 'whitefeller' name of the Nyungar guide Beban who pointed it out. In late spring and summer, when Aboriginal people burnt off the season's grass and undergrowth in order to aid their hunting, they were promoting the growth of fresh grass and giving the country that open park-like appearance that appealed to newcomers from Britain in search of good pasture. As Sylvia Hallam writes, it was the *work* of generations of Aboriginal people that created an environment that European settlers found attractive.[2]

British interest in Western Australia stirred only in the 1820s, more than thirty years after the occupation of New South Wales. Ex-convict sealers and American whalers working their way west from the established harpooning grounds in Bass Strait and the Southern Ocean sailed the waters near the present sites of Esperance and Albany by the mid-1820s. Some who came ashore behaved brutally towards the Nyungar. Of greater concern to the authorities in Sydney were reports of French maritime activity in the area. At war for more than twenty years until the final defeat of Napoleon in 1815, Britain and France were still on uneasy terms a decade later. Despite its unpromising reputation, Australia's empty western sector could seem, perhaps groundlessly, a temptation for France's colonial ambitions.[3] In October 1826 the French naval officer Dumont d'Urville landed at King George Sound to examine its botany. But the West was not to become Australia's Quebec. Having discarded the idea of stationing a garrison at Shark Bay on the western extremity of the continent, Governor Ralph Darling of New South Wales decided to assert British sovereignty by staking out a claim on the south coast, where an eye might be kept on the sealers and whalers. Lockyer's garrison set the British imprint on Western Australia.

Fear of the French was not the only spur to official action in those last months of 1826. The New South Wales authorities were lobbied by Captain James Stirling, a mixture of energetic servant of Empire and Scotsman on the make, with relatives in the powerful British East India Company, which still claimed commercial pre-eminence in the Indian Ocean region. Stirling envisaged a new colony in Western Australia with potential for Indian Ocean trade. He would name it 'Hesperia', the land looking west, with overtones of classical myths suggesting fruitfulness. Governor Darling authorised him to explore Western Australia's largest river south of the tropics, the Swan. Accompanied by the botanist Charles Frazer, Stirling visited the Swan for twelve days in early March 1827. At that time of the year, they can hardly have realised the unique character of the flora of Western Australia's South West. At least two-thirds and possibly more than 80 per cent of the species are not known elsewhere. Misled by the tallness of the jarrah forest and by an exceptionally mild summer, they formed very exaggerated ideas of the fertility of the coastal plain without exploring the inferior sandy country on either side of the river. Stirling was no judge of soil quality. It was therefore misleading when he returned to New South Wales and then to Britain with joyful reports of an environment like the most fertile parts of Italy. He was on sounder ground when he suggested that British officers in India and their families might holiday in Western Australia to recuperate their health, but nothing came of the idea.[4]

His propaganda fell on ready ears. Since the end of the Napoleonic wars in 1815, many army and navy officers had retired on half-pay without career prospects. Farm prices were low, and many small landowners faced an uncertain future. Reports from New South Wales suggested that even ex-convicts were succeeding as farmers and graziers. To members of the more respectable classes, the possibilities were tempting. As James Henty of Sussex told his brothers:

> What can we do in England with £10,000 amongst all of us unless indeed we chose to descend many steps in the scale of Society, and which our feelings would ill stand, having at the same time the opportunity of doing as well and perhaps considerably better…under British Dominion and a fine climate.
>
> For the first year or two we shall have to endure privations and hardships which we have not been accustomed to in England. What of that?[5]

Even the Hentys' farm labourers shared their optimism. One of them, Charles Gee, voiced their hopes in rough-hewn verse:

> Now when we come to New Holland I hope that soon will be
> All will send home to England, and happy there wee be
> With plenty of provishons, boys, and plenty for to do,
> So hear is health to Henty and all his joyful crew.
> So hear is off to New Holland if God will spare our lives,
> All with little children, hower sweethearts and hower wives.[6]

Unlike the colonies of eastern Australia, the Swan River would be free of the convict taint. Investors and settlers responded eagerly to the news that 40 acres (16.2 hectares) would be granted for every £3 invested in cash or goods. Although the British Government was unwilling to spend money on the new colony, it made no objections to attempts by private enterprise, and its publicity further exaggerated Stirling's already over-optimistic propaganda. Many scrambled for early access to the Swan River Colony. One ambitious syndicate was promoted by a cousin of the British Home Secretary, Sir Robert Peel. Thomas Peel sought support from a group of investors already speculating in New South Wales, and when they reneged he found generous but unpublicised backing from an ex-convict merchant, Solomon Levey.[7] At the end of 1828 Stirling was appointed Lieutenant-Governor of Western Australia, and the first settlers left England in February 1829. Western Australia was the first agricultural colony attempted in the British Empire for nearly a century, and the first in Australia to be envisaged from the outset as a society of families. As one of the colony's first medical men put it:

> *If we can imagine the population of one of the parishes of England mixed with a sprinkling of half-pay officers and some gentlemen from the East and West Indies, and a few cockneys, put down on the shores of a wilderness, we shall have some idea of the Founders of this interesting society.*

He compared Western Australia's First Fleet to Noah's Ark.[8]

Few of the settlers can have guessed how great a gamble they were taking. They arrived in June 1829 to the dismal onset of a rainy winter. No advance party had been sent to make essential preparations. No land had been allocated nor buildings erected, nor had any steps been taken to come to terms with the Nyungar. The settlers were dumped with their possessions on Garden Island and later on the beaches north of the Swan. Stirling's energetic Surveyor-General, John Septimus Roe, at once went to work laying out the town sites of Fremantle, Perth and Guildford, and marking out land along the Swan. He and his staff worked under constant pressure from impatient settlers. Roe's straight lines drawn across the lands of the Mooro and the Beeloo survive today in some of the longer streets of Perth's eastern suburbs. Most blocks combined a small stretch of river frontage and a long tract of the less fertile hinterland. To the lifelong resentment of some settlers, the best land on the upper Swan was allocated to Stirling, Roe and a few favoured friends and officials.[9] The location of their holdings may have helped to determine the site of the colony's capital, Perth, but so did access to fresh water and river transport, fine views of the Darling Scarp and—comfort for an isolated people—the shelter offered by Mount Eliza from hostile naval bombardment. Perth was founded on the north shore of the Swan on 12 August 1829 with the apt symbolism of the felling of a tree. The biggest investor, Thomas Peel, arrived too late to claim his original grant, and had to accept a large estate south of Fremantle. It was poor land and Peel was a useless manager. His settlers suffered severe privations; some died. Peel lingered for more than thirty years, a model of broken-down gentility.[10] Destitution and misery were common. 'That man who declared this country good deserves hanging nine times over', declared Eliza Shaw, though her husband was one of that class of whom Henry Trigg wrote in February 1830:

> *We have a great number of half-pay officers and their familys. They are but ill suited to rough it, and when they arrive expect to have eggs, ham, mutton chops and rump steaks in every corner.*[11]

Instead, for the first year of settlement they lived mainly on the salt pork, ship's biscuits and other hard fare brought out from England. Some contracted scurvy. Most of the first comers camped under canvas for months, disturbed by rats, fleas, flies and mosquitoes.

Many of the early investors brought with them servants indentured for a contract of either five or seven years. Within two years most of those indentures were broken or annulled by the Governor. Cash was in short supply in the colony, and so many landowners could not afford to pay their labour force. 'Masters here are only in name', exclaimed George Fletcher Moore, 'they are the slaves of their indentured servants'. As one employer put it, 'Almost every settler is obliged to dismiss his indentured servants for idleness, disobedience to orders, or drunkenness, and so soon as they obtain their liberty they embark for either Hobart or Sydney'.[12] Master and servant legislation enabled magistrates to punish defaulting workers with fines or imprisonment, and these laws remained in force until 1892, but they did little to improve the productivity of the work force, or their living standards. Incompetent workers were hardly worth keeping, and skilled workers (there were only ninety-two out of a total work force of 788 as late as 1837) found they could do better for themselves on the open market. Some of the unskilled were reduced to petty crime. In a generally law-abiding community, it was notable that the majority of crimes were larcenies of food or items of clothing committed by members of the labouring class.[13]

Those settlers who fared best tended to be practical yeoman farmers who had given their enterprise forethought. The Hardey and Clarkson families, Yorkshire Methodists who arrived in February 1830 in their own ship, the *Tranby*, brought with them a prefabricated house that they could erect in Fremantle before taking up their land grants. Establishing himself at a peninsula on the Swan River about four kilometres east of the township of Perth, Joseph Hardey at once busied himself with growing produce for the local market, built the colony's second windmill, invested his profits in property, and was soon a respected confidant of Governor Stirling.[14] Other families, such as the Hentys, soon despaired of success and went off to Van Diemen's Land, whence they would find a fresh opportunity as pioneers of what is now Victoria. Departures from the colony offset natural increase. Between 1830 and 1833 the non-Aboriginal population stagnated at around 1,800, and although a small intake of migrants in 1834 pushed the number up over 2,000, it stayed close to that figure for the rest of the decade.

The first hope of improvement came in the spring of 1830 when Ensign Robert Dale crossed the Darling Scarp and found better country along the Avon River (the upper part of the Swan). In January 1831 Captain Thomas Bannister blazed an overland route between the Swan River and Albany. But in 1831 the Colonial Office imposed a minimum price of five shillings an acre (0.4 hectare) on land sales in all colonies. Investors lost interest in Western Australia. Whereas half a million hectares was alienated between 1829 and 1831, barely 100,000 was sold between 1832 and 1837. Inexcusably, after forty years of contact between Aboriginal people and settlers in eastern Australia, Stirling made no recognition of Indigenous land rights.

The garrison at King George Sound, who encroached comparatively little on the land, lived amicably with the Nyungar, who continued to exercise authority in the region at least until 1842. At the Swan River a cycle of killings and reprisals began within two years, largely because of Aboriginal attacks on introduced livestock grazing on their traditional lands. The Advocate-General, George Fletcher Moore, admitted wryly that 'perhaps these uninformed creatures think they have as good a right to our swine as we have to their kangaroos', but this did not stop him and his fellow colonists from taking strong measures in defence of their property.[15] During Stirling's absence from the colony between 1832 and 1834, relations deteriorated. The killing of unoffending Aborigines provoked the killing of unoffending settlers. In 1833 a senior Nyungar, Midgegooroo, was executed by firing squad before an approving crowd. Two teenage brothers hoping for a reward treacherously killed his son

Yagan later in 1833. If Stirling had fallen into Nyungar hands, he would probably not have fared as badly. As the novelist Anthony Trollope reflected forty years later: 'These black savages were savage warriors and not murderers; and we too, after a fashion, were warriors, very high-handed and with great odds in our favour, and not calm administrators of impartial laws'.[16]

The Binjarup Nyungar of the Murray River district, about 80 kilometres south of Perth, continued to offer defiance. Early in 1834 they raided Perth's first flourmill on the south side of the river, their leader Calyute threatening to kill the caretaker, George Shenton. Soldiers trapped Calyute and his companions. He was given sixty lashes with a knotted cord, with lesser punishments for several of his companions. On his release from gaol, Calyute took the lead in hostilities against Thomas Peel, who was encroaching on his people's lands. Two of the soldiers guarding Peel's property were ambushed and one was killed. This episode of frontier warfare ended in October 1834 with the battle of Pinjarra, when Stirling led a military detachment in a dawn raid that resulted in the deaths of more than twenty Nyungar. Calyute and the remainder of his people offered no further resistance, but Lieutenant Bunbury, visiting the region in 1836, wrote: 'The young men, who are very friendly themselves, tell us that we shall never be quite safe or on good terms with their tribe while the old people are still alive'.[17]

Sporadic episodes of violence were balanced by long periods of coexistence and even cooperation. If one settler at a Guildford meeting in 1837 could propose a war of extermination against the Aboriginal people, his views were not shared by the responsible authorities. Stirling was unhappy about the continued use of the military as a peacekeeping force and wanted to establish a civilian constabulary, but his executive council baulked at the expense. He used the colony's first Foundation Day ceremony, on 1 June 1835, as an occasion for reconciliation, with a Nyungar corroboree as its centrepiece. The government promised 'to visit every act of injustice or violence on the Natives with utmost severity'. The Perth Gazette lamented, 'Too much blood has already been spilt in the warfare between the whites and the blacks, and we are afraid the destruction of the Aborigines has been in the ratio of 10 to 1'. By 1840 the Swan Valley was 'pacified', and Aboriginal people were employed in jobs such as shepherding. Until the convict period, some regularly served as mailmen. Aboriginal leaders accepted designation as 'constables', and a Wesleyan mission school was endeavouring to give the children a Christian education. The frontier of violence had shifted to the Avon Valley. Not without opposition, Stirling's successor, Governor John Hutt, extended to Aboriginal people the right of testifying in civil and criminal courts, but their protection under British law was still uncertain.[18]

Mistrust remained under the surface. For hundreds of years Europeans had thrilled to legends of children spirited away by alien forces, but they seemed a little nearer reality in this raw and ambiguous environment. In the first summer of European settlement, it was widely believed that a small child who was lost in the bush, John 'Bonny' Dutton, must have been stolen away by Aborigines. The government had to issue a notice cautioning settlers against vigilante action, and before long a party of Nyungar restored the boy unharmed to his parents. They had merely wished to show their bush colleagues what a white child looked like. For several decades afterwards, in contrast to modern usage, the term 'stolen children' reflected a fear among settler mothers that the 'black men' would take away their little ones. Eliza Shaw and George Fletcher Moore both wrote of it as a matter of course. Ted Lewington, who lived well into the twentieth century, believed that around 1850 an Aborigine had snatched a baby from his mother's arms and run away, only to drop the child when shots were fired after him. Two decades or so later, the girls of the prosperous Shenton family of Crawley House (now the site of The University of Western Australia) still listened to stories of white children abducted by the 'dark people'.[19]

Conflict with Aboriginal people justified the presence in the colony of a detachment of British troops, supplied by a commissariat whose demands for accommodation, transport and food provided a vital stimulus to the local economy. As Pamela Statham-Drew has pointed out, expenditure on the military guard far exceeded actual export earnings for most of the colony's first twenty-one years.[20] Despite its early reluctance, the British Government was after all funding Stirling's dream. Other sources of capital were few. A handful of Fremantle merchants such as Lionel Samson and George Leake, as agents for local landowners and shopkeepers, advanced them credit. Outside investors were not tempted while the thriving whaling and wool industries of eastern Australia offered strong competition.

James Cameron has argued that despite their inexperience of conditions elsewhere in Australia, the first generation of settlers showed good judgment in selecting country, and adapted well to their new environment.

> *Western Australia was so remote in fact that little information on viable forms of production or suitable methods of land management filtered in from other colonies and...such information as did come was of little relevance or use.*[21]

Although John Septimus Roe led exploring parties to the south in the spring of 1835 and eastward a year later, they found no reliable pastoral country. In 1839 George Grey and his companions, having survived shipwreck near the present site of Kalbarri, walked 600 kilometres to Perth. In the early stages of their journey, they noted Yamatji wells, tracks and grounds showing evidence of systematic yam cultivation. Grey thought this country gave high promise for future European settlement. Further south the party suffered privations in poorly watered coastal country, and this discouraged northward expansion for several years.[22]

Within the settled districts, landowners and their shepherds learned their husbandry through trial and error. Western Australia's first substantial pressure group was its Agricultural Society, founded in 1831 as a medium for exchanging information about the new environment. By the end of 1833 a bountiful harvest from 240 hectares under crop put an end to food rationing, and the following year the first agricultural show was held at Guildford. Enough grain was grown for self-sufficiency by 1835, but sluggish local demand discouraged expansion. Shortages continued. In June 1837 Moore wrote: 'We are most anxiously looking for a vessel from England. There is neither salt, nor foreign flour, nor candles nor soap in the colony'—though he added that there was enough local produce to avert any sense of crisis. In the same year, the Government Resident at Albany reported, 'there is not a pound of meat as well as flour to be purchased in the settlement'.[23]

Wool-growing progressed more slowly. Although 8,000 sheep were introduced in 1829–30, losses through toxic native plants meant that there was only the same number in 1836. Flocks built up to nearly 45,000 in 1841, when wool exports were valued at £3,000. But such progress was puny when it was estimated that in one year American whalers netted £30,000 from their catch in Western Australian waters. Local entrepreneurs began shore-based whaling at Albany in 1836 and Fremantle in 1837, but failed to match their competitors. However, until the 1860s the American whalers proved welcome trading partners for the South West settlers, whose foodstuffs they purchased in return for commodities such as clothes, tools and books.[24] The most encouraging sign of economic progress was the establishment of the Bank of Western Australia in 1837, largely backed by Fremantle merchants. When this was taken over by the Bank of Australasia in 1841, local investors drove it out of business by forming the Western Australian Bank, which was to survive until 1926. This spirit of self-confidence was fed by a modest growth in commerce. In 1840, for the first time, a ship sailed for London with a cargo made up entirely of colonial produce.

Stirling left the colony in January 1839, never to return. In the experienced eyes of a Colonial Office under-secretary, 'Sir James administered the Government of Western Australia with very remarkable ability and temper and with more success than the inherent improvidence of that scheme of Colonisation would have justified any one in expecting'.[25] In the struggle for survival, Stirling's original vision of a gentry colony stood no chance. Some aspiring families followed the Hentys to the fairer prospects of eastern Australia; others drifted into alcoholic obscurity. More worked their land with family labour and held on for better times, but their children were already being shaped by the environment into something tougher and, in many cases, more barbarised. The five Bussell brothers, pioneers of the Vasse district, personified the variety of responses with which the would-be gentry of the first generation met the pressures of the environment. The oldest brother, John, always retained the humane and scholarly values of his background in an English vicarage, even when in later life financial reverses compelled him to turn schoolmaster. The youngest, Alfred, only 13 years old when he arrived in Western Australia, adapted resourcefully to the bush, married a robust young woman without social pretensions, and survived as a thoroughly acclimatised pioneer grazier in the Margaret River district. But some of the intermediate brothers went badly to pieces in the alien environment. Charles Bussell fathered a child on a servant girl and treated her shabbily. The pervading fear of Aboriginal hostility pushed Lenox Bussell into shooting dead an 8-year-old Nyungar girl who had been taken under the family roof. He went unpunished, but when he died at the age of 30 he was deemed of unsound mind.[26] By contrast, the Bussells' neighbour, Georgiana Molloy, attuned quickly to the bush of the South West. A pious young wife of a retired military officer, busy with motherhood (she eventually died in childbirth), she found time to study and classify the botany of a region offering more new and unknown species than any comparable quarter of the globe, and to communicate those findings to appreciative scholars in Britain. She was exceptional.[27]

English traditions of deference wilted in the colonial environment. A newly arrived clergyman might assert that 'Society will never work unless there is a situation for each class according to God's ordinance', but within a few years he was compelled to recognise that the son of two of his servants, well dressed and with a horse of his own, looked 'more a gentleman than many who are truly such'.[28] In Western Australia the clergy were not numerous enough to dominate colonial society, nor were they supported by the infrastructure of tradition and property built up over centuries by the Church of England in the Mother Country. The first Anglican colonial chaplain, John Burdett Wittenoom, was more effective as schoolmaster than as spiritual leader. The second Anglican priest, the Italian-born Dr Giustiniani, left after antagonising the colonists by upholding Aboriginal rights too strongly. Two more Anglican clergy arrived in 1841, and the original Perth church, a modest building walled with mud-brick and rushes that doubled as the courtroom, was replaced by a more substantial edifice in 1845. At Picton the most effective of the early clergy, John Ramsden Wollaston, had to build his own church assisted by his sons. Anglicans had the advantage of their status as the official church, but other branches of Christianity also found a place in Western Australia. The Wesleyans had a church in Perth by 1842; the Congregationalists in 1846. A Catholic bishop, John Brady, arrived in December 1843, followed by several parties of religious.[29]

The transmission of metropolitan culture to the colony largely rested with this handful of clergy and a few educated officials such as George

Fletcher Moore. Somewhat desperately the colonists tried to preserve the decorums and the social rituals of English provincial society. On the monarch's birthday, Government House dispensed modest hospitality and the soldiers paraded. There were dances such as the one when Moore lifted the spirits of his hearers with a song, 'Western Australia for Me', set to the tune of an Irish ballad. By July 1839 a group of citizens put on the colony's first theatrical performance, a musical farce, Love à la Militaire, before an appreciative audience. Wittenoom, a keen amateur cellist, arranged musical evenings.[30] Despite these displays of harmony and consensus, the tensions of a pioneer community kept breaking through. Although only one fatal duel is recorded from the first decade of settlement, there were endless quarrels and lawsuits: over trespass by a neighbour's pig, over a boat borrowed and not returned, over angry words exchanged late at night in taverns. It was all petty, but such incidents enlivened the monotony and provided matter for two Perth newspapers by 1840.

If Perth seemed a remote outpost of European civilisation, the country districts endured a more than Siberian isolation. A member of the Logue family, taken in 1837 as a boy of 11 from Perth to the Avon Valley, never saw the ocean for the next thirteen years. Then on an overlanding trip he climbed a high hill in order to catch a distant glimpse. Eliza Brown, wife of one of the most considerable landowners in the York district, lived in a thatched shed warmed in winter by a pan of coals. The hundred kilometres separating her from Perth seemed limitless to a woman nursing a small child. She was, she wrote to her relatives in England, 'without the common necessities of life'.[31] The isolation of the whole colony was underlined in 1841 when Edward John Eyre, with another Englishman and three Aborigines, set out to overland from South Australia to Albany. His arrival after gruelling adventures, worn out and emaciated, was the result of great good luck and the bush skills of his one surviving companion, the Aborigine Wylie. Eyre became a hero, but his fate confirmed Western Australia's reputation as the most isolated settlement in the world's most isolated continent.[32]

Nevertheless, by the time of Eyre's expedition Western Australia seemed modestly on the move. The colonists were taking the first steps towards understanding their environment. After many sheep were lost through an unidentified poison plant, the experienced botanist-farmer James Drummond identified the culprit as the York pea, a gastrolobium. The Perth Agricultural Society was joined in 1840 by the York Agricultural Society and in 1842 by a Vineyard Society, each trying to promote good practice among the colony's farmers.[33] The pastoral frontier in the South West was gradually expanding, despite the unease of Governor John Hutt (1839–46), who believed that his instructions required him to check the spread of squatting because of the potential cost to the government of providing infrastructure. Although over-shadowed by American competitors, offshore whalers operated from Fremantle and from several bases on the south coast. Open-boat whaling lasted at Cheyne Beach, east of Albany, until 1879, providing employment for Nyungar men as well as Europeans.[34]

Western Australia's modest improvements were overshadowed in the eyes of British investors by the new colonies at Port Phillip, South Australia and New Zealand. Those enterprises reflected the influence of Edward Gibbon Wakefield, whose theories were as yet untainted by practical experience. He inspired the investors who in 1839 planned the formation of the Western Australian Company to develop the land around Leschenault Inlet, 150 kilometres south of Fremantle. Plans were devised for a settlement called Australind, its name reflecting the persisting hope of trade with India and Southeast Asia. Then the promoters lost confidence and dithered over alternative sites before deciding on Australind after all. Investors withdrew their capital, and, although nearly 450 migrants arrived under its auspices in 1841–43, the venture came to be regarded as another Western Australian failure. However, Australind's impact on the colony's human capital was momentous. The Australind colonists included its leader, Marshall Waller Clifton, ancestor of a notable line of public servants, politicians, architects and artists; John Ramsden Wollaston, the first Anglican archdeacon and author of journals throwing a valuable light on colonial conditions; Dr John Ferguson, colonial surgeon for many years, who built the colony's first substantial hospital and founded a Swan Valley winery that has lasted to this day; and the forebears of three notable Premiers, Forrest, Newton Moore and Mitchell.[35]

Four hundred more migrants came during the early 1840s, either independently or under the auspices of the Perth Agricultural Society.

Others were sent out under official assisted immigration schemes, including the first harbingers of convictism. Several parties of juvenile offenders from the Parkhurst penitentiary were despatched by the British Government between 1842 and 1851. One 15-year-old, John Gavan, became the first non-Aboriginal resident to be hanged for murder. He was taken in a cart for execution at the Round House at Fremantle, and many years later his victim's brother remembered the finale:

> He wanted to know if it was going to hurt to be hanged and they told him it wouldn't hurt. It wouldn't take long. Then he started to take off the new pair of boots with which he had been fitted out for his trial. When told he need not do that he said 'I don't want my nice boots to be spoiled'. They were probably the first boots he ever had. And the last.[36]

The official responsible for the Parkhurst boys, John Scholes, probably owed his lapse into alcoholism to the trauma of this case. Most of the Parkhurst boys seem to have given little trouble, but imperceptibly the Swan River Colony was edging into the culture of convictism.

The influx of immigrants stimulated economic activity and property values, but when it ceased in 1843 a slump followed. Business confidence faltered; Charles Bussell and his brother Alfred held 'Much conversation about future prospects and lamentations at the dark and cheerless void that lay before us'.[37] Others responded with a number of new initiatives, modest of necessity but enough to diversify the economy. The Legislative Council in 1844 mounted what would be the first of many campaigns exhorting Western Australians to buy locally. Others looked to East and South Asia for export markets. In 1844 horses were exported for the first time to India, thus beginning a trade in cavalry remounts in which some settler families such as the Brockmans specialised for many years. Next year a small experimental cargo of sandalwood was despatched to India, stimulating landowners and merchants to develop a direct trade with China. Communications were uncertain. When the Hong Kong merchants Jardine, Matheson & Co. wrote to W. E. Stockley in Perth, it took nine months for the letter to reach him and ten months for his reply to return via Bombay, but the Western Australian Bank in 1846 appointed Jardine, Matheson to act as its agents in Hong Kong and China.

Wool remained the leading export commodity, though squeezed by dull markets. Most of the accessible country in the South West and the Avon Valley was now under occupation. Some of it was already showing signs of soil exhaustion, and introduced exotics such as double-gees and capeweed were beginning to infest the local pastures. The quest for 'better country further out' stimulated several expeditions to the eastward, the last by Roe in 1848 extending east of Esperance, but little was found to attract settlement. Permanent water was scarce. There was little good grass in the forest land, and a good deal of country was infested with poisonous plants.[38] By this time Roe was over 50. His best work was done as mentor to younger men, notably the Gregory brothers who, arriving in the colony as children in 1829, grew up as proficient colonial bushmen able to adapt English technology and saddlery to the demands of the Australian environment. In the spring of 1846 Augustus, Francis and Charles Gregory followed Grey's reports and spent seven weeks examining Yamatji country 500 kilometres north of Perth. They returned with reports of good grazing land and a seam of coal on the Irwin River. This news prompted some Avon Valley landowners to back Augustus Gregory in leading a second expedition in 1848.[39] This party mapped the lower course of the Murchison River and reported traces of lead in the Chapman Valley. The country was thrown open for settlement and its port at Geraldton was named for Governor Charles Fitzgerald, who attended its foundation. During this visit he was lucky to escape with his life when a Yamatji warrior put a spear through the fleshy part of his leg; like Governor Phillip in the first years of settlement in New South Wales, Fitzgerald may have been enduring payback for the offences of another European. Undiscouraged, several Avon Valley graziers such as the Burges and Brown families took up properties in the region.

The occupation of new country was not in itself enough to ensure growth. Pastoralists complained of the scarcity and cost of labour, perhaps unjustifiably, but shepherding was a hard, monotonous life, and more could be made by sandalwood-cutting. Shepherds were often either alcoholic deadbeats who could get nothing better, or poor youngsters such as Walter Padbury, orphaned at 10 years old and keen to accumulate experience and modest capital. Padbury soon progressed out of shepherding into butchering, and thence to the career as businessman and investor that would bring him in time to the status of Perth's first local philanthropist.[40] From the 1840s, some properties employed Aboriginal shepherds. Conflicting stories survive about their treatment. In the hinterland of Albany, two shepherds were accused of flogging the back and testicles of an Aboriginal fellow worker suspected of theft. The *Perth Gazette* thought it 'one of the most horrible and brutal cases brought before a court of justice'. The accused were sentenced to three years' hard labour. Immediately below this report is the case of three Aborigines found guilty of stealing a sheep. They were each given seven years' transportation to Rottnest.[41] Against this can be told the story of Mary Elizabeth Garratt in the same district, who found herself about to give birth at a time when everyone was away from the homestead except for one Nyungar woman, herself heavily pregnant. Mrs Garratt had her baby with the help of her companion, and then acted as the other woman's midwife. 'Within three days both women were in the saddle assisting with the mustering.'[42]

It was taken for granted that marriage and childbearing were the natural destiny of colonial women. Married in their late teens, many were still having children when the first grandchild arrived. If widowed, a woman with children lost no time in securing another husband for the sake of economic security. Ann Farmer was by no means exceptional. In February 1832, at 25 years of age, she was left a widow with four young sons when her husband, a private in the 63rd Regiment, drowned in the Swan River. By the end of June she was married again to William Watson, the innkeeper at Redcliffe, by whom she had five more children. Six months after his death in May 1843, she took a third husband.[43] Some families tried to manage their fecundity. The nine sons of William and Margaret Forrest were born at regular intervals of between twenty-one and thirty months, suggesting a regime where the conception of one child occurred only after the previous one was weaned at around the age of twelve months. Western Australia was usually considered a healthy environment for raising children, although accidents were frequent. Georgiana Molloy and Eliza Shaw were among the better-known women to lose little boys through drowning while temporarily unsupervised.[44] A census of Western Australia's 4,622 non-Aboriginal inhabitants in 1848 showed that 2,487, or more than half, were under 14. Margaret Anderson has calculated that in the late 1840s, 64 per cent of Western Australian families included seven or more children, reflecting and enhancing the youthfulness of the settler population. And the population was healthy; in 1842 a medical officer reported:

> *Measles, small pox, typhoid, or puerperal fevers, or any of those dire diseases to which the Mother country is subject, are here unknown. Among the diseases most prevalent, I may mention ophthalmia, and a mild form of dysentery, both of which prove but trifling, if common care be taken, and proper remedies applied...*[45]

The pastoralists still complained of labour shortages, real or imagined. Led by the Fremantle merchants, financiers of much colonial enterprise, and abetted by the York Agricultural Society (itself losing momentum, though including some influential colonists among its number), the pastoral lobby sought a bold remedy for its labour problems: the admission of convicts. The timing was fortunate. Australia's eastern colonies, having outgrown their need for convict labour, had repudiated transportation, and in 1848–49 were vigorously resisting British Government moves to renew the practice. Within Western Australia the desperation felt by many veteran settlers was voiced by George Fletcher Moore:

> *The whole aspect of the colony seems to be unhinged...the gentry are going down the hill most fearfully, their own servants, the working men and butchers, public house-keepers and retail dealers, are rising on the ruin of others.*[46]

With minimal public consultation, the Legislative Council endorsed the pastoralists' plea for convict labour, and the Colonial Office soon responded, as it suited its plans. So it was that on 1 June 1850, precisely twenty-one years after Stirling founded the Swan River Colony as a society of free citizens, the first chain-gangs disembarked from the *Scindian* to provide Western Australia with a labour force of unwilling immigrants. The pastoralist Gerald de Courcy Lefroy, who happened to be in Fremantle, thought them a fine set of men much superior to their guards, and would have engaged some on the spot if regulations had permitted it.[47]

Convictism was to transform Western Australia. Until 1850 the history of the colony was the history of the south-western corner. The inhabitants of the large remainder of Western Australia continued to lead a traditional life that left no written records, though they must have known something of the disruption and dispossession of the Nyungar and Yamatji communities. Often short of resources, neglected by private investors and the British authorities, the shabby, genteel Swan River Colony could grow only slowly until the convict system brought increased manpower and capital. Just because Western Australia was now a penal colony, imperial authority would increase its reach and range of activities. In the three decades after 1850, the process of land taking would accelerate. Although Western Australia would continue to lag behind the other Australasian colonies, the settler imprint would deepen, the conquest of Aboriginal communities would spread across the colony, and the pioneers would consolidate their grip on the land—and in the process the land would consolidate its grip on the settlers.

2

Convictism and its legacy, 1850–1879

Between 1850 and 1868, 9,668 male convicts arrived in Western Australia at a cost to the British Government of more than £2 million. This investment of capital and labour was the economic salvation of Western Australia in two decades when the counter-attraction of gold in Victoria and New South Wales was at its most powerful. (As it was, despite official discouragement, probably as many as one-third of the convicts who served their sentences, as well as many free settlers, slipped off to the eastern colonies. A few ex-convicts found their way to destinations as exotic as Callao and Mauritius.) The convicts provided a home market for Western Australian produce, but they contributed even more as labour and as a substitute for advanced technology. Some have argued that the arrival of the convicts undercut the conditions of free labourers by reducing their bargaining power, and Lefroy of Walebing recorded that wages dropped by half after the arrival of ticket-of-leave men in the district. Quarrels soon flared in pubs between bond and free. Many free labourers left the Toodyay district, but the quality of the newcomers was often unsatisfactory. One farmer complained of his ticket-of-leave employee: 'he did not understand throwing dung from a cart'. The animosity was slow to die down. Well into the 1860s, other workers despised the convicts as a form of 'scab' labour. In the event, a significant number of the pre-1850 working class were among the employers of ticket-of-leave men.[1]

Even the convicts retained memories of English traditions of working-class protest. In 1859 a steamship company agent at Albany antagonised the coal lumpers, mostly ticket-of-leave men, by threatening to replace them with Victorian labour. They sent him an anonymous letter threatening to destroy him and the coal heap if he did not leave Albany, but gave him three months' grace 'rather than have the blood of such a low despicable fellow on our hands'. The distinction between 'bond' and 'free' overtook class for a while as a marker in society. As Sir Paul Hasluck put it, 'In the very early years there had been distinctions between gentry and working classes, but with the transportation of convicts…the circle gathered in all those who were truly among the early settlers'.[2]

While serving the first part of their sentences, convicts were employed on public works, although it was almost always necessary to supplement them with skilled workmen from the free labour market. The system resulted in several prized historic buildings, among them Fremantle Gaol, the Perth Town Hall, Government House, the Governor's summer residence on Rottnest (now a hotel popularly known as 'The Quokka Arms'), the Colonial Hospital (now part of the Royal Perth Hospital complex) and, finest of all, the first part of the Fremantle Asylum, now a museum and art gallery. The two last buildings marked a welcome advance in social services. At the Colonial Hospital Dr John Ferguson was a pioneer in the use of chloroform as an anaesthetic. The Asylum was a boon for the psychiatrically disturbed, who previously could only be accommodated in prison cells. An afflicted patient whose family could not afford to pay for care might be sent home, as Cecilia Hardy was returned to her husband in the Murray district; in 1869 she wandered away into the bush and died of thirst. For those living outside the towns, accident or illness remained hazardous. In 1861, when a young Pinjarra landowner accidentally shot himself in the neck, he had to mount his horse and gallop 80 kilometres to Perth for medical attention. Less mobile patients endured a slow and jolting journey by cart, during which their condition often deteriorated. Gradually, as funds became available, the infirmaries attached to rural convict depots were upgraded to government hospitals.[3]

Isolation was not yet conquered, but improvement came with convict labour. The colony's communications system was upgraded. Crowley has estimated that 239 bridges were built or repaired and 920 kilometres of road constructed by 1863, but travel was still slow. In 1852 the arrival of the P & O steamer *Australian* at Albany began nearly half a century when that port would serve as Western Australia's gateway to the rest of the world, but the last stages of the journey to Perth remained tedious. In the same year, the Perth–Albany road was improved to provide an alternative to the hazardous sea lanes around Cape Leeuwin, but it remained a rough bush track. The fastest mail coach achieved only 6 kilometres an hour and took at least four days, heralding its arrival in Perth with the flourish of a post-horn. For most travellers, the journey meant a week of bumpy travel in a three-horse cart, camping out at night, with an awning provided for female passengers.[4]

After a period of good conduct, convicts on ticket-of-leave could be hired as wage labourers in the private work force. Although colonial employers seldom admitted it, this did much to relieve the labour shortages of former years. Even the smaller farmers and tradespeople benefited from hiring a few ex-convicts. Bigger pastoralists kept up a steady demand for shepherds, though not on the scale of the magnates of New South Wales. One of Western Australia's greatest entrepreneurs, the York pastoralist and merchant John Henry Monger, employed sixty-three ticket-of-leave men between 1852 and 1871. Monger was the leading dealer in the sandalwood trade, which provided a living for many ex-convicts and which, after a revival in 1857, steadily contributed to the colony's export income, peaking at between £63,000 and £70,000 annually in 1873–76. Ex-convicts also worked in the timber industry, although the hardwood forests of the South West were at first found difficult of access. Progress quickened in the 1860s after Henry Yelverton erected the colony's first steam sawmill at Quindalup near Busselton.[5]

Few ex-convicts won through to riches. One was Daniel Connor, who was transported from Ireland for sheep stealing. Beginning after his release as a pedlar with a pack on his back, Connor scraped together enough capital to set up as the miller at Toodyay. He lent money to local landowners and claimed his due in hard seasons, investing the surplus in real estate in Perth. He educated his family well. Two sons studied medicine at Trinity College, Dublin, and returned to Perth. One, under the name O'Connor, became the hero of the 1893 smallpox epidemic, and went into politics. A son-in-law, the publican Timothy Quinlan, became Member for Toodyay and Speaker. The old man died in 1898, a benefactor to the Catholic Church. To this day the family owns valuable real estate in Perth's central business district, and his descendants include respected lawyers and physicians. But Connor remained an exception to his class and era.[6]

During the 1850s and early 1860s, it sometimes seemed that convict transportation brought fewer social problems to Western Australia than anticipated. In the country districts a Resident Magistrate, a factotum who, like the prefect in a French provincial town, took responsibility for almost every form of government activity, represented authority. He was supported by a handful of police, members of a force established in 1851 and in its early years recruited to a large extent from sons of the pre-1850 labouring class, such as the Gee family.[7] They encountered a good deal of petty theft and drunkenness, but no organised resistance. Officials commented bemusedly on the good behaviour of road gangs at such depots as Freshwater Bay (now Claremont). 'The settlers sleep with their doors unlocked', commented a visiting Melbourne journalist, 'and they may safely do so'. In 1863 the *Perth Gazette* could editorialise, 'This country may be traversed from end to end without fear of the bushranger, as in New South Wales or Victoria, and it is but rarely we have to record any outrage upon human life'. Violence was yet lurking in such a society. The same newspaper carried the story of two assigned convicts, John Johnstone and Thomas Just, working in a surveyor's camp in the York district. They fell to boasting which of them could eat and drink the most, and quarrelled. Johnstone shot Just through the heart, then went to his tent and cut his own throat from ear to ear.[8]

Conditions apparently deteriorated after the arrival of Dr John Stephen Hampton, Governor from 1862 to 1868. Hampton, a veteran of the Van Diemen's Land penal settlement, was harsher and more interventionist than his predecessors, perhaps because the convicts sent from Britain at that time were thought to contain a higher proportion of hardened offenders. During his regime, ninety-six convicts were sentenced to a total of 6,599 lashes.[9] More ticket-of-leave men lapsed into delinquency than in earlier years. Social problems seemed to multiply in the later 1860s. Alcoholism, already a prominent feature of colonial life among all classes, increased further. An unbalanced gender ratio led to sexual crime, including a good deal of child molestation; three child rapists were hanged during the 1860s. Some escapees turned bushranger, though none achieved the notoriety of Starlight or Mad Dog Morgan in New South Wales. The best remembered, Joseph Bolitho Johns ('Moondyne Joe'), owed his fame to his skill in escaping several times from close confinement. In March 1867 the young woman who would later become Lady Forrest wrote to a friend, 'All about this part of the world people are in a great state of excitement for Moondine Joe is out again, the policemen out in every direction, but everyone else takes his part, especially all the ladies'. (He was recaptured in the cellars on the Houghton vineyard in the act of applying the tap to a cask.) During his lifetime, some thought him 'an overrated celebrity', but one of Western Australia's few authentic popular ballads remembered him at the expense of the nepotist Governor Hampton:

The Governor's son has got the pip
The Governor's got the measles
For Moondyne Joe has give 'em the slip
Pop goes the weasel![10]

Western Australians would have liked to imagine that their convicts were harmless scallywags like Moondyne Joe, but such squibs concealed fear that if the convicts combined to defy authority they might overwhelm the respectable citizens. In old age, Ted Lewington asserted that around 1860 the prisoners in Fremantle Gaol planned a mass breakout, and were restrained only by a line of pensioner guards with fixed bayonets. The story may not have been true, but it reflected a powerful anxiety persisting among the settler community. At the end of the transportation period in 1867–68, the arrival of Irish Fenian political prisoners generated panic lest they break out with the help of American privateers and seize control of Fremantle.[11] One Fenian, John Boyle O'Reilly, who got away with the help of an American whaler, took a subtler revenge by publishing a novel, *Moondyne*, portraying Western Australia as a realm of surrealistically Gothic horror.[12]

Authority was buttressed by the forces of religion and education. The Sisters of Mercy, who arrived in 1846, founded a convent that set cultural standards for Catholic and Protestant young women alike. A party of French missionaries in the Albany hinterland failed to adapt to their new environment, but in 1846 the Spanish Benedictines led by Dom José Serra and Dom Rosendo Salvado established missions at Subiaco, near Perth, and at New Norcia, 150 kilometres northward. They were to leave an important stamp on the colony. Events soon thrust them into leadership of the Catholic community. Bishop Brady had proved a muddled and quarrelsome administrator, and was removed in 1852. His successors were first Serra, then the ascetic Martin Griver, both Spaniards. Consequently, while sectarianism was never absent from nineteenth-century Western Australia, Catholicism was not as inflamed by Ireland's grievances as in many parts of eastern Australia. It proved easier to encourage the practical tolerance desirable among the small population of a remote colony.

Salvado at New Norcia, particularly, built up widespread respect among the non-Catholic community. Modern critics have sometimes found him authoritarian and paternalistic, and he certainly inherited the European tradition that abbots should be great landowners, but many of his attitudes were enlightened.[13] For more than fifty years, until his death in 1900, he upheld the Spanish missionary tradition that all races had the capacity for Christian education. Young Indigenous males might be trained for the priesthood; unhappily, the first Aboriginal acolytes sent to Rome could not survive European winters, and the experiment was not repeated. Young women might be taught the same range of skills as their settler counterparts, and even more. When the telegraph came to Western Australia, the first female operator and postmistress at New Norcia was an Aboriginal woman, Mary Ellen Cupar, and when she succumbed to tuberculosis in 1875 she was replaced by another, Sarah Ninak.[14] The New Norcia mission did not stand aloof from English culture. With the coaching of the young English-educated Protestant landowner Henry Bruce Lefroy, the New Norcia Aborigines put together Western Australia's most formidable cricket team during the 1870s. New Norcia in its early decades offered an important contradiction to the myth of Aboriginal backwardness.

The Church of England remained the main faith of the official and propertied classes. The first generation of Anglican clergy were troubled at the colonial tendency to skip churchgoing, although it is arguable that the lives of 'a large number of colonists centred around a domestic setting where prayer, Scripture and even hymn-singing could occur in a comfortable environment without the need for clergy'.[15] Archdeacon Wollaston was also concerned for the souls and welfare of Aboriginal Western Australians, though his remedy took the form of removing children from their parents to a mission at Albany, Annesfield.[16] This venture survived until 1871, and like New Norcia produced some impressive examples of Aboriginal capability, including women. Both Wollaston and Wittenoom were dead by 1857 when leadership passed to the first Anglican bishop, Matthew Hale. He established a high school that from 1858 to 1872 offered a sound education to the generation of colonial-born youths who would provide leadership to Western Australia at the end of the nineteenth century.[17] Though most of these pupils came from well-off families, there was also room for able lads of modest background, among them three of the sons of the Bunbury miller William Forrest. Western Australia early established a myth of opportunity open to talent, at least male talent, but it was also tacitly expected that those who succeeded in climbing the ladder of opportunity would merge imperceptibly into the established ruling circles. If 'you might never take William Forrest for a toff', John, Alexander and David Forrest would fit in easily as powerful and respected figures in their society.[18]

Gradually the number of respectable artisans, clerks and tradespeople was growing, some recruited from the pensioner guards, some from the second generation of colonial-born, others from the minority of ex-convicts who managed to marry respectably (some to young Irishwomen imported to redress the colony's gender imbalance). Their habits of thrift were encouraged by the founding of the Perth Building Society in 1862 and a post office savings bank in 1863. The stock of currency improved, but in country districts barter survived for many years among those who found an order on Monger's more negotiable than a golden sovereign. From 1866 the monopoly of the Western Australian Bank was challenged by the branch offices of competitors from Melbourne and Sydney, first the National Bank, then the Bank of New South Wales.[19] This growing demand for credit reflected the improving prosperity of merchants and farmers, themselves benefiting from the sustained improvement in local demand that came from the convicts.

Between 1850 and 1865 the value of wool exports rose from £15,000 to £102,000, before receding slightly for the next five years. This growth must be kept in perspective. Even in 1870 Western Australia produced only 1 per cent of Australia's wool exports, most of it inferior to fleeces from the eastern colonies.[20] Between 1850 and 1870 the area under crop went from 3,200 to 20,000 hectares, and livestock numbers grew nearly as fast. Over 400 kilometres north of Perth, the Greenough and Geraldton districts opened up with hopes that a grain-growing yeomanry would be partnered by the development of the colony's first mineral fields, the lead and copper of the Northampton district. During the 1860s, base metals contributed an average of £14,000 annually to Western Australia's export income, but transport cost inhibited growth. In an imaginative application of new technology, the proprietors of the Geraldine mine imported one of the first traction engines to carry ore from the mine to Port Gregory, but it broke down irreparably on the primitive tracks over the sandplain.[21]

This was not the only sign that isolation might spur Western Australians to technological innovation. An 1829 settler, Alfred Carson, and an American immigrant, Solomon Cook, were both notable for their work with steam engines. In 1852 Cook's steam mill at York was reported as grinding enough flour to supply most of the district's needs. Shortly afterwards, he installed engines in several passenger and cargo boats plying on the Swan River, and in 1862 produced a threshing machine adapting Ridley's South Australian prototype for local conditions.[22] His namesake George Cook, a free emigrant who arrived in 1854 and was appointed government coachmaker, was also noted for his steam engines and working models. His inventions included an alarm clock that activated a tea-making device, but there was no scope for its commercial development. James Coates Fleming, a young merchant transported for forgery in 1864, possessed the skills essential for creating Western Australia's first telegraph line in 1869. In the undercapitalised and underpopulated colony of the 1860s, none reaped an adequate reward for his ingenuity.[23]

For the present, sheep and cattle remained the mainstay of Western Australia, and climate and geography determined the spread of the pastoralists. An almost total lack of summer rainfall constrained expansion east of the Avon Valley. What later became the Wheatbelt was held in large grazing licences by entrepreneurs such as Monger of York, whose shepherds followed the sandalwood tracks to garner a few months' winter feed before lack of water forced them back to the settled districts. From the 1850s some small graziers established themselves in the southern country between Kojonup and Albany, but the cost of overland freight ate into their scanty profits. Hence settlement tended to spread close to the coast. When the Dempster and Moir families became the first settlers of the Esperance district in the late 1860s, they relied mainly on communication by sea.[24]

The main thrust of colonisation went north, encouraged by an Australia-wide surge towards the tropics following the establishment of an autonomous Queensland in 1859. Frank Gregory made a reconnoitre of the Gascoyne district in 1858 and conducted a major expedition in the Pilbara region in 1861, returning with favourable reports of its pastures. A number of second-generation Western Australian pastoralists took up land in the Pilbara between 1863 and 1866. They were joined by several parties of Victorian investors whose plans for settling what is now the Kimberley district were made remotely, based on the illusions of map grazing. Only one group, the Camden Harbour Association, attempted for a few months in 1864–65 to found a settlement, but soon succumbed to the harsh environment. The survivors retired to the Pilbara district, where they managed to establish themselves with several more parties from Victoria and South Australia and to spread into the Ashburton district.[25]

This occupation of the North West brought the settlers into a new phase of conflict with the Aboriginal inhabitants. In the settled South West, the fabric of Nyungar society was shattered by the measles epidemic of 1860, which swept ferociously through a population whose earlier isolation had left them vulnerable to exotic diseases. Many years later, Ralph Ashworth remembered how as a boy coming into York he saw 'fifteen or sixteen blacks lying dead and their mates too weak to bury them...There were hundreds of blacks before then, but that was the end of them'.[26] This may have fostered the tendency to think conveniently of the Aboriginal people as 'a dying race', but there was nothing moribund about the Indigenous response to the occupation of the North West. Their readiness to fight back was probably sharpened by previous encounters with Indonesian seafarers. The Worora claimed the ousting of the Camden Harbour settlement as a victory, and their hostility certainly contributed to the sense of pessimism that led the settlers to quit. Further south at Roebuck Bay (later the site of Broome), Sub-Inspector Frederick Panter and two companions were speared in the night in Yawuru country. A reprisal party led by the young colonial Maitland Brown killed eighteen Aboriginal people. Brown's monument still stands in a Fremantle park as a memorial to the episode, though with a second inscription added in 1989 putting the Aboriginal perspective. Further conflicts included the *Flying Foam* confrontation in 1868, when dramatic reprisals avenged the spearing of another policeman, as well as several less publicised affrays.[27]

Despite E. T. Hooley's feat in overlanding sheep from the settled districts to the Pilbara in 1866, only a handful of South West stockmen imitated him. The sea continued to be the main line of communication between the Swan River and the North West, bringing good profits to Fremantle shipowners. Meanwhile, from 1868 the North West pastoral industry was buttressed by offshore pearling, an activity that provided an outlet for the energies of the wilder younger sons of Western Australian landed families. Several squatters such as the Sholl brothers profited by exploiting the forced labour of Aboriginal divers, many of them women. Even after legislation was passed in 1871 to regulate these practices, Aborigines for several hundred kilometres around were recruited into the pastoral and pearling industries by methods that the authorities in Perth were powerless to regulate effectively. Greater professionalism was attempted by one of the arrivals from Victoria, Charles Broadhurst, who recruited several hundred Malayan divers under contract in 1874–75, but most of them soon went home. Most pearlers considered that Aboriginals 'were less expensive, while at the same time they are said to be more expert in procuring shells than the Malays'. By 1876 exports from pearling were valued at £75,000 annually, second only to wool. It was not surprising that, despite exposures in the press, little was done to curb the exploitation of Aboriginal people by pastoralists and pearlers.[28]

By using Aboriginal labour as shepherds, the expanding pastoral industry had less need of a convict work force. Despite its role in improving Western Australia's very modest export performance, convict transportation lost favour during the 1860s. The British Government baulked at indefinitely subsidising the unpromising colony, while even the

Western Australian elite grew perturbed at the social problems arising from the convict presence. Besides, the rest of Australia, now a potential source of migration and investment, looked unkindly on a colony still wallowing in the convictism that the east had outgrown. In 1863 the British garrison was withdrawn. For the rest of the century the colony's main defence force consisted of amateur companies of volunteer riflemen who served with varying degrees of efficiency and enthusiasm.[29] Two years later the decision was taken to cease transportation from the beginning of 1868. This did not mean an end to the British Government's financial responsibilities: not until 1886 was the number of convicts serving out their sentences small enough for the local authorities to agree to shoulder the cost of their upkeep. But it was a sign that, economically and politically, Western Australians were edging towards greater self-reliance.

This sense of self-reliance was encouraged by the reform of the Legislative Council. Previously this body consisted of a majority of officials to whom the Governor might add a few prominent citizens, but in 1867 the council was enlarged to comprise six officials and six nominees. With unexpected enlightenment, Governor Hampton agreed that the six nominees should be elected by property-owners. The success of this experiment was followed in 1870 with the council's enlargement to twelve elected members and six nominees, as well as such officials as the Colonial Secretary and the Surveyor-General. As in the past, these officials constituted the Executive Council from which a Governor was expected to take advice, though as in the past it was the Governor who had the last word. Membership of the Legislative Council was confined to adult males with a substantial property qualification, so that throughout the 1870s and most of the 1880s Legislative Councillors were almost all influential landowners and merchants. In the 1870s they reflected the growing dominance of the pastoral interest, as well as the shift in the colony's financial centre of gravity from Fremantle to Perth. Many of them were members of the Weld Club, founded by a group of officials in 1871 as a meeting place for the colony's elite. In its early years it was a necessarily more modest counterpart to the Melbourne Club and the Australian Club in Sydney, for until improved transport made Perth easier of access some pastoralists chose not to join. These men and their wives could expect to be invited to the new convict-built Government

House, for Western Australia's hierarchy was defining itself along lines similar to those of many nineteenth-century British colonies.[30] Governor Frederick Weld, for whom the club was named, brought to his post between 1869 and 1875 not only practical experience as a New Zealand grazier and politician but also a background from among England's oldest Catholic gentry—a change from the middle-class Hampton.

In its first session the reformed Legislative Council showed commendable activity, so that Governor Weld could exclaim of the colony, 'At last she moves'. Local government was established with the setting up of municipalities and road boards throughout the settled areas. Financed by grudging ratepayers, these bodies could seldom afford to provide even the most basic amenities. Initiative nevertheless showed itself even in those unpromising circumstances. When encroaching sand drift threatened to overwhelm Geraldton, the Resident Magistrate, Maitland Brown, mobilised local farmers and convict labour in an enterprising landcare project. The dunes were covered with cut brush and planted with acacia and melaleuca. The government gave approval and provided funds in 1870. Visiting Geraldton in 1875, Governor Weld was impressed with the success of this early essay in environmental management.[31]

Perth itself was prettily situated, and the Cape lilac trees along St Georges Terrace presented a fine sight in springtime; but its street lighting came only in the 1870s, and even then consisted of lamp-posts at the main intersections smokily fuelled by whale oil. Only the central streets of Perth were macadamised, pedestrians elsewhere plodding through black sand. Winter flooding, especially in June 1872, damaged property and scattered rubbish indiscriminately, and so high priority was given to the filling in of swamps and the provision of efficient drains. As for sanitation, many households lacked cesspits of any sort, and even the new Town Hall's water-closets were a source of filth and stench.[32] In the smaller country towns, conditions were, if anything, more primitive.

The worthy citizens who served on the municipal councils also provided membership of the boards of education created to oversee the colony's school system. The *Education Act* of 1871, with a practical prudence encouraged by the Catholic Governor Weld, provided that private (mainly Catholic) schools as well as government schools would be funded from the public purse. Thus the colony avoided a cause of sectarian strife that troubled much of eastern Australia at that time. Parties or factions of the kind developing in eastern Australian parliaments were as yet unknown in Western Australia. Governors might still overrule the Legislative Council or defer its legislation for the Colonial Office's consideration. In 1875 there was a short-lived agitation for complete self-government, but Western Australia's population and resources were as yet too small for London to take the demand seriously. Western Australia in the 1870s, with 18,000 settler inhabitants and probably at least as many Aborigines, was one of the most insignificant and remote corners of the British Empire—so insignificant that when Queen Victoria's son, Alfred, Duke of Edinburgh, visited the Australian colonies in the *Galatea* in 1867–68, his party forgot to call at Western Australia and had to make a perfunctory visit a year later. In the hierarchy of governorships appointed by the Colonial Office, Western Australia sat somewhere between the Falkland Islands and Trinidad.

One or two members of the gentry class whom Stirling had hoped to attract settled in the colony in those years. James Lee Steere, a merchant navy captain of ancient lineage, met and married Catherine Leake, the belle of Perth, took up an estate in the South West and entered politics in much the spirit of a squire serving on the parish vestry. Sir Alexander Cockburn-Campbell, a needy Scottish baronet, accepted the commissionership of police and later the resident magistracy of Albany, and his son Sir Thomas, after turning newspaper proprietor and editor, entered politics.[33] Families of less aristocratic origins tried to keep up the gentry style, but there were not enough of them and they were not rich enough to leave a lasting imprint on their community. The British-born older generation deplored the coarsening effect of the colonial environment. Charlotte Bussell complained that colonial ladies could talk of nothing except 'Bulls, Horses, Pigs, Sheep, and Sheep ointment, Branding etc'. This made them 'the most uninteresting companions possible...and therefore the gentlemen are advised to marry true Britishers—that they may have something superior'.[34] When widowed, she went to live in Paris.

Besides, the miasma of its recent convict past lingered over Western Australian society. For many years after 1868, men out late at night in Perth could expect the challenge of 'Bond or free?' Visiting the colony in 1872, Anthony Trollope saw many who struck him as looking like 'old lags', but added that although they were much given to drink, there were remarkably few crimes of violence. However, 'the convict flavour was over everything…Men who never were convicts come under suspicion of having been so, and men who were convicts are striving to escape from it'. Around the same time, the wife of the Anglican clergyman at York, Janet Millett, forecast that because many ex-convicts were unmarried, the felonry would 'not make so large a mark upon the future population as might naturally be expected'. In the bush some ended their days in solitude. The police occurrence books for York and Beverley in the late 1870s record the stories of a number of ex-convicts found wandering in the bush alone, destitute and starving. Some were accommodated in an institution at the foot of Mount Eliza, a sufficient distance from the pubs of central Perth for an old man on foot to work up a good thirst.[35] Many ex-convicts, however, became family men, including a significant number with children by Aboriginal partners. Prejudice died hard. As late as 1879, Governor Sir Harry Ord commented on 'the line drawn by the free population towards even the most worthy of the convict class', although in his view 'amongst the convicts many excellent colonists have been brought to these shores'. But a senior police officer spoke of

> upwards of 1,400 expirees…who are simply a burden to the colony—idle loafers, and apparently busy rogues, who owing to their drunken and thieving propensities, require constant police supervision from years end to years end.[36]

While agreeing that 'the presence of expirees led to a distinction between the bond and free', Paul Hasluck argued that this ceased when 'The gold rush of the eighteen-nineties made the distinction between true Sandgropers and "tothersiders"'. A readiness to blot out the penal legacy could be seen in a court case of July 1898, when a retired York farmer who had been transported to the colony in 1856 sued a hotelkeeper for calling him a convict and a horse-thief. Chief Justice Onslow awarded damages of £250 to the plaintiff since he had never been convicted of stealing horses and should not have been upbraided for his past after forty years of good conduct.[37] It was many years before old settlers in country towns such as York and Pingelly ceased to say of other old families, 'You know, their grandfather didn't pay his own fare', but in Perth and the larger centres such distinctions could be forgotten well before the last convict died in 1938. In Tasmania, Peter Bolger has written, old emancipists and their families tried to purge the stigma of convictism by being more 'normal', more patriotic and more conservative than free settlers. It may well have been the same in Western Australia.[38]

At the height of convictism in the 1860s, law and order remained a major preoccupation. At the pinnacle of the law stood the first Chief Justice, appointed in 1861, Archibald Burt. Conservative and conscientious, he brought from a youth in the slave societies of the West Indies a keen awareness of the importance of maintaining order and deference in a society with many second-class citizens of uncertain loyalty to the forces of authority.[39] Perth's two long-established newspapers, the *Perth Gazette*, with a somewhat critical attitude towards Government House, and the more conservative *Inquirer*, were joined by a Fremantle competitor in 1867, the *Herald*. Operated by two ex-clergymen transported for the educated man's crime of forgery, the *Herald* spoke for the emancipists, striking an irreverent note with its columnist 'An Old Sandalwood Cutter', a pen-name concealing the disgraced aristocrat William Beresford.[40] When Burt moved to discipline the press in 1870, it was, however, the *Inquirer* and the *Perth Gazette* that suffered. A rising young lawyer, Stephen Henry Parker, perhaps the brightest of all Bishop Hale's graduates and a bold rider at race meetings, got into trouble with the bench for criticising proceedings taken against one of his ex-convict clients. Stung by Burt's reproach, he vented his anger in the press, with the result that both editor-proprietors were charged with contempt of court, one fined and the other imprisoned. Parker himself escaped with a £50 fine. The vulnerable management of the *Herald* contented itself with the dumb insolence of a blank column.[41]

This case showed that the government and the courts would brook no serious challenge to their authority. Burt showed his independence in a number of cases during the 1870s. In 1872, with Weld's support, he sentenced a young pastoralist from a prominent family to five years' imprisonment for killing an Aborigine. After energetic lobbying by spokesmen for the pastoral interests, the Colonial Office reduced the sentence to one year. Burt was consoled with a knighthood. A few years later he was implacable in passing sentence of death on a pastoralist convicted of shooting his wife. It was a harrowing case over which two juries disagreed and a third, empanelled from passers-by brought in from the street, could be brought to a decision only by the judge's warning that there were perhaps not enough respectable citizens in Perth to panel a fourth jury. Appeals for clemency on the grounds of diminished responsibility were dismissed, although many believed that the accused was not executed but smuggled overseas.[42]

Burt's verdicts may be seen as reflecting the need for legal control of the use of violence on the pastoral frontier, an issue on which modern historians sharply disagree. Frank Wittenoom, who as a young man during the 1870s helped to establish a number of sheep stations on the upper Murchison, wrote in old age some fairly candid reminiscences in language more acceptable in his day than ours. He told of a lonely life on a monotonous diet of mutton and damper, and took it for granted that the local Aboriginal people were inferior, but not contemptible. He saw himself as firm but just, and would not allow his shepherds to bully or thrash Aborigines or to impose themselves on unwilling women.

> Of course one always wore a revolver, it was part of one's dress, not that it was often necessary to use it, but I am convinced that the fact of it hanging on one's belt saved a lot of argument and trouble with the niggers.

Several times when confronted with Aboriginal men whom he regarded as troublemakers, he took some pains to deliver them to the police, knowing that they would be sentenced to a gaol term at Rottnest, and after serving their sentences perhaps be retained as trackers or police aides far away from their own country. But in time his patience wore thin, and by 1882 he was advising a visiting magistrate that all police should be withdrawn from the district. This would leave settlers 'to deal with the matter in their own way' and 'if half-a-dozen of the worst ringleaders were shot it would soon "put an end to the whole affair"'. The pressures of an outback environment warped the moral codes of many settlers in ways not easily intelligible to an urban reader in the twenty-first century.[43]

Western Australia was not destined to remain merely a pastoral frontier. A tiny trickle of investment was appearing from Victoria. One or two Melbourne speculators were venturing into suburban real estate as early as 1868, but the main attraction for Victorian money was the timber industry. This led to the construction of the colony's first private railways, the non-passenger timber lines at Lockeville, near Busselton (1871), and from Jarrahdale to Rockingham (1872). Stockmen traversing the South West went many miles out of their way to gaze on the wonder of technology, the steam locomotive. In 1872 Charles Broadhurst imported the colony's first steamship, the *Xantho*, but it had been poorly maintained and serviced by its previous owners and was soon a wreck.[44] The government then contracted passenger and mail services to 'a tub of a steamer', the *Georgette*, which was to figure in 1876 in two of Western Australia's most mythic events. In March, when six Fenian convicts escaped in a boat to the safety of the visiting American merchantman *Catalpa*, the *Georgette* sailed in pursuit only to be rebuffed by the Yankee skipper and return empty-handed. The ballad-makers sang:

> *Come all you screw-warders and jailers,*
> *Remember Perth regatta day,*
> *Take care of the rest of your Fenians*
> *Or the Yankees will steal them away.*[45]

In December 1876 the *Georgette* fell victim to the dangerous seas north of Cape Leeuwin. Generations of Western Australian schoolchildren were taught the story of the 16-year-old Grace Bussell (and less often of the Aboriginal stockman Sam Isaacs), who rode into the raging ocean with a line by means of which many of the passengers could be brought to safety.[46]

Fear of American intentions was fanned in June 1876 when workers at the guano deposits of the Lacepede Islands in the North West were disturbed by two intruders sent by the United States consul in Melbourne to raise the Stars and Stripes. Police despatched from Roebourne dislodged them, and when the British Government complained to Washington the United States authorities disowned the annexation and stated that the consul's action was unauthorised. In 1880 a Geraldton newspaper reported that the Marquis de Rays, a grandiose French aristocrat, intended to take advantage of the emptiness of Western Australia's north by establishing a colony there, to be called Port Breton. Eventually, the marquis took his luckless colonists to New Britain, off the coast of New Guinea, where the enterprise soon failed. But Western Australians remained fearful. In the summer of 1881–82, reports of an unidentified whaling boat were enough for Governor Robinson to call out the volunteer militia.[47] Western Australians felt pressure to develop their isolated colony before some alien force challenged them.

If the attraction of outside investment depended on better communications, the main achievement of the 1870s was the coming of the telegraph. A local syndicate opened the first line, between Fremantle and Perth, in 1869, but the operators had to sell out to the government in 1871. It was not the last time that the public sector had to take over from unsuccessful private enterprise. Thus the government took responsibility for linking the local system to South Australia and, by the way of Charles Todd's overland line, to the world beyond. Roe's last significant decision before retiring as Surveyor-General at the end of 1870 was to commission his two promising pupils John and Alexander Forrest to take a party across the Nullarbor assessing the route that a telegraph line might follow. A better bushman and more careful in his preparations than Eyre had been, John Forrest won acclaim by his successful conduct of the enterprise. Again with his brother and with his valued Nyungar guide Tommy Windich, Forrest led a second transcontinental expedition across the centre in 1874. This earned them the sort of popular prestige that in our day comes to young men and women as successful Olympic athletes or tennis stars. Like the Gregorys before them, the Forrests were thorough professionals who planned their moves carefully in advance, saved their men from avoidable privations, kept hostilities to a minimum with the Aboriginal people through whose country they passed, and succeeded in their goals. Outside Western Australia their achievement is largely ignored in favour of tragic incompetents such as Burke and Wills.[48]

The telegraph line was completed along the Forrests' route in 1877 and gave an immediate stimulus to business. In 1878 a Fremantle entrepreneur, James Lilly, initiated a regular steamship service to the eastern colonies, and major overseas shipping companies such as the P & O and Orient lines soon joined him, using the safe harbour at Albany for their port of call. Timber exports continued to rise, passing £60,000 in 1878. This year saw the arrival of the Adelaide entrepreneur M. C. Davies, who exported the first karri in 1879. The example of the timber industry stirred the government into authorising the first public railways. Between 1874 and 1879 a 54-kilometre line inched its way from Geraldton to Northampton, arriving too late to be of much use to the lead and copper mines that it was meant to serve. In 1879 a start was made on the Eastern Railway, which in the next six years would stretch 144 kilometres from Fremantle to York, to the benefit of the Avon Valley primary producers.

Despite these omens of change, progress still seemed torpid as Western Australians celebrated the fiftieth anniversary of their colony in 1879. It was encouraging that sheep numbers doubled during the 1870s, in 1879 passing one million, and in 1880 pushing the value of wool exports above £300,000 for the first time. This was still barely 2 per cent of the total Australian clip, and because of problems of technology and distance the quality of Western Australian wool lagged behind the national average. Wheat-growing was retarded by the slow-growing local market, several outbreaks of rust, and poor practice. The last was usually blamed on farmer conservatism, but even the most progressive were held back by lack of capital. Visiting the colony in 1872, Anthony Trollope considered Western Australian farming

> atrociously bad…Men continue to crop the same ground with the same crops year after year without manuring it, and when the weeds come thicker than the corn they simply leave it. Machinery has not been introduced. Seed is wasted, and farmers thresh their corn with flails on the roads after the old Irish fashion.[49]

As for the vineyards that might have flourished in so Mediterranean a climate, Trollope wrote:

> I will not take it upon myself to say I drank West Australian wine with delight. I took it with awe and trembling and in very small quantities. But we all know that the art of making wine does not arise in a day.[50]

Pearling, timber and the reviving export industries in sandalwood and cavalry horses each made their modest contribution, but none could produce the multiplier effect of gold to act as a major engine of growth. If the West was to catch up with the more fortunate eastern colonies, it must match them with discoveries of gold; but in 1863 Edward Hargreaves, trading on his reputation as the pioneer prospector of New South Wales, had assured the government, after a tour of the South West, that no gold would be found in Western Australia. Without gold it was hard to imagine how to entice substantial investment to what some called 'the Cinderella colony'. Nearly a decade after Governor Weld had proclaimed that the colony was on the move, pessimism lingered. 'I think seriously of the future', Alfred Hillman confided to his diary in 1879, 'and do not see how we can be anything more than we are at present, progressing so slowly as to be a by-word and a reproach amongst all the Australian Colonies'.[51]

3

'At last she moves', 1879–1894

The fortunate agent of change was Alexander Forrest. Like his brother John, Alexander Forrest was a notable specimen of the colonial second generation, no longer traumatised by emigration, aware of their country's resources, and eager for their development. In 1879 he led an expedition across the northern breadth of Western Australia, naming the Kimberley district and the Ord River. He estimated that his party had discovered at least 20 million hectares of first-class pastoral land, and hinted at prospects for gold. He was rewarded with a land grant, though the authorities were less forthcoming when a Nyungar member of his party, Tommy Dower, asked for a 4-hectare block outside Perth as a camping site for the remnant of his people.[1] Coming at a moment when Melbourne and Sydney investors were on the lookout for fresh speculations, giving renewed attention to the tropical North and New Guinea, Forrest's report provoked a flood of applications for country. Manipulation of the process of allocating pastoral leases favoured the Western Australian sheepmen, who concentrated on the Fitzroy Valley in the West Kimberley, but applications swarmed in from Victoria, New South Wales, Queensland and England, including one from a duke. Although many of these speculators threw up their leases without stocking them, between 1883 and 1885 several parties of overlanders such as the Duracks and the Macdonalds trekked beef cattle long distances across northern Australia into the Kimberley district.[2] Their occupation would be fiercely contested by the Aboriginal inhabitants, and their new properties were far from established markets, but the example of Queensland suggested that pastoral settlement could soon be followed by mineral discoveries and the arrival of meat-hungry diggers. They also sought overseas markets. Before the end of the 1880s, trial shipments of cattle went to Southeast Asia from Derby, Wyndham and Darwin.[3]

The hope of northern development fostered lively interest in transcontinental railways. In the United States and Canada, bold private investors were spanning North America with railways, attracted by generous grants of land on either side of the new lines. During the 1870s, South Australian syndicates dreamed of a line to Darwin, and in 1881 Queensland's Thomas McIlwraith sketched ambitious schemes to link Brisbane with the Gulf of Carpentaria. Not to be outdone, in 1882 two Western Australian squatter-politicians put up a proposal for a land-grant railway between Perth and the Kimberley district. This got nowhere, but it heralded several schemes for land-grant railways joining Perth with Melbourne and Sydney. The most persistent of the transcontinental projectors was a Sydney merchant, Anthony Hordern, who used Alexander Forrest as his agent and surveyor. In the tradition of the entrepreneurs who dreamed great dreams for Western Australia, he also spoke of founding a university and an agricultural college, butter and cheese factories and a winery. In 1884 he was awarded a contract to build a land-grant railway from Albany to the government railway terminus at York (later altered to Beverley) and introduce 1,200 British migrants. In 1886 a London-based syndicate was authorised to build a line from Geraldton to Guildford, 13 kilometres east of Perth, on the existing railway to York.[4]

Under Governor Sir Frederick Napier Broome (1883–89), the colonial government increased its borrowing to fund several small extensions to the government railways, as well as expanding the telegraph system northward to link with a submarine cable to Java and thence to Europe. This doubled the colony's public debt to £1.367 million in 1890—about the limit of government borrowing that could prudently be undertaken without a rapid acceleration of Western Australia's economic growth. This public investment produced a modest multiplier effect. Exports in 1881 exceeded £500,000 for the first time, wool accounting for half, with the pearling and timber industries also making substantial contributions. By 1886 the railways to Northampton and York were benefiting settlers in the Chapman and Avon valleys, respectively. Improved freights gave better access to such materials as fencing wire and—a belated innovation first imported in 1879—corrugated iron.

Agriculture nevertheless made sluggish progress. The area under crop, 35,560 hectares in 1880, increased by about 10 per cent in the next decade, though with marked fluctuations from year to year. Farmers dependent on the goodwill of storekeepers and merchants and the uncertainty of seasons could not invest in improvements, even the replenishment of their land by manuring. A few imported bone dust from Adelaide, but the cost, at £12 a ton, was prohibitive. Although C. E. Broadhurst began the systematic exploitation of the guano deposits of the Abrolhos in 1883, much of it was exported, for only a minority of Western Australian farmers had the capital or the initiative to enrich their wheatfields from that source. Rust or smut blighted crops in some seasons. In the Busselton region, farmers bemoaned the wasting diseases that sickened their herds of cattle, for it would be half a century before scientists began to identify the trace elements lacking in the apparently promising coastal soils. A minority of better-off farmers could afford new technologies. North of Bunbury the Hayward and Rose families kept in touch with agricultural innovation in Suffolk, the English county of their origins, and were among the first whose dairies used mechanical separators. William Glover put up the first wire fence in the Kojonup district in March 1882, but the expense of cartage deterred some neighbours from imitating him.[5]

Isolation bred conservatism. A Victorian traveller, meeting the Scottish pioneer Andrew Muir in the Hay River district north-west of Albany, heard 'a very contented picture of his quiet and monotonous existence'. He and his colonial-born son showed ingenuity in adapting traditional Scottish ploughs to local conditions, and in using bush timber to build hurdles for sheepfolds, but when the younger Muir retired after seventy years on the land, he had to admit that the scrub on his property was denser than in his youth and much of the pasture eaten out. In the same district, Prue Arber, on her own with an infant at the age of 18, kept her independence by using her skills at shepherding to build up a respectable flock and landholdings. Although she lived well into the twentieth century, she never kept up with improving technologies of wool-growing and relied on her dogs and some homemade wooden yokes to control her flock. On her annual shopping trips to Albany with her wool cheque, she presented a determinedly old-fashioned figure in crinoline bodice, fitted white apron and straw hat.[6]

Prue Arber was only one of a generation of resourceful women compelled by the practicalities of rural life to contradict the stereotype of the genteel Victorian lady for which Charlotte Bussell (also a resourceful farmer) had yearned. The women of the Muir family joined the men in hunting kangaroos, for they 'were well able to take part in a long vigorous ride and be in at the kill, even if fitted out with long skirts and side saddles'. When Elizabeth Treasure married Constable Tom Flanagan at Albany in 1886, a local rhymester celebrated the bride as possessing all the valuable rural qualities:

> Riding a buck-jumper, driving a gig,
>   Milking a cow, feeding the pig,
> Nursing the baby, quick out of bed,
>   Deft hand at a cake, a pudding or bread,
> Smart at the needle, neat in her dress,
>   Kind to the poor and all in distress.[7]

Jane Adams, a colonial-born farmer's daughter married at 17 in 1868, settled with her husband in 1875 at 'Mangowine', a large pastoral lease 150 kilometres east of Toodyay. They built a mud-brick cottage beside a soak and cleared a few hectares to grow wheat, fruit and vegetables and run poultry and a cow. There Jane reared eleven children and looked after the property on the frequent occasions that her husband was away with sheep or travelling as a scab inspector. For a few years after the discovery of the Yilgarn goldfield in 1888, she and her husband kept a wayside inn, with Jane and her daughters baking dozens of loaves of bread twice daily. When her husband died in 1895, leaving her with young children, she won the contract for the local mail run and operated it with her teenage son. For later comers, she was a role model.[8]

Jane Adams's story was not unusual in a technological backwater such as Western Australia where farmers relied on family labour. Although primary education was in theory compulsory from 1871, the authorities were often lenient about truancy when children were required to help with ploughing and harvesting. Charles Crowther, Member for Greenough, voiced a common attitude when he complained that education transformed 'the young who in the future were to recruit the ranks of the physical labourers of Western Australia, into clerks'. But although an urban journalist could see the Greenough flats as a 'perfect garden of Ceres teeming with riches of vegetable gold', in reality 'Most Greenoughites were poor and the local economy ran on a barter system. This was not helped by a succession of natural disasters including fire, flood, drought, crop disease and all sorts of infestations...' Such hardships bred a conservative attitude to risk and enterprise. A visiting woman journalist in 1895 found rural Western Australians 'generous, impulsive, quick to form friendships, and industrious enough, but unfortunately not always in the interests of real progress. What their fathers have done before them, they do and teach their children'. She was particularly struck by their failure to improve their diets by growing fruit and vegetables.[9]

Some of the more enterprising South West families hoped to find their fortunes in the North West and the Kimberley. For a while the hope seemed justified. Between 1883 and 1886 the pearling industry received a boost with the development of the new port of Broome. At first Governor Broome complained that he had given his name to a mere dummy township inhabited only by the tenants of three graves, but the pearlers now had the technology to work the deep deposits of Roebuck Bay with Japanese and Indonesian divers. Before the end of the decade, Broome was a multicultural boomtown like no other in Western Australia.[10] Meanwhile, prospectors were probing the Kimberley district, and late in 1885 a payable find was reported at Halls Creek. The news provided a rush of perhaps 1,500 diggers during 1886, mainly from Queensland.

Then the bubbles burst. Halls Creek proved a disappointment. Anthony Hordern succumbed to sunstroke in the Red Sea just before construction commenced on the Albany railway in 1886. His successor, the Western Australian Land Company, could not find work for its first shipload of migrants, abandoning them on the jetty at Albany, and was allowed to cease importing them. Early in 1888 the contractors for the Midland Railway ran short of funds, to the financial embarrassment of several prominent citizens, including S. H. Parker. At the same time, disastrous floods hit the Greenough farmers. Once again Western Australia's economic vulnerability was exposed, and once again the bright promises of visionary entrepreneurs such as Hordern were shown to be hollow.

This crisis tested the mettle of the Legislative Council as shapers of the colony's economic policy. In the early 1880s its record had been at best chequered. As one editor put it, 'the House is not blessed with many representatives who are fitted to be ministers of finance'. In 1879 the veteran Colonial Treasurer, Anthony O'Grady Lefroy, revealed a deficit of nearly £80,000 due entirely to the defective arithmetic of his department's account-keeping. This stimulated the Legislative Council to set up a standing financial committee, which proved a good school of budget management for some of the colony's leading politicians.[11] Nevertheless, its senior elected members were unconvinced when Stephen Henry Parker, now Member for Perth, argued year after year for the grant of responsible government. Their doubts had some justification, as for several years in the mid-1880s Western Australia's small governing elite was tearing itself apart in a series of spectacular but largely trivial quarrels.

Part of the trouble lay with Governor Broome's personality. He seemed a promising appointment because, like Weld before him, he was a vigorous man in his early forties with practical experience in the New Zealand pastoral industry. Unfortunately, he was hasty and quarrelsome, and he soon fell foul of the colony's two leading legal officers, the Chief Justice, Alexander Onslow, and the Attorney-General, Alfred Hensman, by requesting their advice on matters that they thought fell outside their responsibilities. Both were newcomers to Western Australia but they found an ally with local prestige in the first colonial-born member of the Executive Council, John Forrest, who was appointed Surveyor-General in 1883. The Executive Council was dubbed a 'bear-garden', and things got worse after Broome suspended Hensman in March 1886.[12] These squabbles were gleefully reported by a press no longer inhibited by the restraints once accepted in an ex-convict colony. Readership was expanding, with an increasing literacy recognised by the establishment of a public reference library in 1887 supplementing older literary institutions.

In 1882 the Stirling brothers, proprietors of the *Inquirer*, launched the *Daily News*, Perth's first daily paper. The rival *Western Australian Times* (formerly the *Perth Gazette*) reinvented itself as a daily under the name of *The West Australian* in 1885, and launched a weekly, the *Western Mail*. For more than sixty years, the *Western Mail*, aided by the expansion of the railway system, would become essential reading for rural Western Australians, its popularity enhanced by its practical usefulness in publicising new farming technologies and practices. A humorous weekly, the *Possum*, failed to survive the economic downturn in 1888. It was briefly revived as the *WA Bulletin* in 1890 but shared little rapport with its Sydney namesake. When the Sydney *Bulletin* announced, 'The talented Henry Lawson is going to Western Australia', the Perth journal inquired, 'Who's Henry Lawson?'[13] Meanwhile, between 1877 and 1890 York, Geraldton, Albany and Bunbury all acquired their own local newspapers. The telegraph enabled them to bring their readers news from all corners of the world, as well as keeping them up to date with the latest political moves in Perth. Broome and his officials manoeuvred before a Western Australian public better informed than at any previous time.

Of Perth's two daily newspapers, the *Daily News* tended to side with Broome's critics, but *The West Australian* took his part and showed little enthusiasm for self-government. Its principal owner, the native-born Charles Harper, was a cool conservative whose one passion in life was the intelligent promotion of agriculture, but his business manager, and editor from 1887, Winthrop Hackett, was in those years a more contentious character. Scion of the Anglo-Irish Protestant ascendancy and ally of the conservative North West squatters, Hackett weathered more than one libel case during his first years as editor. None created more furore than his prosecution by an even more controversial figure, the Anglican missionary John Brown Gribble. Already notable as the only man to stand up to Ned Kelly at the Jerilderie raid, Gribble was known for his work among Aboriginal people when he was appointed to the Gascoyne district in 1885. He was soon outraged by what he saw as the maltreatment of Aborigines by the local pastoralists, and became so unpopular that he had to leave the district, narrowly escaping violence. He published *Dark Deeds in a Sunny Land*, in which his allegations of cruelty provoked Hackett, himself a failed Gascoyne squatter, to describe Gribble editorially as 'a lying, canting humbug'. The embattled missionary gained no support from his bishop, Henry Parry, who was preoccupied with the completion of a new cathedral and could not afford to antagonise influential Western Australians. Instead, Gribble sued Harper and Hackett for libel. Although a good deal of disturbing evidence was tendered during the trial in June 1887, the judges found in favour of the defendants. Defeated, Gribble left Western Australia. An ex-convict, David Carley, who supported Gribble's allegations, was easily discredited. Dissenters and troublemakers were not welcomed in Western Australia.[14]

Meanwhile, the advocates of self-government took advantage of the increasing self-confidence encouraged by economic progress. They founded a Reform Association in December 1886 and recruited several members of the Legislative Council. The cause won unprecedented support in July 1887 after Parker presented a numerously signed petition on behalf of his Perth constituents, and the Legislative Council agreed to the principle of responsible government by thirteen votes to four. This stimulated the more businesslike members of the Legislative Council to demonstrate the role that they expected of an autonomous parliament. During the summer of 1887–88 Alexander Forrest successfully introduced a number of measures for tariff protection on locally grown primary produce. In the same parliamentary session, a commission was set up to report on Western Australia's agriculture. Consisting of five of the colony's most experienced primary producers chaired by H. W. Venn, this inquiry would provide a solid basis for future growth.[15]

Thus Western Australia was reaching for political maturity at a time when the second and third generations were beginning to feel comfortable in their environment. Townspeople like the banker Alfred Hillman took pleasure in the apparently limitless spread of the everlastings in the country behind Geraldton in an early September after good rainfall. When the English botanical painter Marianne North visited the colony in 1880 because of the profusion of little-known wildflowers in the South West, she gave encouragement to Margaret Forrest and her friend the Victorian Ellis Rowan. Nine years later Rowan and Forrest would put on the first formal art exhibition ever staged in Perth, its popular theme the native flowers of the colony.[16] After 1886 Perth families took advantage of the railway to picnic in the Darling Range, and some lovers of the open air took up properties there, among them the Parker family, Justice Stone, and Governor Broome's official secretary, the Honorable Josceline Amherst.

Names such as these might suggest the gentry tradition that Stirling had dreamed of establishing, but such a dream was further from reality than ever. Snobbery there was; in 1892 a visiting clergyman found that

> Government officials, professional men, the descendants of the first colonists and others form a quasi aristocracy, and any attempt on the part of a newcomer to treat all colonists on the same level proved itself a mistake.[17]

Western Australia was simply not nearly rich enough to nurture the kind of dynasties typified by the Barr Smiths and Bonythons in Adelaide or the Manifolds and Clarkes of the Western District of Victoria. To the extent that Western Australian communities possessed elites, they consisted of self-made men and their families who had prospered more than their peers and imitated English gentility as an index of their achievement. 'The merchant princes of Fremantle', who through successful trade and shipping formed a snug coterie managing the affairs of the port, have left their monument in the late nineteenth and early twentieth century facades and buildings that to this day distinguish the west end of Fremantle.[18] But their authority was never absolute. Even in their heyday, from 1870 to 1900, they met a persistent tradition of proletarian and democratic challenge, first voiced by the ex-convict writers of the *Herald*, later by the lumpers and railway workshops employees who made up an increasingly significant share of the Fremantle work force. In 1887 the community was set agog by the exploits of the 'Fremantle bushranger', Thomas Hughes, a young hoodlum who, after shooting a policeman, remained at large in the bush outside Perth for many weeks before arrest and conviction. 'He was a young West Australian born and bred, and as such the physical prowess, the dexterity and perfect mastery of bush lore he had shown won him the instinctive sympathy of the masses.'[19] The outlaw was not hanged, surviving after imprisonment to a bucolic old age, but the episode showed that law and order could not count on working-class youth. In an era when Victoria bred the Kelly gang and Sydney the larrikin 'pushes', Western Australia did not want to seem backward in identifying juvenile delinquency, and in 1880 the Legislative Council had passed an act punishing disorderly conduct, such as insulting passing females or making too much noise, with up to six months' gaol.[20] Town life was fostering social tensions.

Several country towns in the late nineteenth century seemed dominated by one family or individual. In his Avon Valley home town, John Henry Monger, merchant, sandalwood dealer and pastoralist, was so conspicuous a citizen that he was known as 'the Duke of York'. When he died in February 1892, the local paper described his last weeks in great detail: how he had seemed to recuperate after a trip east, how a special train had taken him from Albany to York, how his condition had soon deteriorated, and how he had breathed his last one morning at his residence, 'Faversham House', surrounded by his wife, nine children, and surviving brothers. As the report put it:

> the weary wheels which had revolved for three score years stood still, and he sank quietly away repeating the words 'Jesu, lover of my soul', in the presence…of the whole of the members of his family.[21]

Another special train brought Sir John Forrest and many more up from Perth for the funeral. But Monger had not been able to ensure that the route for the colony's most important railway, linking the Avon Valley to the goldfields, passed through York. Instead, the choice fell on Northam, where the local member of parliament, George Throssell, had distinguished himself by his loyal support for the Forrest ministry. Orphaned quite young and handicapped by deafness, Throssell by diligence and shrewdness outpaced all his business competitors to earn the nickname of 'the lion of Northam'.[22] In Katanning the miller and produce merchant Frederick Henry Piesse cast such a long shadow over his community that after his death they erected a statue to him. Like Monger and Throssell, he built a fine house overlooking the town, and when he went home for lunch in his carriage his wife would be waiting to pull off his boots when he alighted.[23] None of these men had gentry origins. Monger was the son of a sawyer, Throssell of a pensioner guard, Piesse of a police officer whose promotion was blocked because he was thought not quite a gentleman. Nor did they found dynasties. Each had a son who went bankrupt within a decade of the old man's death. To be a member of 'an old family' in Western Australia was not a guarantee of economic or social status.

Not that Western Australia in the 1880s was becoming a working-man's paradise. Especially in rural districts, the old master and servant legislation still governed relations between employees and bosses. Shepherds and farm workers considered unsatisfactory by their employers could be taken before a magistrate and fined and in some cases imprisoned with hard labour for a week or a month. When Governor Broome's officials tried to decriminalise breach of contract by employees and otherwise to reform the law in 1884, they found themselves opposed by every member of the Legislative Council. One or two, such as Parker, who commented that Western Australia was 'a police ridden society', opposed because the reform did not go far enough. The great majority simply rejected any reduction in the power of employers.[24] Yet the spirit of deference was on the wane, not only among the townspeople who applauded Tom Hughes but even in York of all places. Here the distinction between old families and ex-convicts stood out so sharply that, according to tradition, the custom had arisen at the annual ball of drawing a chalk line down the centre of the hall. On one side the working class and agricultural labourers might dance, with the other side reserved for the 'silvertails'. In 1887 the working-class lads took their partners and danced irresistibly across the line, and if class distinctions did not vanish from York they became less blatant.[25]

Fremantle, Perth and, to a lesser extent, Albany were also open to democratising influences from the eastern colonies. Trade unionism arrived by this route. Between 1883 and 1889 a number of craft unions mobilised carpenters and joiners, railwaymen, printers and bootmakers into a movement that pressed for an eight-hour working day. Some industries conceded this reform in 1890 and 1891, but it was far from widespread, and the trade union movement was not yet strong enough for vigorous strike action. Meanwhile, in 1889 the waterside workers organised themselves into the Fremantle Lumpers Union. This soon proved itself a forceful organisation, with strong local roots, and the union became an essential element in the formation of a Trades and Labour Council in 1892.[26]

Another less obviously political import was 'Victorian' football (now Australian Rules). In the early 1880s, members of the Bateman and Burt families who had been sent to school at Adelaide returned proclaiming the superiority of the Victorian game over all other forms of football. Young Western Australians were soon persuaded, as other codes such as rugby had been too short a time in the colony to become entrenched. From 1885 three teams, Fremantle, Rovers and Victorians, played regular fixtures. In early years, play was often rough and the spectators rougher. After one match in Fremantle in 1891, the ringleader of a crowd who invaded the ground, Tom Marshall, was sentenced to twenty-four hours' imprisonment for riotous behaviour, and on his release was carried through the streets of the port by enthusiastic fans. Sport was soon linked with local politics. An ex-convict's son, Marshall was already a town councillor and co-founder of the Fremantle Lumpers Union, and a few years later would scandalise the respectable by winning a seat in the Legislative Council—from which he was soon removed by a providential bankruptcy. Another who took a provocative part in the affray but was not arrested was Walter James. Son of a publican's widow and himself able enough to qualify in law, James would enter parliament at the same time as Marshall, but survived to become Premier while still under 40.[27] Even before the colony was irrevocably transformed by gold, there were signs that men of property might not have it all their own way in a self-governing Western Australia.

Governor Broome released the genie from the bottle in September 1887, when after months of squabbling he took the controversial step of suspending Onslow as Chief Justice on the grounds that he had released official correspondence to the press. Crying tyranny, a mob urged on by Hensman and Alexander Forrest that night burnt Broome in effigy in a Perth street. The British Government overruled Broome, sending instructions in May 1888 for Onslow's reinstatement. In the same month, at a by-election for the Perth constituency, a veteran Irish radical lawyer, John Horgan, narrowly defeated the conservative Septimus Burt. Horgan ran a lively campaign denouncing the 'six hungry families' who, he claimed, dominated Western Australian society, and dubbing the Weld Club a 'pot house'. Even Bishop Salvado was abused as a land-grabber.[28] Horgan lasted only eight months in the Legislative Council, and during that time the solid men rallied. Confident that the voters wanted sound stewardship of the colony's economy rather than the fireworks of urban democrats, during the constitutional debates of 1888–89 rural conservatives ensured that the electorate under responsible government would be biased in favour of the North West and the country districts. The framers of Western Australia's constitution were fighting on two fronts, since as well as holding the local radicals in check they were fending off the well-meant suggestions of the Colonial Office. London officialdom thought that a non-Aboriginal population of merely 40,000 needed only one house of parliament rather than two, and could never manage one-third of an entire continent; might not the Kimberley and the North West be excised? Both these ideas were successfully resisted, and the right to vote was confined to men of at least modest property. It was not yet certain whether Western Australia's economic future would recover sufficiently to provide a stable basis for property-owners and aspiring democrats alike.[29]

Optimists soon found cause for hope. Some of the prospectors attracted by the gold of Halls Creek stayed in the West and were rewarded by further discoveries in 1887–88. In the Pilbara a treasured local legend says that the glint of gold was first seen when young Jimmy Withnell picked up a stone to shy at a crow. Credit for the discovery of the Yilgarn goldfield went to a recently arrived English speculator, Henry Anstey, but it should have gone to the experienced diggers whom he grubstaked. The first major find on the Murchison, at Nannine, was made by a group of prospectors guided by Richard Robson, an English jackeroo who never thought of staking a claim for himself (though he later made money in the carrying business before embarking on a brief but eventful parliamentary career). From such accidental beginnings came a series of moderately thriving goldfields.[30] By 1889 gold exports were valued at £58,874, ranking third after wool and timber. Revival followed. In 1889 the Albany railway was opened for traffic. A year later the Midland line resumed with a reconstructed company and, after tortuous negotiations with the government, was completed in 1894. Government expenditure on railways and telegraphs reached a new peak of £3.7 million in 1889, thus anticipating the entrepreneurial role that the state would undertake in the 1890s, and setting a precedent for Western Australian governments during the twentieth century. Prominent citizens of Perth set up a stock exchange in 1888 and a chamber of commerce in 1890. Even agriculture revived, perhaps stimulated by the Legislative Council's protective tariffs. In 1889 more land was planted for wheat than ever before: more than 14,000 hectares.

In the face of this progress, the British Government swallowed its doubts about the viability of so vast and underpopulated a colony. After lobbying by a delegation from the Legislative Council, generously supported by Governor Broome, the British Parliament agreed to the grant of self-government except for Aboriginal policy, where misgivings still lingered after the Gribble affair. One per cent of Western Australia's revenue was set aside for Aboriginal welfare, administered by an Aborigines Protection Board who would report to London. Inevitably, Western Australians took offence at this restriction on their sovereignty, with its implication that they could not be trusted to deal justly with the Indigenous minority. The board, manned largely by elderly colonists of limited political clout, turned out to have little effect. As government revenue rose during the 1890s, 1 per cent was regarded as far in excess of Aboriginal needs. In 1897, by a manoeuvre that some later saw as open to legal challenge, the Colonial Office was persuaded to abolish the board and the 1 per cent obligation with as little publicity as possible.[31] For all other purposes, Western Australia was put constitutionally on equal terms with the other Australasian colonies.

Sir William Robinson, Governor of Western Australia for the third time, formally proclaimed self-government on his arrival on 21 October 1890. Proclamation Day joined the calendar of Western Australian public holidays until discontinued by a cost-cutting government shortly after World War I, without provoking much public complaint—surprisingly for a community that would shortly vote for secession. At the time, the ceremony was remarkable mostly for its encouragement to the colony's few creative artists. Sir William himself was a prolific composer, and his song 'Unfurl the Flag' was sung by hundreds of schoolchildren to mark the great occasion. Henry Clay, the colony's nearest approach to a poet, composed an anthem: 'Arouse Thee, Westralia'. But Western Australia's cultural achievements were as yet few. Of Clay it has been written that 'his principal works are less conspicuous for their colonial subject-matter than for their romantically nostalgic images of a settled social order'. He himself acknowledged that 'The pioneers of local literature in a small community should prepare to encounter special difficulties and a probable harvest of loss'.[32] Music fared better through the interest of the colony's leading men of law. When Edward Stone founded the

Perth Musical Union in 1880, his colleagues Onslow, who possessed a fine bass voice, and Hensman, a talented violinist and conductor, soon reinforced him. For about a decade the union strove to educate Perth audiences, although the most commercially successful season recorded at that time was of Gilbert and Sullivan's *Iolanthe*, which played to full houses in 1891. Its political satire probably appealed to a public with its own new parliament.[33]

Western Australia's legislature consisted of two houses. The Legislative Assembly, the lower house, originally of thirty members, would be elected by a property-owning franchise, soon amended in 1893 to an amount low enough to give the vote to almost all adults except women, bankrupts, clergymen, Aborigines and idiots. Property-owners would be entitled to vote for an upper house, the Legislative Council, with twenty-four members chosen from eight provinces, but until the colony's non-Aboriginal population reached 60,000 (it stood at 46,000 in 1890) the council would have a smaller membership nominated by the Governor on advice from his ministers. Intended as a house of review to check the imprudence of democracy, the Legislative Council had the power to overrule even the financial legislation of the Legislative Assembly. Its members, although for many years preserving the fiction of belonging to no political party, were weighted towards conservatism. However, it was in the Legislative Assembly that the Premier and his ministers would have to command a majority. Because Western Australia had no organised political parties, it might have been expected that, like every other Australian colony, the early years of its parliament would see a series of unstable, short-lived governments as factions based on local and personal ties shifted and regrouped. This did not happen. After elections late in 1890, the Surveyor-General, John Forrest, became first Premier and remained uninterruptedly in office for ten years. This was a record unsurpassed in Australian politics until the late 1940s.[34]

Because of this continuity, Sir John Forrest (he was knighted in 1891) enjoyed unusual scope to impose his stamp on public policy. Unlike the 1880s, divisive personality clashes no longer dominated public life. Onslow and Hensman sat quietly on the Supreme Court bench, and in his early years of office Forrest's cabinet were a loyal team. There was no politician to challenge him, indeed no formal leader of the Opposition until 1894.

The two members sometimes seen as filling that role, S. H. Parker and M. F. A. Canning, were soon muzzled by the gift of office. They may be acquitted of cynical opportunism, since nearly all colonial politicians shared the same goals of encouraging investment and immigration, promoting rural industries, and extending public works. They differed from Forrest mainly over the pace at which it was safe to pursue these goals. A local hero of forceful temperament, Forrest's record as explorer and surveyor gave him authority in his assessments of Western Australia's potential. His blunt manner masked an ability to absorb and internalise the ideas of others. He was a canny reader of the political odds, adept at reconciling diverse interests. Many of the policies identified with him reflected trends already evident. Governor Broome had broken with earlier conservatism in borrowing for developmental purposes. The Venn commission, when it reported in 1891, anticipated many of Forrest's measures for advancing agriculture. Forrest's achievement lay in providing an attractive environment for investors, promptly undertaking the provision of public works and infrastructure, and creating an image of stability that meant that capital would flow into Western Australia even when the credit of the rest of the continent was tarnished by the 1893 financial crisis.[35]

Forrest possessed a remarkable clarity about policy aims. His goals included the fostering of Western Australian agriculture, the centralisation of the colony's transport system on the Perth–Fremantle metropolitan area, and eventually the construction of a transcontinental railway integrating the West with the rest of Australia. In the absence of resident capitalists, it would be the government's responsibility to raise the loans required to provide the necessary infrastructure for economic growth. Forrest could hardly have foreseen the good fortune that within a very short time would follow the discovery of the Coolgardie–Kalgoorlie goldfields, but he could claim credit for the political stability and managerial skill that would turn those discoveries to advantage.

His first priority was agriculture. The Venn commission reported that Western Australia had only recently matured into a cash market: 'up to within a few years ago the agriculturalist had at best only a precarious market, a mixture of barter and tardy cash'. Many who wished to be farmers lacked capital. Forrest responded by passing legislation in 1893 based on the homestead legislation of North America. Any applicant who resided on the land, cleared it, and met a minimum target of improvements each year would be entitled to a free grant of 160 acres (almost 65 hectares). He followed this in 1895 by the creation of a state-owned Agricultural Bank to extend credit to farmers on easy terms, thus meeting a need that private banks had been unwilling to fulfil. A pragmatic sceptic about private enterprise, Forrest in 1896 bought out the Western Australian Land Company, which owned the Albany railway, because it was failing to develop the promising country between Beverley and Albany quickly enough. Between 1895 and 1900, Western Australia's acreage under wheat more than trebled, though not yet producing enough for the local market. Confidence blossomed. Forrest's Minister for Lands, George Throssell, asserted in 1897 that '160 acres and a wife was all that was required to make the majority of Perth young men happy'. Technological advance in milling also helped. The first roller mills were introduced in 1890, and two years later the Piesse brothers of Katanning introduced electricity. Power surplus to their mill's needs was made available to local householders, who became Western Australia's first domestic users of electricity.[36]

Forrest was backed by a civil service of no more than mediocre calibre, but early in his premiership he made an outstanding appointment as Engineer-in-Chief, Charles Yelverton O'Connor, with twenty-five years of New Zealand experience behind him. His impact in Western Australia stands comparison with Brunel's in the United Kingdom.[37] O'Connor's first assignment was the creation of a safe harbour for Fremantle. Even after the completion of the railway between Albany and Perth, it was unsatisfactory that the colony's main port should lie more than 500 kilometres from the capital city. As a large number of nineteenth-century shipwrecks attested to, the approaches to Fremantle were notoriously unsafe.[38] Most authorities saw the solution in the development of Cockburn Sound, to the south of Fremantle, and it took O'Connor some time to persuade Forrest to find an alternative in an artificial harbour at Fremantle itself. This entailed removing the bar at the mouth of the Swan River, dredging extensively, and creating an inner harbour with wharves along either side of the river mouth. It also called for the removal of the railway workshops from Fremantle to a new site at Midland Junction, east of Guildford, which met with strong resistance from Fremantle landowners and businessmen.

Not for the last time, Sir John Forrest backed O'Connor's judgment against all comers. This meant government expenditure on a heroic scale. It has been calculated that of £17.7 million spent on Western Australian bridges and harbours between 1892 and 1900, Fremantle harbour took the lion's share. Its underfunded rival, Albany, grew resentful, and as late as 1900 listened appreciatively when a parliamentary candidate told them that the first major flood on the Swan River would ruin Fremantle Harbour.[39] It was by far the most costly government project authorised thus far, and took until 1899 to complete. During that time of unprecedented boom, great inconvenience would be caused by bottlenecks in Fremantle. Some tended to blame the local combine of shipping agents for their woes, and in 1892 the American Captain Nathan Shaw touched eloquence when he reported:

> It is a terrible place, no place to put a vessel, no shelter whatsoever...Any man who would come a second time is a damned ass. Still blowing a heavy gale, I was never so sick of a place in my life, and may the curse of Christ rest on Fremantle and every son-of-a-bitch in it. God damn them all.[40]

The captain was unfortunate, for he came in a week when Western Australia was convulsed by momentous news. In September 1892 Arthur Bayley and William Ford announced their discovery of gold at Coolgardie, 180 kilometres east of Southern Cross. 'We gathered nuggets like spuds in a paddock', said Ford. The richest find so far, Coolgardie was eclipsed nine months later when Paddy Hannan and his mates located gold at Kalgoorlie, 40 kilometres further east, thus stimulating the series of discoveries that unveiled the 'Golden Mile' between Kalgoorlie and Boulder. Many smaller finds kept expectation high for several years. The timing was perfect. In eastern Australia, because of the widespread recession, unemployment was high and industrial strife common. In 1894 alone, 25,000 men decided to try their luck in the West, most of them from Victoria and South Australia. Although a few enterprising spirits came overland by foot or bicycle, most travelled by sea, landing at Esperance,

Albany or Fremantle and tramping several hundred kilometres to the goldfields. Despite the risks of dysentery, typhoid and mining accidents, they soon created dozens of new communities in the arid interior. They came so quickly and in such numbers that the Wongi inhabitants were soon swept aside and reduced to the status of fringe-dwellers.[41]

At the same time, because of a lull in South African goldmining and the collapse of world silver prices, British investors were on the lookout for new speculations. At first they were wary of the overcapitalised Coolgardie goldmines, and 70 per cent of early flotations were left with underwriters. Late in 1894 a group of speculators led by Colonel J. T. North (who had grown rich on Chilean nitrate) made a killing by promoting the Londonderry and Wealth of Nations mines on the London stock market. The Londonderry was floated for £700,000, of which only £50,000 was earmarked for working the mine, the rest going to the vendors and promoters. Both properties turned out to be almost valueless, but before the bad news could depress the market the Great Boulder, leading mine on the Golden Mile, was found to yield rich deposits at depth. Enthusiasm rekindled. In 1894 sixty Western Australian goldmining companies were listed, representing an investment of probably £18 million. Only one-fifth of these survived until the turn of the century, but they were enough for a most valuable capital inflow into Western Australia.[42]

Many shareholders lost heavily. One editor considered there was no equal to 'the bogus financeering and the charlatan engineering which was the motive force behind the Western Australia boom of 1895', while the *Financial Times* wrote of 'the waste and extravagance which one sees throughout Western Australia'. Prominent among the promoters of Western Australian goldmines were notorious scamps such as Whitaker Wright, veteran of twenty years of American speculation, and Horatio Bottomley, a bankrupt publisher who, despite mining inexperience, soon mastered the knack of fudging balance sheets and watering capital. If London punters continued to rush for Western Australian shares, it was partly because a few properties came under honest and efficient management and paid consistent dividends. The Great Boulder, managed for many years by Richard Hamilton, paid its shareholders dividends equal to the value of 60 per cent of gold production. From 1896 a firm of mine managers and engineers, Bewick Moreing, brought a much-needed, though often ruthless, professionalism to the Western Australian goldfields. Its staff included a very able young American, Herbert Hoover, who was to be President of the United States between 1929 and 1933. He made a better reputation as engineer than he would as President, setting a model of economical management that restored the fortunes of many mines, though often at the cost of retrenching staff.[43] Unfortunately, it would be many years before the law caught up with the Bottomleys and Wrights of the London share market. Scandals continued, but so did the myth of 'the Golden West'.

From the Western Australian point of view, all this profligate investment was almost entirely beneficial. Unlike the eastern colonies, the Western Australian goldfields were not rich in alluvial gold, the 'poor man's gold' that attracted numerous prospectors and provided the venture capital to grubstake further exploration. J. W. McCarty has argued that 'it was the indiscriminate British purchase of undeveloped outcrops which assumed the role of parent alluvial fields', providing the basis for development in Western Australia.[44] Perth businessmen such as Sir George Shenton and Alexander Forrest throve as middlemen between prospecting syndicates and London capitalists, and their profits shored up many commercial projects and land subdivisions. The bonanza was especially timely as a prop for the pastoral industry. Falling wool prices were accompanied by a drought in the North West between 1890 and 1892, which apparently wiped out a quarter of Western Australia's 2.5 million sheep. In 1893 wool gave way to gold as the colony's major export. Compensation came with the arrival of thousands of diggers, whose hunger for mutton and beef could be met by local graziers protected from outside competition by tariffs. Farmers prospered equally, while the carrying trade, builders and the owners of rental properties in Perth made windfall profits. Banks and insurance companies based in London or Melbourne made haste to set up branches in Western Australia. Governor Sir Frederick Weld, who died in 1891, had not lived quite long enough to see the fulfilment of his prophecy. At last Western Australia was moving.

4

The Golden West, 1895–1905

The Forrest government sought long-term benefits from Western Australia's sudden prosperity, among them the provision of infrastructure for future growth. No Australian colonial government ever acted more promptly in bringing public works to new goldfields. Southern Cross, 370 kilometres east of Perth, had railway and telegraph in 1892, within four years of its establishment. Coolgardie, Kalgoorlie and all the major centres of the Murchison goldfield were connected by telegraph in 1894, and Coolgardie and Kalgoorlie had their railway by 1896. The Forrest government was taking a gamble on the permanency of the goldfields, but without such amenities it was unlikely that miners or investors would linger in the hot, dusty environment. As it was, permanent buildings and substantial public offices soon gave a satisfyingly urban look to the main streets of leading goldfields towns. Although Coolgardie's main street was twice devastated by fire, the town for three months in 1899 hosted an 'International Mining and Industrial Exhibition' attended by more than 60,000 visitors who gazed at the products resulting from the wonderful progress of fewer than seven crowded years.

The massive influx of newcomers was absorbed with comparatively little social disruption. A commissioner of police might complain that 'the tide of emigration from the East has brought us in its flood a large proportion of criminals', but in fact the goldfields were not overwhelmed by frontier violence, although the police were under-resourced. In a settlement on the road between Northam and the goldfields, 'law-breakers were sometimes chained to the hotel verandah posts pending despatch by train to Northam for trial', and a carrier delivering stores up the railway line 'became used to carrying a revolver to protect himself while dealing with a rough workforce and collecting payment of accounts in gold sovereigns', but there was very little actual gunplay.[1] Violence was most likely to flare over religious antagonisms, on a scale previously unknown in Western Australia. Catholics and Protestants clashed when the Orangemen paraded in Coolgardie in July 1897, and in 1901 police had to draw their revolvers to quell a more unruly disturbance of the same kind at Southern Cross.[2] Yet in general, the goldfields from the beginning were a surprisingly orderly community.

Water was the big problem. Domestic users wanted it, the hygiene to counter diseases such as dysentery and typhoid depended on it, and above all mining technology made voracious demands for it. If the water shortage earned profits for the 'Afghan' camel drivers, whose beasts of burden carried a good deal of freight in the early years of the goldfields, it led to difficulties in servicing the steam locomotives once the railways came. The landscapes around the goldfields towns were bare and arid, since all the available timber was soon felled to feed the furnaces of the processing plants, and the windswept goldfields towns endured a constant problem with dust. The Murchison and Coolgardie–Kalgoorlie goldfields were situated in country with an annual but irregular rainfall of 250 millimetres. How could they be supplied?

By the beginning of 1896, C. Y. O'Connor had undertaken to construct a 560-kilometre pipeline from Mundaring, on the Helena River in the Darling Range behind Perth, to Coolgardie and Kalgoorlie. Nowhere in the world had such a project been attempted on this scale. Carping critics were numerous, but the pipeline concept must have fired some Western Australian imaginations, if we judge by later competition for the scheme's authorship. To the end of his long life, the mining entrepreneur Nat Harper claimed the honour, and some Perth feminists liked to give the credit to Lady Forrest, but in the upshot Forrest's political courage and O'Connor's professional skills were the essential ingredients of success.[3] Forrest may have been buoyed up by his habitual optimism, but he was also mindful of the benefits that a pipeline could bring to the 'waterless waste' between the Avon Valley and Coolgardie. 'The best portions of that country will be ringbarked and occupied by graziers, and in some instances probably by farmers.'[4] It was a modest forecast in the light of the expansion of wheat-growing that was soon to follow.

Geoffrey Blainey has argued that O'Connor overstated the water problem in Kalgoorlie and its hinterland by using inadequate rainfall statistics and overestimating the cost of condensing the locally available salt water. He suggests that Broken Hill, founded in arid country ten years earlier than Kalgoorlie, provided a model of how a mining community could supply its industrial needs by building dams and distilling the salt water found at depth in mineshafts. Others have supplemented this argument. Perhaps the conquest of typhoid on the goldfields owed as much to skilled nursing and to sound public health policies as to the coming of the pipeline. Also it has been convincingly argued that the residents of Kalgoorlie and smaller towns were 'already building a water conserving culture', with gardens adapted to local conditions. Even after the coming of the pipeline, dust storms fanned by the indiscriminate clearing of timber for many kilometres around were to envelop Kalgoorlie until reafforestation in the 1970s. Nevertheless, Western Australians have taken pride in 'the golden pipeline' for a century. 'O'Connor succeeded in pushing the limits of the technology of his day', said a modern engineer.[5] The people of Kalgoorlie and Boulder gave credit to the pipeline for their parks, swimming pools and efficient fire brigade service. Mundaring Weir water was essential for the permanent development of the city as a large residential regional centre, as well as the smaller towns en route. It seems no coincidence that industrial strife and militancy were less common in Kalgoorlie than in Broken Hill, though water was not the only factor.

Bold public works had to compete with the great strains placed on Western Australia's social services by a population increase of more than 400 per cent between 1891 and 1901. Nowhere was the pressure felt more than in the colony's education system, already suffering from what has been described as 'parsimony and discrimination'.[6] Ill-paid teachers worked in often substandard classrooms with children of a wide range of ages and ability. There were only two fee-paying high schools for boys and one, closed in 1887, for girls. Rich families sent their sons for higher education to Adelaide or Melbourne, or, less often, to English public schools. With an increase in school enrolments from 5,000 in 1890 to more than 25,000 in 1901, the situation bordered on the chaotic. The government gradually took a grip on the crisis with the creation of the Education Department in 1893 and the appointment in 1896, as director and inspector-general, of the London-trained Cyril Jackson. A young dynamo, Jackson in six years provided Western Australia's schools with their first solid foundations. The number of state primary schools trebled, the imposition of school fees and the payment of teachers by results were abolished, and specialist institutions were set up, including the Perth Technical School, a progressively coeducational teachers' training college at Claremont, and schools for the blind and deaf and dumb.[7]

Parallel with the increase in state schools went the growth of the Catholic education system. In 1895, after a protracted wrangle, the government ceased to fund private (largely Catholic) schools, partly to fall into line with the other Australian colonies but also as a result of a campaign by Protestants who found a spokesman in Winthrop Hackett. Forrest kept the critics at bay as long as possible, partly to win the Catholic vote but also because he believed 'that all churches are languishing in this colony; nearly all of them were in debt and had the greatest difficulty in finding money to carry on their work'.[8] The Catholic bishop, Matthew Gibney, responded with a herculean program of building, recruiting staff from Ireland. The Presentation and Dominican sisters set up convent schools in the country towns and goldfields; the Christian and Marist brothers saw to the needs of the boys and groomed the brightest for white-collar occupations—another contribution to the Western Australian belief in opportunity for male talent. Other denominations followed on a lesser scale, concentrating on secondary education for the better-off. Guildford Grammar School dates from the initiative of Charles Harper in 1895; Scotch College, from 1897. A mushroom growth of small private schools mostly failed to survive, but one of the most successful, Miss Parnell's Claremont Girls' High School, throve to provide the nucleus for the modern St Hilda's. In 1901 an Anglican sisterhood founded Perth College for Girls, with the Methodist Ladies College following in 1907.[9]

In these years the churches consolidated their role as the government's essential auxiliary in providing social welfare. The Anglicans and the Catholics had managed orphanages near Perth since 1868, but demand escalated as thousands arrived during the 1890s. In the belief that children fared better away from an inner-city environment, the Anglicans established a home at Parkerville in the Darling Range, and

the Catholics founded Clontarf on the Canning River. To supplement
the overburdened public hospital system in Perth and the goldfields came
Catholic and Anglican sisterhoods, while in 1902 the Sisters of the Good
Shepherd arrived to establish a refuge for handicapped or wayward young
women—waywardness embracing anything from a life of prostitution
to parental exasperation. Juvenile delinquency and drink were also two
major concerns for a newcomer to the provision of social welfare, the
Salvation Army, which, although at first regarded askance, soon won
community acceptance. In 1899 the Forrest government granted it more
than 11,000 hectares for an industrial school at Collie for youths at risk.[10]

In addition to promoting welfare, the churches also stretched their
resources to provide places of worship in the rapidly growing suburbs
and country towns. The recruitment of clergy was a constant problem.
Old ethnicities were reinforced as Bishop Gibney's efforts in Ireland
were matched by those of the Anglican bishop Charles Riley to attract
young Englishmen, preferably university graduates with a stamp of
'muscular Christianity'. For many families, churchgoing attested to
respectability. On Sundays, Stephen Henry Parker and his wife, parents
of a numerous family, 'led a procession of frock coats, voluminous skirts
and picture hats to St George's Cathedral'. They were unique only in
their social prominence.[11]

Sunday afternoons could be devoted to healthy recreation. The
Forrest government enhanced Perth's cultural amenities with a public art
gallery built in 1895 and zoological gardens opened in 1898, both of them
benefiting from the energising influence of Winthrop Hackett. The Art
Gallery of Western Australia fared better in its early years than it would
for another half-century, with a purchase fund three times as large as
that of its Victorian counterpart and a policy of acquiring contemporary
Australian works such as Frederick McCubbin's *Down on his Luck*.[12]
Middle-class Western Australians, in increasing numbers, spent their
leisure in tennis, golf, or yachting on the Swan River. Commercial
spectator sports were not permitted to disturb the Sabbath calm, but
the working class kicked footballs or played scratch games of cricket,
and many enjoyed Perth's beaches, although it would be some years
into the twentieth century before the segregation of men and women
swimmers came to an end.

The majority of the new arrivals who crowded into Western Australia during the 1890s hoped to establish homes of their own with families. Often the breadwinner arrived first, sending for wife and children as soon as he had saved enough money, though for some the sociability of the pub put that ideal into jeopardy. Others, such as the father of the future Governor-General William McKell, never sent for their families at all, but in some cases settled down with a new partner.[13] Even when reunited, families often endured a period of living in tents or other makeshift quarters. The building trade could not keep up with demand, although reinforced by hundreds of carpenters, bricklayers and other skilled artisans thrown out of work by the collapse of the Victorian land boom. During the 1890s, Perth's rents were probably the highest of any Australian capital. Many newcomers eventually built their own houses, simple four-roomed weatherboard cottages roofed with corrugated iron, often with a detached kitchen and laundry. At the rear of the property, a sentry-box earth-closet provided sanitation, though some houses lacked even this amenity. The backyard served as playground for the children, and space for a fowl yard to provide eggs and the occasional Sunday dinner, and often a fruit tree or two—lemon, almond or loquat. Most houses, even in working-class suburbs, had a central passage and verandahs for coolness. Terrace houses were few. For those who could afford it, brick was favoured over weatherboard as a building material, though only the more affluent chose orange Marseilles tiles instead of iron roofing. A patchwork of councils created haphazardly during the 1890s did their best to maintain standards, but they were too under-resourced to do much.[14]

In the Perth metropolitan area, the demand for housing brought into being a string of suburbs along the Fremantle–Perth railway, as well as Bayswater, Bassendean and Midland to the east, and North and South Perth. Unfortunately, no new suburban railways were built to service this growth. Two gas companies provided power, and a private entrepreneur's electricity plant served part of the western suburbs, but it was 1899 before central Perth got electricity and tramways, one year later than Kalgoorlie. Private enterprise also supplied central Perth with piped water after 1891, but the quality was poor and the supply unevenly distributed. The great growth in population during the 1890s strained the system almost to breaking point. Inadequate waste disposal and water supply were blamed for an upsurge in typhoid. In 1895, 566 cases were reported in Perth, of whom seventy died. The Forrest government purchased the waterworks in 1896, but the situation deteriorated further during the following summer, especially in new and working-class suburbs where pipes had not been laid and housewives had to rely on a few wells and an irregular municipal water cart. A visiting Melbourne journalist commented that Perth was as dirty as the worst of Asian ports: 'It would be no use hosing Perth; it requires to be blown up and not rebuilt'. Only in 1898, when chairmanship of the board of management passed to the ex-Wesleyan minister and temperance advocate William 'Water on the brain' Traylen, were the reservoirs enlarged and mains extended to the most built-up areas.[15]

Because of the importance of Western Australian forests in ensuring a pure water supply, Traylen was an early advocate of their conservation, but his pleas fell largely on deaf ears. In 1896 the Forrest government created a Department of Woods and Forests, with the highly experienced John Ednie-Brown as its head, but Ednie-Brown's brief focused on the production of marketable timber. Although he energetically initiated the planting of softwoods and sandalwood, he did little to challenge the existing emphasis on exploiting the jarrah and karri resources of the South West, and in the 1890s, under the entrepreneurship of M. C. Davies and others, this trade was reaching its zenith. From Bunbury, from Davies's own ports at Hamelin Bay and Flinders Bay, millions of cubic feet of felled timber departed each year, bringing an export income of more than £500,000 by the turn of the century. Western Australians felt pride that jetties made of their timber defied the teredos of India, and the swarming traffic of the City of London rumbled along streets supported by the former giants of the South West.[16]

Native timber seemed a reliable source of fuel and energy at this time of strong economic growth. On the Kalgoorlie goldfields, mining machinery would soon have ground to a halt but for the consumption of an estimated million and a half tonnes of salmon gum and other timbers annually in the boilers and steam engines of deep mines.[17] The extension of underground mining called for reliable timber props. Cheap firewood warmed the hearth and fuelled the kitchens and laundries of private homes across Western Australia; many families collected their own. Coal had been sought since the earliest years of settlement, but the only commercially viable deposit, located at Collie by Arthur Perrin in 1883 and David Hay in 1888, was of second-rate quality. It was nevertheless good enough for the Western Australian railways, and by 1898 three Collie mines were at work, with an assured local market.[18] The South West was developing a considerable mining sector, since from 1888 useful deposits of tin were worked at Greenbushes, 70 kilometres south-east of Bunbury, and in 1899 there was a short-lived gold rush at Donnybrook. Nowhere yet was there a satisfactory answer to the need for cheap fuel and energy to underpin future industrial growth, and this would remain a central question in Western Australia for many years into the twentieth century.

Even without such a source of energy, the gold rush gave a great stimulus to local manufacturing. Curiously little of this progress resulted from investment by those who had won spectacular wealth on the goldfields. The newly rich tended to reinvest in real estate and further mining ventures rather than capitalising new industries. Several squandered their gains on conspicuous consumption. William Brookman, an Adelaide bankrupt who rose to wealth through the Great Boulder bonanza, 'bought much land, acquired a country estate, a seaside cottage, a private yacht, and a motor car and lived in a town mansion with a suite of liveried servants'.[19] He claimed to have secured the investment of £35 million in Western Australia and established fifty-two mines. He became a member of the Legislative Council and briefly Mayor of Perth, with sweeping ambitions for his adopted city, but by 1904 he was poor once more. A more public-spirited character, Alfred Morgans, was briefly Premier. He owned a steam yacht, on which he entertained the justices of the High Court on their first visit to Perth in 1903, and tried to acclimatise fallow deer on his grazing property in the Porongurups, but saved little for his old age. Another Great Boulder investor, Eugenio Vanzetti, like Anthony Hordern before him, dreamed of forming a colony of 300 Italian farmers and vignerons, and actually settled twenty-five peasants on an estate near Northam. In 1898 he opened Perth's finest cafe, the Alhambra, and promoted companies to crush and transport ore from the goldfields. Then his overstretched empire collapsed, leaving a residue of anti-Italian feeling that prompted a royal commission in 1904.[20]

Most industrial progress resulted from more modest enterprises. By the financial year 1900–01, Western Australia's manufacturing output stood at £3,562 million, or about 5.5 per cent of the Australian total. Crowley has calculated that by 1904, 'Some 13,000 people were employed in tanneries, soap and candle works, brickyards, lime kilns, flourmills, aerated-water and cordial factories, boot and leather shops, and in gasworks'.[21] These years saw the establishment of family firms specialising in construction materials and engineering, such as Bunnings, Mallochs and Tomlinsons, who would enjoy local prominence for decades. Such factories, nearly all on a modest scale, could be found in many country towns, as well as scattered among the houses in the Perth metropolitan area. A good deal of simple agricultural machinery was manufactured locally, some of it innovatively adapted for regional conditions. One or two enterprising attempts were made at the use of local resources, such as Jonah Parker of Dangin's venture into the manufacture of eucalyptus oil for several years in the 1890s. Inventive citizens of Western Australia in those years included William Hancock, government electrical engineer and pioneer of radiology; Herbert Akroyd Stuart, probably the inventor of the diesel engine; and, a little later, Alfred Alcock, who produced a working model of a hovercraft in 1921 but lacked financial backing.[22] As in Victoria, it looked as if the gold rush might be followed by industrial advance, provided that, as in Victoria, the infant industries enjoyed substantial tariff protection. This was not to be. By choosing to enter the common market of a federated Australian Commonwealth as a founder member on 1 January 1901, Western Australians gave themselves access to many future benefits, but they doomed their secondary industries to decades of stagnation.

It was by no means inevitable that Western Australia would join the Commonwealth. New Zealand stayed out, partly because Australia was too distant. The metropolitan area of Western Australia was even further away by sea from Sydney and Melbourne. Both colonies, as well as Fiji, were invited to join when a loosely knit Federal Council was set up in 1883. The Federal Council met every two years in Hobart to discuss matters of common concern and, when policies were agreed, to recommend them to the individual colonial parliaments. Its influence was limited because some colonies, notably New South Wales, did not join. Western Australia was among the most faithful in attending during the council's decade and a half of activity, perhaps because membership of such a body reduced the sense of isolation. This did not mean that any closer scheme of federation would be welcomed. In 1891 Western Australia took part in the first federal convention, but most of the seven Western Australian delegates, strangers to the politicians of other colonies and conscious of inexperience, said little in debate. One of them, Winthrop Hackett, told Edmund Barton that Forrest was the only leading Western Australian interested even in exploring the subject. Otherwise, he wrote, 'the feeling against amounts almost to madness'.[23]

Because Western Australia eventually voted by a large majority to enter the Commonwealth, 'the feeling against' has often been dismissed as the reaction of stick-in-the-mud 'sandgropers'. No doubt Western Australia contained many rural conservatives for whom even Sir John Forrest's reforms were too disturbing. But it was realistic to wonder whether Western Australia's industries, newly founded in the wake of the gold rush boom, could vie with longer-established competitors in eastern Australia, just as it was worrying that in any federation a remote and underpopulated Western Australia would lie far from the centres of economic and political power in the south-east. Although the draft constitution of 1891 annoyed Melbourne democrats by providing for a Senate in which each state would elect an equal number of members, it also left ultimate financial control in the House of Representatives, where Victoria and New South Wales would dominate. In any case, during the next few years Western Australia was too preoccupied with the gold rush, and the other colonies with their economic recession, to give much attention to constitutional reform.

In 1895 a conference of Australian premiers agreed that a second federal convention should take place. Instead of being nominated by the colonial parliaments, as in 1891, the delegates would be elected by the voters at large. Forrest and his ministers thought so much democracy unsafe at a time when the influx of newcomers to the goldfields made the outcome of a popular election uncertain. Queensland was also dubious, and at the Federal Council of January 1897 the Queensland

and Western Australian delegates made an unsuccessful proposal for the election of delegates to the Federal Council. This would have given that body a popular mandate but its decisions would still have to be ratified by the individual colonies or state parliaments, whereas there was no such check on the federal parliament under the untried draft constitution of 1891. The Western Australian Parliament then chose ten of their number, headed by Forrest, to attend the three sessions of the second federal convention in 1897–98. There they made a strong push to dump the mild restrictions on the Senate's powers agreed at the 1891 convention but were narrowly defeated because Queensland, who would have supported them, failed to send a delegation.[24] In the remaining sessions of the convention, none of the delegates except Forrest made a major contribution to debate, but their votes were essential in securing the acceptance of industrial arbitration as a federal power.[25] Only one concession was made to Western Australian interests. Instead of losing tariff protection overnight as a result of entering federation, Western Australia would be allowed to scale down its duties over five years until they were eventually eliminated.

Meanwhile, the Western Australian elections of 1897 returned Forrest comfortably for a third term. The Opposition, formally organised since 1895 under the locally born lawyer George Leake, was reinforced by a few goldfields members, but as yet political organisation on the Kalgoorlie and Murchison fields was neither strong nor polarised against the Forrest ministry. This changed in March 1898, when the ministry made a clumsy attempt to alter the alluvial mining regulations in a way that disadvantaged working prospectors. Confronted at his next visit to Kalgoorlie by a crowd of several thousand angry diggers, Forrest mishandled the situation. Although he escaped to his train with nothing worse than an accidental poke in the ribs from an umbrella, the incident was termed a riot. Political antagonism grew between the recently arrived 'tothersiders' and the 'ancient colonists'. Inspired by editors such as John Kirwan of the *Kalgoorlie Miner* and the longhaired radical Fred Vosper, the goldfields brooded on grievances. The railways were expensive and inefficient and centralised on Fremantle instead of using the closer port of Esperance. The tariffs on meat and produce hit the pockets of the goldfields consumers. The political system was rigged so that the pastoral north, with only a few dozen voters to each constituency, had as many seats in the Legislative Assembly as the goldfields with their thousands. Militancy stirred.[26]

Against this background, many Western Australians were understandably nervous about federating with an eastern Australia sympathetic to the 'tothersiders'. Forrest himself continued to assert that if Western Australia could make good terms, including the promise of a transcontinental railway, it should join the Commonwealth, but few of his colleagues and supporters were persuaded. If he lost some conservative supporters, Forrest meanwhile shored up his ministry by placating the urban liberals and the working class. Many of the food tariffs were cut in 1898. During 1899 and 1900 several measures of social reform were enacted. In 1899, having opposed three previous attempts, Forrest accepted a proposal to give some women the vote, thus endorsing an innovation adopted in few parts of the world and by New Zealand and South Australia alone among the Australasian colonies. Some saw this as opportunism, since women were more numerous in the conservative long-settled parts of Western Australia than on the goldfields.[27]

Other changes, however, suggest a genuine, if paternalistic, commitment in Forrest to social reform, as well as a concern to woo working-class voters. In 1898 the rights of workmen to secure their wages from tardy employers were much improved, with a proviso that manual workers were to be paid weekly unless an agreed written contract specified otherwise. Working hours in shops were limited, with a mandatory Saturday half-holiday. A 'truck' act passed in 1899 restricted the long-established practice of paying workers with goods from the company store rather than in cash. Although in earlier decades, when coin was in short supply, this had been a convenient means of paying workers in isolated communities such as the timber townships, employers could too easily exploit the system by overcharging. After a major waterside strike in 1899, Forrest pushed through the establishment of a court of industrial arbitration in 1900, even though this provoked the resignation of one of his cabinet. This did not entirely safeguard trade union officials—as late as October 1900 the secretary of the Shop Assistants' Union was imprisoned under the 1825 *Conspiracy Act* for urging workers to boycott hotels employing Asian labour—but it was an advance on the old masters and servants legislation. Even some democrats such as Vosper, although persistently critical of the Forrest government, began to argue that social reform could be effected more easily in an autonomous Western Australia than in a Commonwealth dominated by the businessmen of Melbourne and Sydney.[28]

The pressure on Western Australia mounted after mid-1899. By this time, the four south-eastern colonies had agreed to federate, and in September Queensland voted to join them. This left the West as the odd one out. Forrest submitted a proposal to parliament to authorise two plebiscites, one inviting the voters to endorse the proposed federal constitution as it stood, and the other supporting federation subject to four conditions, of which the construction of a transcontinental railway was at the head. The conservative Legislative Council rejected both plebiscites, leaving Forrest little room to manoeuvre. Building on an idea that had been in the wind for some time, the *Kalgoorlie Miner* and other goldfields media began to push the concept of 'Separation for Federation', the creation of a new autonomous colony that would join the Commonwealth. A 'monster meeting' at Coolgardie in December 1899 agreed to send a delegation to London to seek the support of the British Colonial Office. Shortly afterwards, the inhabitants of Albany, with a sure sense of parody, set up a movement of their own for the secession of their region as a reprisal for the Forrest government's bias towards Fremantle. Neither demand found favour with the British authorities, but the fear of goldfields secession was enough to push some waverers, such as Winthrop Hackett, into supporting Western Australia's entry into the Commonwealth as a founder member.[29]

Hackett's shift was important, as *The West Australian* was now establishing itself as the colony's leading newspaper. Sobering into conservatism, Hackett's editorials, though generally supportive of the Forrest government, did much to promote the myth of consensus as the desirable state of mind for Western Australians. In 1896 a potential rival emerged in the *Morning Herald*, a Perth daily pitching its appeal to 'tothersider' readers, but it never challenged the *West*'s pre-eminence. It was eventually purchased by the Catholic Church and shut down in 1909 after an ill-judged decision not to publish racing information. The *Inquirer* ceased publication in 1901, and its stablemate the *Daily News* found a niche as an afternoon daily, less formal than *The West Australian*. Fred Vosper moved down from the goldfields in 1897 to help establish the *Sunday Times*, a crusading, not to say muckraking, weekly modelled on John Norton's Sydney *Truth*. The *Sunday Times* and the Kalgoorlie *Sun*, established in 1898, bombarded the Forrest government and its associates with accusations of corruption, sometimes with exaggeration but often with the zeal of outsiders attacking the easygoing cronyism of a small-town elite suddenly rolling in money. The Governor, Sir Gerard Smith, was recalled to London when the press revealed that he had been promoting dubious goldfields properties: 'I can't have my governors booming mines', wrote Joseph Chamberlain, the Secretary of State for Colonies.[30] The critics were at their most aggressive early in 1900, when the independent Member for Geraldton, Richard Robson, was moved at a banquet to declare the Western Australian Government 'rotten and corrupt'. This offended the upholders of consensus. 'We don't want this firebrand coming among us', exclaimed Alexander Forrest, one of the main targets.[31] A select committee found Robson's charges unproven, and he resigned to leave Western Australia and join the South African police force, but the mud stuck. Later in 1900 the Opposition came within eight votes of toppling the Forrest ministry on a motion of no confidence.

Until *The West Australian* changed its mind, no major Perth newspaper supported federation. The proposed Commonwealth was not democratic enough for the *Sunday Times* and not careful enough of Western Australian interests for the others. The *Morning Herald*, through its leader writers Archibald Sanderson and Hal Colebatch, argued that as largely a primary producer, Western Australia stood to lose by integrating its economy with the tariff-protected industries of south-eastern Australia.[32] Thus originated a strand of 'dry' economic thought favouring minimal tariffs and limited government intervention in the economy, which through Colebatch, John Stone, John Hyde and others would form a persistent counterpoint to Australia's major economic orthodoxies during the twentieth century.

When the colony's politicians accepted the inevitable and scheduled a plebiscite on federation for the end of July 1900, it turned out that Hackett had gauged the public mood correctly. Among the mining communities of the goldfields and the North West, sentiment was solid for federation, and enough newcomers from the east had now settled in the Perth–Fremantle metropolitan area to swing a 'Yes' vote in those electorates. Rural Western Australia, with its preponderance of old 'sandgroper' families, strongly opposed the change, but the numbers lay with the city and the goldfields, and by 44,800 votes to 19,691 the verdict was 'Yes'. Rueful local patriots asserted that Forrest was pressured into federation by the British Government, but there is no evidence for this. The voters of Western Australia, including for the first time women, judged that the risks of staying out were greater than the hazards of joining the Commonwealth. If the inaugural celebrations on 1 January 1901 were somewhat muted in Perth, there were brass bands in Kalgoorlie and Boulder. Sir John Forrest was away in Sydney, taking his oath as a member of the first federal cabinet as a preliminary to the new career on the national stage that would take him tantalisingly close to the prime ministership of Australia and to the House of Lords.

He went just in time. New forces were arising to challenge old paternalism. During the 1890s, the status of women was advancing. It was only in 1892 that, at the third attempt, S. H. Parker succeeded in removing the law that compelled women at marriage to surrender all their property to their husband. In the same year, the first feminine pressure group came into being with the formation of a Perth branch of the Women's Christian Temperance Union. In a society where alcoholism was prevalent among all classes and a great harm to family values, this was a major social issue. In ensuing years a number of Perth's most prominent women, including Lady Onslow and on occasion Lady Forrest, formed themselves into a pressure group urging action on a number of social issues. Largely through such efforts, a home for unmarried mothers was established in 1894, supplementing the work of the Ministering Children's League founded three years earlier. Formally united in the Karrakatta Club, founded in 1895, but often banding together informally, these women perfected the art of lobbying. If women were awarded the vote in 1899 in the hope that they would prove a conservative influence, they could also be expected to keep male politicians keenly alert to matters of social conscience.[33]

The organised working class was also making its presence felt politically. During the boom years of the gold rush between 1892 and 1896, the Trades and Labour Council languished, as few spared energy for the labour movement. By 1897 city building workers had staged the colony's first abortive attempt at a major strike, and a builder was returned to the Legislative Assembly with a somewhat vague mandate as a labour representative. In 1899 the waterside workers staged a more successful five-week strike, eventually resolved by an arbitration tribunal comprising the Anglican and Catholic bishops and the chairman of the Methodist Conference. On the goldfields, workers with experience of unionism in Victoria and South Australia formed a separate vigorous Trades and Labour Council. The most powerful union, the Australian Workers Association, in April 1899 convened a congress at Coolgardie that brought the two regional trade union movements together. Their pressure did much to stimulate Forrest's compulsory arbitration legislation of 1900, and their influence showed at the elections for the first Commonwealth Parliament in March 1901, when two Labor Party men were returned to the Senate and two to the House of Representatives.[34]

At the state elections of 1901 (the first held since the introduction of a salary payment for members of parliament), six Labor members, all but one from the goldfields, found themselves holding the balance of power between George Throssell, Forrest's successor as Premier, and the less conservative Opposition, whom they supported. George Leake formed a ministry in May 1901 and, with one short break, precariously held office until his unexpected death in June 1902. He was succeeded by Walter James, probably Western Australia's nearest approach to a Deakinite liberal. Already notable as the foremost parliamentary advocate of votes for women, James put forward several constructive measures, including the opening of a school of mines in Kalgoorlie and the setting aside of a substantial amount of land as a university endowment. In 1903 he pushed through a *Prisons Act* improving the conditions in gaols. Building on the report of a parliamentary select committee of 1900 dominated by Frederic Vosper, the James government also legislated for substantial reforms in mental health care, including the building of a specialist institution at Claremont.[35] James was less successful with his industrial legislation because of obstruction by what he termed the 'Hippopotami of the upper house', while he was challenged from the other flank by an increasingly confident Labor Party. Because of the timely concessions

6

7

8

9   Convict stone-breakers sketched in Perth, 1867.

10   The Convict Establishment and officers' quarters, Fremantle, around 1870.

11   Fremantle Asylum for lunatics and aged women, now the Fremantle Arts Centre, taken in the 1870s.

12   Government House parade; Governor Hampton presents commissions to officers
      of the Western Australian Volunteers, 1863.

13   Bishop Hale's Perth Boys' School in St Georges Terrace, 1861.

14   Port George IV, site of the unsuccessful Camden Harbour settlement, 1864.

15   The eight members of Alexander Forrest's 1879 expedition to the Kimberley district.

16

17

18

16 Some things never change: the Weld Club in the 1890s.

17 A merchant prince of Fremantle: James Lilly 'father of Western Australian shipping' in the 1890s.

18 Governor Broome and official party arrive at Guildford for the turning of the first sod of the Midland Railway, 1886.

19 The *Arabella* loading wool from bullock wagons at Condon in the North-West, around 1895.

20 Sandalwood piled for shipment, possibly at Bluff Point near Geraldton.

made to them by the Forrest and James governments, Labor in Western Australia had not learned enough militancy to frighten away potential voters. A number of the old Forrest party aligned themselves behind James as the lesser evil, but after the 1904 election Labor numbers were much enlarged, so that the balance of power now lay with a handful of former Forrest supporters calling themselves the Independent Party. They decided in August 1904 to support a Labor government led by Henry Daglish. His team, inexperienced and divided by rifts between goldfields and city representatives, fell apart within twelve months. After the election in October 1905, it seemed that Western Australia was reverting to a classic two-party system, with a non-Labor government led by C. H. Rason confronting a diminished Labor Opposition.

These years of political musical chairs contrasted with the stability under Forrest, but in most respects there was a surprisingly high degree of continuity of policy between ministries. To a large extent, Forrest's blueprints were still guiding policy, especially regarding lands and agriculture. Inevitably, this fundamental continuity was disguised beneath noisy political skirmishing, whose chief victim was not a politician but the Engineer-in-Chief, C. Y. O'Connor. Incited by the *Sunday Times*, the Leake government set up a royal commission looking for corruption in the running of the goldfields pipeline scheme. O'Connor was not implicated but he may have been over-trusting of his subordinates. The pressure preyed on him and he committed a dramatic suicide.[36] Ten months later, on a blazing Kalgoorlie afternoon in January 1903, Sir John Forrest opened the scheme amid bipartisan rejoicings. 'The town was gaily decorated and lit with innumerable electric lights', reported a visitor; 'it was a wonderful gala night marred it is true by a murder and several accidents'.[37]

Perhaps in reaction to the experience of federation, the state governments in those years created a number of icons symbolising Western Australia's distinct political identity. A badly needed Supreme Court building was completed in 1903. Next year a half-completed Parliament House in West Perth was opened on the hill where Yellagonga of the Mooro used to camp in that era (still remembered by a few) when Governor Stirling and his company were newcomers. On a different level of self-assertion, the Western Australian Government embarked on the erection of a fence stretching more than 1,800 kilometres from Condon, near Onslow, to the south coast near Esperance, for the purpose of keeping out the hordes of introduced rabbits infesting the Eastern States. But no fence is proof against fools who leave gates open, and although a second and a third supplementary rabbit-proof fence followed, the scheme was a failure. In January 1903, even before the first fence was completed, a farmer at Cunderdin 150 kilometres east of Perth killed a rabbit and 'spoke glowingly of the relish he had for it for Sunday dinner'.[38] He was the first of many who would find 'underground mutton' a welcome addition to their diet in hard times. Within a few years, rabbits fed and cavorted throughout the agricultural South West, leaving the fence as a symbolic barrier to whatever plagues and nuisances might emanate from eastern Australia. Local pride was flattered when a Western Australian horse, Blue Spec, won the Melbourne Cup in 1905, but this was not enough to remove underlying sources of tension.

As Western Australia's tariff barriers against imports from the east vanished in 1906, the public mood soured, and in that year the Legislative Assembly resolved by nineteen votes to thirteen to seek secession from the Commonwealth.[39] The state government shelved the resolution, and for more than twenty years secession lay largely dormant as a political issue. It was never quite extinct, and its appeal is readily understood. After control by the remote British Government until 1890, Western Australians had only ten years of managing their own affairs, and those ten years chanced to coincide with the colony's most exciting and invigorating spurt of growth on all fronts. Then the West yielded authority to a federal government based in Melbourne, and later in Canberra, dominated by politicians and public servants with no innate sympathy for Western Australian perspectives. If the level of irritation with remote control was stimulated enough, Western Australians would remember the heady years of autonomy as evidence that they could do better on their own.

At least membership of the Australian Commonwealth enabled Western Australia to exclude unwanted immigrants more efficiently. Previously, the colonial government had not been overzealous in excluding non-European immigration, beyond profiting by experience elsewhere in Australia and imposing, ahead of any strife, a ban against Chinese on the goldfields. In the pearling industry, the Chinese were excluded from owning boats, but the Malays working in the fleet since the 1870s were reinforced after the introduction of deep-sea diving by Japanese, as well as some Indonesian and Filipino labour. Perth and the larger towns were home to a number of Chinese market gardeners, greengrocers, laundrymen and restaurateurs who provided useful service for many years. Most were without wives and families and expected in their old age to return to their native province. On the goldfields, Japanese prostitutes assuaged the sexual needs of all comers. 'Afghan' camel drivers, whom even the racist editors of the *Coolgardie Miner* would have accepted if they had not set a precedent for other non-Europeans, diversified into a number of other callings, including the provision of Perth's first nightwatchman service. None of these minorities settled in sufficient numbers to stir serious hostility, but as early as 1895 an Anti-Asiatic League at Coolgardie was calling for a ban on further alien immigration. By 1897 several members of parliament were demanding a total ban on the entry of non-Europeans into Western Australia. Knowing that the British authorities would not support this because of their Indian empire, Forrest preferred to adopt the 'Natal dictation test' fashioned in South Africa, requiring that any new arrival undergo a dictation test in any European language. This measure effectively stopped nearly all non-European immigration, except for some special arrangements for the pearling fleet, and formed a model for the Commonwealth's White Australia Policy in 1901.[40]

Sir John Forrest never tired of praising Western Australia as an outpost of the great British Empire, and demographically he was justified. At the 1901 census, 95 per cent of those counted had family origins in Great Britain and Ireland. Among the small minorities were several groups who would prove forerunners of significant elements in a future Western Australia. From 1890 a few dozen Greeks, mostly but not entirely from the Island of Castellorizo, settled in and around Perth. The goldfields attracted a modest but steady influx of Dalmatian Croats and Italians, some of whom became timbercutters and others mineworkers. One of these men, Modeste Varischetti, won fame in 1907 by surviving nine days after being trapped in an air-pocket deep in the unexpectedly flooded Lake View mine. Deep-sea apparatus was rushed from Perth to ensure his recovery, and in honour of his rescuer most Western

Australians surnamed Hughes were dubbed for decades afterwards with the nickname 'Diver'. As yet the presence of such minorities was not seen as presenting much risk of racial disharmony.[41]

Marginalised and intractable, there remained the question of Western Australia's Indigenous population. Even their numbers were uncertain, informed guesses varying from 15,000 to 30,000. Many considered that they conformed to the stereotype of a dying race. Daisy Bates, observing the process with ghoulish philanthropy, produced a graphic account of Fanny Balbek, whom she described as 'the last full-blood Mooro', stalking through houses and backyards as she followed the tracks travelled by her people before the city of Perth existed. In the South West, many Nyungar families, some with a settler parent or grandparent, kept a precarious independence through working as domestics, farmhands, fencers or horsebreakers. A few possessed small properties that they tried to work as well as they might without access to loans or capital. They were thwarted by the old prejudice that Aboriginal people 'did not know the value of money', just as their children were often blocked from attending primary school on the pretext that they could not be educated beyond a certain age or, in some cases, that other parents objected.[42]

Outside the South West and the goldfields, Aborigines could not be written off so easily. In the Murchison, Gascoyne and Pilbara districts, Aboriginal labour was a mainstay of the pastoral industry, though even after a generation of servitude their fidelity was not taken for granted. In 1906 the Marble Bar policeman reported that the district's Aborigines had acquired firearms and would quit work—a curious anticipation of the Pindan movement forty years later—but it was just a rumour.[43] Unlike the Maoris of New Zealand, hardly any Indigenous Australians used guns in resisting encroachment on their lands, although in the Kimberley district frontier conflict was still very much alive. Between 1894 and 1897, the former police tracker Jandamarra (alias Pigeon) took the leading part in Bunuba resistance to encroachment on their lands in the King Leopold Ranges, and this resistance was successful until Jandamarra and many others were killed.[44] The authorities, while rejecting the claim of pastoralists to the right to inflict their own justice, sent police to control the areas of conflict. Zeal for making arrests was fostered by the practice of paying constables a cash allowance for rations for Aborigines in custody. This at least provided an incentive for keeping suspects alive, and on the whole the police had an interest in reducing the level of frontier violence. From time to time, a file of inland Aborigines yoked by neck-chains would appear in Derby or Wyndham for trial for cattle-killing. Usually a term of exile in imprisonment on Rottnest followed. This reduced but did not eliminate unofficial episodes of racial homicide along the Ord. Nor was it enough to silence critics such as Walter Malcolmson, who published a series of letters in the London *Times* in 1901 that gave readers in the Mother Country a low opinion of Western Australian humanity. The James government responded by inviting the Queensland Chief Protector of Aborigines, a noted ethnographer, Walter Roth, to conduct a royal commission on the condition of Aboriginal Western Australians. Roth's report, tabled in 1905, recommended that reserves should be formed where Aboriginal people might be settled as wards of state. Intended as a protective measure, the Roth report would lead in practice to legislation that for more than half a century would block any hope of citizenship rights or equality of status for Western Australia's Aboriginal minority.[45]

So it was that Western Australians came to define themselves at the beginning of the twentieth century. They chose to share no identity with the Aboriginal inhabitants of their land and were perplexed at how to deal with people of mixed origin. They had no welcome for the inhabitants of those regions of Southeast and East Asia closest to them geographically, and little for immigrants from those Mediterranean countries of similar climate whose culture might have offered some enrichment of their own. Western Australians knew themselves to be citizens of their own state, of the federated Australian Commonwealth and of a wider British Empire. For many it is a fair guess that the first and last of these allegiances stood higher than their membership of a united Australia, as although the number of adult Western Australians born in Victoria and South Australia considerably exceeded the native 'sandgropers', it was not yet certain how many of the 'tothersiders' would settle permanently. Ironically, the year in which the pipeline reached Kalgoorlie was also the year when gold production peaked in Western Australia. After 1903 the returns began to fall, mushroom townships began to lose people and buildings, and departures from Western Australia increased until in

1907 they exceeded new arrivals. If Western Australia was not to lose many more, some compelling attraction must be found to keep them. To a generation brought up on the myth of a bold yeomanry, the answer was obvious. Heedless of environmental factors that they did not understand, Western Australia's public men invested their hopes in agriculture and, above all, in the farming of wheat.

5

Optimism dismayed, 1905–1918

The credit or otherwise for opening up the Western Australian Wheatbelt is usually given to two Bunbury men who grew up in the shadow and example of Sir John Forrest, replicating his agricultural enthusiasms, his blunt style of leadership, even his thickset physique. Newton Moore, a surveyor, was Premier from May 1906 to September 1910. His colleague, James Mitchell, a bank manager, less judicious in assessing country but even more zealous, served with him as Minister for Lands and Agriculture. Unlike Forrest, neither on taking office had any personal experience of the world outside Western Australia, and they took for granted the local orthodoxy that bringing land under cultivation was the noblest work of man. Their timing was singularly blessed. In 1901 William Farrer, after years of experiment, produced a drought-resistant variety of wheat, Federation, suitable for areas such as the inland South West, with a winter rainfall of between 250 and 400 millimetres. At the same time, a number of firms led by Cuming Smith began the aggressive marketing of superphosphate, a cheaper and more convenient fertiliser than the dwindling stock of locally produced guano. This facilitated wheat-growing on the large tracts of sandplain and scrubplain east of the Avon River. Where Forrest had predicted that, with reliable water, this country would support graziers and 'probably farmers', a more optimistic scenario could now be plotted.

Since 1892 a few farmers had already ventured beyond the Avon Valley, and the completion of the Coolgardie pipeline promised a valuable supplement to its uncertain water supplies. Unlike New South Wales and Victoria, where entrenched squatters put up fierce resistance to the inroads of 'cocky' farmers, the pastoral leases east of the Avon had been used only for winter grazing and were resumed without provoking claims for heavy compensation. Smallholders such as Jane Adams of 'Mangowine' were allowed to select freehold homestead blocks.[1]

Responding to more realistic estimates of carrying capacity, the authorities increased the standard size of a farming block from the 160 acres (65 hectares) of Forrest's legislation to 1,000 acres (405 hectares) of first-class land or 2,000 acres (810 hectares) of second-class. Novice farmers could draw on advice from an expanded state Department of Agriculture led by competent directors William Lowrie (1908–12) and George Sutton (1912–37). For many, especially after the Department of Agriculture's journal ceased publication in 1909, the most important source of information remained the *Western Mail* and its respected agricultural editor, Catton Grasby. In each district, care was taken to distribute land fairly among applicants, who had to pass the scrutiny of a Land Board of experienced farmers. Ex-miners from Kalgoorlie or the Murchison competed with retrenched civil servants, government-sponsored unemployed labourers, and younger sons of South Australian farming families looking for opportunities no longer easy in their own state. Not a few city businessmen, among them two mayors of Perth, John Henry Prowse and Sydney Stubbs, saw in middle age the chance of a second career. The new lands attracted a multinational work force to an extent that might surprise modern readers. The population of Quairading in its early years included Germans, Scandinavians, Croats, Italians, a Turkish labourer, a Greek fishmonger, Indian hawkers and several Chinese. In 1906–08 the Italian consul in Perth proposed to sponsor groups from northern Italy to settle in the Great Southern region, but the state government threw cold water on the plan, mistrusting the Italians' political leanings.[2]

Every contract surveyor in Western Australia and their teams found employment mapping out land for subdivision into farms. At first Crown land near existing railway lines was surveyed for settlement. As demand grew, successive governments laid a network of railways stretching eastward. Between 1904 and 1919, government railways increased from less than 2,500 kilometres to 5,600. All the new farming communities clamoured for railways, and politicians were judged by their skill in securing them. The narrow-gauge lines were built cheaply and hastily, using sleepers of local timber; sometimes the gangs constructing the railway from York to Bruce Rock achieved a mile (1.6 kilometres) a day. This stored up problems of maintenance for the future, as well as making for slow services. For decades the Western Australian Government Railways acronym, WAGR, was construed as 'Walk and Go Rapidly'. As well, steam locomotives sometimes threw out sparks that set fire to pastures and crops, and required large quantities of water, thus increasing demand in a region not well provided by nature.

Few pondered how the water resources of the Wheatbelt would be affected by the clearing of so many thousands of hectares of salmon gum, York gum and gimlet from the face of the land, but the warning signs began early. By 1910 the Blackwood River at Bridgetown had become too brackish for use in steam locomotives, the result of clearing around its upstream headwaters in the wheat country. Eager for quick returns and conforming to government regulations, pioneer farmers chopped down as many trees as they could in the shortest possible time. With axe alone, a strong, skilful worker could clear up to an acre a day (about 0.4 of a hectare), although the process of stacking and burning was a much slower job. All through the expanding wheat frontier, burning operations in late summer 'darkened the sky with smoke by day and left myriads of twinkling log-fires at night'.[3]

Timber was everywhere regarded as a crop to be harvested before the long-term cultivation of pasture and fields of grain turned Western Australia into an acceptable model of agricultural landscapes. Few questioned the exploitation of the superb hardwoods of the South West. It was an index of community attitudes that while competent directors of agriculture oversaw the opening of the Wheatbelt, the position of conservator of forests was left unfilled for seventeen years after the death of Ednie-Brown in 1899. Sailing ships crowded Bunbury harbour for cargoes of timber for several years after the turn of the century, but the jarrah and karri industries were encountering problems. After storms pounded his port at Hamelin Bay in 1899 and 1900, M. C. Davies was no longer paramount in the industry, meeting competition from the railway contractors C. and E. Millar and other rivals. In 1902 'Little Napoleon', Henry Teesdale Smith, the Western Australian manager for Millars, brokered the amalgamation of eight timber companies, who became known as 'the Combine'. Their price fixing soon provoked complaint from smaller firms. The wasteful practices of contract sleeper-hewers serving the railways disturbed the conservation-minded. In 1903–04 a royal commission, chaired by the experienced Charles Harper, successfully recommended a stricter and fairer system of permits for timbercutting, but the market continued to decline. The much-enduring timber workers, whose lives already followed the pattern portrayed some years later in Katharine Susannah Prichard's *Working Bullocks*, soon learned militancy. A three-month strike in 1907 gave them a higher minimum wage and recognition of their federal union. The Labor ideal was moving out of the goldfields and suburbs and into the bush. In response to the mobilisation of shearers by the Australian Workers Union, the Pastoralists Association of Western Australia was formed in 1907.[4]

For the first two-thirds of the twentieth century, Western Australia would be dominated by a rural ethos. Of twelve state premiers between 1906 and 1971, none represented a constituency from Perth and its suburbs. Labor drew support from the goldfields and regional ports, while its opponents' strength lay in the agricultural heartland. Government expenditure would give priority to rural infrastructure: first railways, then the provision of primary schools, hospitals, police and other services. Postal communications, telegraphs and, later, telephones were the responsibility of the Commonwealth Government. These taxpayer-funded initiatives, accompanied by the arrival of storekeepers, butchers and bakers, gave population to the townships that sprang up along the railways, usually at intervals of 15 or 20 kilometres—the distance convenient for return journeys between towns in one day by a farming family in a horse and buggy. Without the modern conveniences of telephone, radio and television, isolation pressed hard on the pioneer farmers. Many had to cart water for long distances for even the most basic domestic needs.

Underpinning the expansion of the Wheatbelt lay the overseas credit rating of the State of Western Australia. Despite one or two minor excitements such as the discovery of Paynes Find in 1911 and the Bullfinch rush on the Yilgarn in 1912, the glory days of goldmining were over, but Western Australian governments could still borrow. The vision of Western Australia as a new granary for the British Empire struck a sympathetic chord with London investment houses, although it was only one among a number of agricultural frontiers opening up between 1900 and 1914, competing with Siberia and the western provinces of Canada. Successive agents-general in London, usually ex-premiers, built up a close relationship with the firm of Nivisons, which specialised in placing loans for Australian states. Western Australia's public debt grew from £13 million in 1901 to £34 million in 1914, most of it poured into the development of the Wheatbelt. Nor were the investors the only members of the British public to respond to the promise of Western Australia. The image of the British Empire as lands of opportunity for the young and enterprising never glowed brighter than in the years between 1909 and 1914. Pride in the colonising mission of Empire reinforced perceptions that South Africa, Rhodesia, New Zealand and the prairie provinces of Canada all promised prosperous and healthy futures for the vigorous migrant prepared to work hard and produce the food and primary products that the Old Country required. In this 'swarming of the hive', as British emigration rose to new heights, Western Australia seemed an attractive destination.

In the five years before the outbreak of war in 1914, 30,000 assisted or nominated immigrants, nearly all from the British Isles, arrived to seek their fortunes in 'the Golden West'. The young idealist Kingsley Fairbridge, seeking an environment where boys from the urban slums of Britain might make a new start, found his answer in 1912 by starting a farm colony north of Pinjarra.[5] Many of those who migrated were young, single men, and some remained in Perth to become future leaders of the business community. Tom Ahern from County Cork was to found one of the city's longest-lasting emporia. Harry Hearn from Newcastle was to become a major furniture retailer and member of parliament. Harry Howard from Nottingham was to catch the growing demand for electrical goods and radios in the 1920s and 1930s, ending up as a dominant Lord Mayor of Perth. Most migrants did as expected and went on the land, where their inexperience and lack of local knowledge made a sure recipe for hardship. And not all were young, single men. My grandparents, arriving in 1912 with three children and twelve shillings and sixpence in cash, had to adapt quickly to bush skills to scratch a living in the Pingelly district. After two years, my grandfather went back to his proper job as a clerk and the family survived, the men pleased with their axemanship and the women with a wealth of household skills. But some were less lucky.

A modern economic historian has argued that, instead of sinking borrowed capital into immigration and loss-making railways, it would have been sounder policy for Western Australian governments to back the rehabilitation of the goldmining industry.[6] This would have required a spirit of cooperation new to the hardy individualists who managed the mines of Kalgoorlie and the Murchison. Besides, experience elsewhere in Australia suggested that most mining communities were impermanent, destined for speedy decay when the easily accessible ore gave out. Western Australia seemed no exception. Between 1901 and 1911 the population of towns such as Coolgardie, Broad Arrow and Kanowna fell by half, though few could have predicted that Kanowna, a city of several thousand inhabitants in its prime, with four breweries and six brass bands, would utterly cease to exist by 1960. Weatherboard halls and churches in moribund goldfields communities were taken down for rebuilding in the new country towns and suburbs.

Even Kalgoorlie lost much of its panache. There were still cultural and educational achievements to boast of. Boulder City's brass band twice won the prize as Australia's best. Goldfields primary schools produced scholarship winners. The Sisters of St Joseph provided education fit to launch the career of a world-famous concert pianist, Eileen Joyce. But one by one, professional men and business leaders departed for greener pastures, and Kalgoorlie concentrated on survival. So it happened that unlike eastern Australia, where substantial provincial cities such as Launceston, Rockhampton and Ballarat throve to develop their own distinctive character, Western Australia had little significant urban culture outside the city of Perth. And Perth, now that federation had stunted its potential for secondary industry, was all too well aware that its prosperity and growth depended upon its role as supply and service centre for the farmers.[7]

Retailers attracted to Western Australia by the gold rush of the 1890s carried much of this trade. All of them developed extensive mail-order businesses in response to the expansion of the Wheatbelt. Boans Limited was founded by Harry Boan and his brother, who had begun as kerbside pedlars in Broken Hill. They set up business in 1895 in a single-storey wooden building in an unfashionable and somewhat swampy quarter of Wellington Street, calculating rightly that its situation opposite the central railway station would bring customers from the expanding suburbs. In twenty years, Boans was Perth's leading emporium, manufacturing its own furniture, noted for the elegance of its tea-rooms, and drawing a large clientele from town and country. Nearby, William Baird and his brothers and sisters pitched a successful appeal to rural customers by establishing an enlarged version of the old-fashioned country store, stocking merchandise of every description. A more direct challenge to Boans was offered by the Eastern States–based firm of Foy and Gibson, whose emporium established in 1896 came to cover an entire block between St Georges Terrace and Hay Street. Outstripping all these in its volume of rural trade was the firm of Metters, originating in South Australia. For half a century after 1896, Metters provided the windmills, the wood stoves, the troughs and hardware and much else of the essential infrastructure for country farms and families. It also did good business in the metropolitan area, and in the 1920s, when gas stoves became available, the Metters 'Early Kooka' was a godsend to the housewives who could afford them.[8]

With a not unpleasurable awareness of its status as the most isolated city in the civilised world, Perth in the early years of the twentieth century was an adolescent city, part overgrown country town, part young metropolis. St Georges Terrace, by now established as the main business thoroughfare, boasted an attractive streetscape of office blocks, churches and hotels, none more than a few storeys tall and most reflecting that turn-of-the-century stylistic confidence known as 'Ballarat baroque'. It was not yet a thoroughly urbanised environment. Perth's citizens enjoyed the foresight that had preserved a thousand acres (400 hectares) of secondary bush as Kings Park, immediately to the west of the central business district. They liked to imagine that when the easterly blew strongly on spring mornings, strollers in the Terrace could scent the wildflowers on Darling Range. They spoke less often of the interruption to traffic when drovers walked their livestock through the city streets on the way to market.

This kind of incongruity between the aspirations of a modern city and the survivals of a recent bucolic past was not uncommon. Sir John and Lady Forrest's residence in Hay Street, 'The Bungalow', was an imposing home fit for an elder statesman, but at its rear in Murray Street Aborigines in rags still sat about waiting for a yarn with the old man, and the nearby properties were mean cottages. Some indeed were brothels until around 1905, when the authorities persuaded their operators to move to a less central position. (Around that time, the *Sunday Times* estimated that Perth contained more than sixty brothels.) For the next fifty years, commuters on trains leaving West Perth station could not avoid eyeing a modest collection of single-storey houses of ill repute at one end of Roe Street. At the other end lay the central police headquarters, and from time to time uniformed officers would take a stroll down the street to ensure that the premises were run in an orderly fashion with due regard for hygiene.[9]

Some boasted that Perth had no slums, but in the two hustling decades since the finding of Coolgardie's gold in 1892, the metropolitan area grew hastily, with insufficient planning and a good deal of social stratification. The rich tended to cluster around riverside views. Adelaide Terrace to the east of the central business district was gradually losing favour to the higher environment of West Perth, especially Mount Street. A number of businessmen and semi-retired pastoralists preferred Peppermint Grove and Claremont, riverside suburbs halfway to Fremantle. White-collar workers, artisans and skilled tradesmen could be found in neat weatherboard houses, often owner-built, on quarter-acre blocks in suburbs with reasonable public transport such as Subiaco, Maylands and North Perth. It was easy for recent migrants, accustomed to the less spacious housing of the British Isles, to succumb to the Australian dream of home ownership. Until the establishment of the Commonwealth Bank in 1913, banks were still reluctant to enter the field of housing finance. In their place, the long-established Perth Building Society and more recent cooperatives such as the Starr-Bowkett Society provided the thrifty and provident with credit.[10] Much depended on the capacity of the family breadwinner to avoid death or incapacity, and with the average male life expectancy at 53 years, this was a risk, but it was a risk that many families were prepared to take.

In suburbs of a pronounced working-class character such as Midland Junction and Bassendean, with their high proportion of breadwinners from the railway workshops, or the environs of Fremantle, where waterside workers and their families lived, the urge for owner-occupancy was scarcely weaker. Closer to the centre of Perth, the houses sat on narrower blocks and the streets were meaner. A rookery south of the West Perth railway station would be swept away in the 1920s to provide space for the metropolitan produce markets. In the streets north of the railway, later to be transformed into the modern Northbridge, the ethnic minorities settled. The ageing Chinese were still eyed askance as opium smokers of dubious morality, although the formation of their Chung Wah Association after China became a republic in 1912 suggested a stronger sense of good citizenship. They coexisted peacefully with a growing number of neighbours of Greek or Italian origin.

A driving force promoting the orderly development of Perth was its Town Clerk (chief executive officer) from 1900 to 1944, William Bold.[11] Appointed by a Mayor of limited staying power but grand vision, who spoke of making Perth 'a fairer Athens and a nobler Rome', Bold looked to the examples of Joseph Chamberlain's Birmingham and the English 'Garden City' movement as models for Perth to follow. He was another who doubted the capacity of unregulated private enterprise to plan effectively for the public wellbeing. In 1908 he persuaded the Perth City Council to acquire the Perth Gas Company, which produced both gas and electricity: 'a costly and controversial purchase at the time, it eventually proved a valuable asset to the city'. He hoped also to municipalise Perth's tramway system, but in 1912 the state government outbid the city council. His outstanding ambition was to persuade the state government to legislate for the amalgamation of the metropolitan area's jigsaw of local authorities into a single 'Greater Perth', which, like the London County Council, could practise economies of scale in planning and the provision of services. This ideal has only been achieved once in Australia—in Brisbane in the 1920s—but it was not unrealistic at Perth's stage of development. Governments fixated on rural growth failed to put enough support behind Bold's dream, and although between 1914 and 1917 the suburbs of North Perth, Leederville and Victoria Park were to come in with the Perth City Council, the local government boundaries of Greater Perth remained piecemeal and illogical.[12]

In defining their sense of place, many residents of Perth and its suburbs found local government less important than sporting allegiances, especially in districts with a strong working-class culture. Australian Rules football was dominated by the East Fremantle club in the first decade of the twentieth century, although South Fremantle, with its strong following among waterside workers, often ran close. Before long, challenges came from other teams such as East Perth, owing its origins to local factory workers, and Subiaco, drawing on a strong artisan culture. Curiously, a Midland Junction side, supported by the railway workshops, never did well and failed to survive World War I, though it may be seen as an ancestor of the later Swan Districts club.[13] The professional classes took full advantage of local opportunities for yachting and golf, and all sectors of the community were learning to enjoy the Indian Ocean beaches. Surf lifesaving was established at Cottesloe by 1908, and the old restrictions on mixed-gender bathing crumbled a few years later. Meanwhile, the state government was promoting holiday resorts outside the Perth metropolitan region. Rottnest, although continuing to serve as an Aboriginal prison (and, during the two world wars, as an internment camp for aliens), was beginning to win popularity as a holiday resort. In the South West the government subsidised the construction of a hotel at Yallingup, where honeymoon couples and other tourists might enjoy the scenery and take conducted tours through the nearby caves. After a vigorous campaign urged by the conservationist J. G. Hay, the Stirling Ranges were listed as a national park in 1913.[14]

The state government of this period had inherited from Forrest a tradition of pragmatic intervention in social issues, but the Legislative Council often blocked its efforts. Adhering to the fiction of freedom from party allegiances, its increasingly conservative members resisted Newton Moore's attempts to introduce Western Australia's first land and income taxes in 1907, compromising only with an understanding that rates would be kept low. The ministry's representative in the Legislative Council, James Connolly, meanwhile effected a series of social reforms between 1906 and 1911. To lessen the frontier conflict in the Kimberley district resulting from Aboriginal spearing of cattle, Connolly created a government pastoral station, 'Moola Bulla', where Aborigines were encouraged to settle, with the assurance of adequate provisions. To meet the great strain placed on hospital capacity by cases of tuberculosis, a widespread ailment among ex-miners, a makeshift sanatorium was set up at Coolgardie in 1907. This was to be replaced by a custom-built sanatorium at Wooroloo in the hills east of Perth, but it remained 'a place of "last resort" rather than a curative and educative facility'.[15]

Many of Connolly's initiatives reflected the growing belief among Western Australians in peopling the state with healthy children reared in supportive family environments. The creation of a Department of Child Welfare in 1907 was followed by the establishment of specialised children's courts and a children's hospital (now Princess Margaret Hospital). Connolly also commenced work on a government maternity hospital, later King Edward Memorial Hospital, though it was not completed until 1916. Largely through Connolly's insistence, in 1911–12 Western Australia acquired what was then the most advanced pure foods legislation in Australia. In 1911 Connolly also gave encouragement to the ideas of a Kindergarten Union, promoting the concept of preschool education along lines already established in South Australia. With the support of a number of prominent citizens, the first free kindergarten was opened near the Perth central business district in May 1912. Demand soon ensured that others followed.[16]

Connolly's reforms were supported and often stimulated by a reinvigorated women's movement. Most of its leading figures, such as Edith Cowan, Bessie Rischbieth, Dr Roberta Jull and Lady James, were members of the Karrakatta Club and wives of prominent professional men, and when they spoke on matters of social welfare these women commanded respect. They established the Children's Protection Society in 1906 and its day nursery for the children of working mothers. To improve the coordination of fund-raising and lobbying, most of them joined in forming the Women's Service Guild in 1909 and the Western Australian chapter of the National Council of Women in 1911. Unhappily, the two organisations were to split in 1915 over the policing of venereal disease during World War I. One faction, led by Edith Cowan, supported compulsory notification of the disease and went with the National Council of Women; Bessie Rischbieth and her supporters disagreed and stayed with the Women's Service Guild. Both continued as prominent pressure groups, but perhaps with diminished effect.[17]

Under Moore and his successor, Frank Wilson (Premier 1910–11), plans were made to bring educational opportunity to older children. Stimulated by the state director of education, Cecil Andrews, the government authorised the creation of Perth Modern School, a secondary school whose students would be admitted after qualifying at a state-wide examination taken in the final year of primary school. This was consciously designed as a ladder of opportunity for able children of limited family means, and drew criticism from headmasters of private fee-paying schools, who complained of unfair competition. In the upshot, Perth Modern School set the standards that the private schools tried to emulate.[18]

Tim Dolin, who has analysed the patronage of the Collie Miners Institute library for eighteen months during 1908–09, provides an insight into the cultural values of the families behind Western Australia's schoolchildren. He shows that 392 of the town's residents, about 40 per cent of the adult population, borrowed from the 1,165 books housed in the library. Ninety per cent of those books were novels by the fashionable authors of the day: Rider Haggard, Marie Corelli, E. Phillips Oppenheim and, above all, the Hocking brothers, Wesleyan ministers whose fiction popularised their Methodism. Classics such as Dickens and Thackeray were not especially popular, nor surprisingly was Ethel Turner, although the Australian racing novelist Nat Gould, a precursor of Dick Francis, enjoyed a following. The socially diverse readership—mostly members of coalminers' families—were not strongly Australian in their tastes, but constituted part of a worldwide English-reading community. In both suburban and rural Western Australia, this would remain the pattern until the coming of television.[19]

Meanwhile, in 1909 a royal commission considered the establishment of a university. As its chairman was Winthrop Hackett, who had long been a strong and at times lonely advocate of tertiary education, its findings were positive. In 1911 an Act of Parliament setting up The University of Western Australia was passed, despite criticisms from both extremes in politics. The conservative Sir Edward Wittenoom thought that demand could be met by sending students to the Eastern States, while Rufus Underwood, the Labor Member for Pilbara, asserted that universities bred snobs and drones and that it was easier for a porcupine to walk backwards down a canvas hose than for a university man to achieve anything worthwhile.[20]

In October 1911 Labor gained office with a landslide victory. Some thought this due to a reform of 1907, which extended the Legislative Assembly franchise to all adults over 21. The political tide was flowing to Labor throughout Australia, but in the West it probably gained extra impetus from a dry year on the Wheatbelt, threatening the solvency of many newly established farmers. The largely inexperienced Labor ministry was led by John Scaddan, at 35 the youngest Premier in the state's history: 'rugged, puritanical, pugnacious, chivalrous, dominating' in the eyes of one who knew him.[21]

In many respects, the new government continued the initiatives of its predecessors, now known as the Liberal Party. Secondary school students' fees were abolished, and after the university senate took the decision on Hackett's casting vote, it was agreed that The University of Western Australia, uniquely among its peers in the British Empire, would charge no fees for tuition. These policies, so foreign to modern notions of 'user pays', were upheld with bipartisan support for nearly half a century, even in the harshest economic climate. Western Australians tended to pride themselves on offering opportunity to the talented, pointing to graduates of Perth Modern School such as Dominic and Vincent Serventy, Paul Hasluck and 'Nugget' Coombs as examples of the careers open to young people of modest means. There were limits; even as late as the 1940s, many girls, such as Hazel Masterton (later Hazel Hawke), were not encouraged by their families to seek qualifications that they would probably cease to use after marriage.[22] Some have argued that the majority of entrants to Perth Modern School came from affluent middle-class suburbs, but this is debatable. Children of the watersiders of Fremantle or the railwaymen of Midland may have been discouraged from looking beyond their working-class backgrounds (though exceptions such as the family of the communist maritime unionist Paddy Troy are not hard to find). But inner suburbs such as Maylands, Highgate and North Perth produced scholarship winners in numbers suggesting supportive home environments. Those who missed out on scholarships were not necessarily disadvantaged, as the public secondary schools, Perth Boys and Perth Girls, had first-class head teachers who encouraged their students to explore the nearby State Library and Western Australian Museum.[23]

The Scaddan government also shared its predecessors' enthusiasm for agricultural expansion. Between 1911 and 1916, the area under wheat trebled. Farmers were assisted by easier loans from the Agricultural Bank. More new railways than ever were built. The urban working class benefited from legislation in 1912 that offered government advances for the purchase or erection of workers' homes. More controversially, the Scaddan government increased land and income taxes. The Legislative Council threw out many of the government's proposals, including an attempt to end alienation of Crown land, but it was unable to thwart Scaddan's policy of 'state socialism', to many the most radical of all the Labor government's innovations.

This radicalism did not take the form of nationalising property. All the members of cabinet were small property-owners, several investing in wheat farms. Their initiatives reflected the pragmatic tradition of state intervention, which went back to Forrest rather than a doctrinaire socialism. The government wanted to provide competition for those sectors of private enterprise thought guilty of profiteering at the expense of consumers. This they achieved by setting up businesses funded by loan accounts whose expenditure did not require the Legislative Council's consent. The state entered the sawmilling industry to curb the influence of established timber companies and to provide sleepers for the transcontinental railway, which was at long last under construction. Other state enterprises included an agricultural implement factory, brickworks, fisheries, retail butcheries, hotels, and a dairy supplying pure milk to hospitals. In 1912 a State Shipping Service was established, with four steamers providing competition in the shipment of beef cattle to the metropolitan area from the Kimberley and the Pilbara districts. They were venturing into troubled waters. In March 1912 their main competitor, the Adelaide Steamship Company, lost its finest ship, the *Koombana*, with all hands and passengers in a cyclone off the Pilbara coast. Hardly a trace of wreckage was found, and for many Western Australians its disappearance left a more lasting impact than the wreck of the *Titanic* would do a few weeks later.[24]

Undeniably, consumers benefited from many of the Scaddan government's initiatives, but its management was amateurish and provided ammunition for critics who objected to state enterprise. Accounting and quality control were often defective and the government incurred losses. These increased after the creation of an Industries Assistance Board to cushion the financial impact of the 1914 drought by distributing seed wheat, superphosphate and fodder to those who were struggling. The board, according to its critics, 'undoubtedly saved the wheat belt, but in doing so was guilty of every sin in the agricultural and adminis-trative calendar'. By 1915–16, the last year of Scaddan's term of office, the government deficit was big enough to earn him the nickname of 'Gone-a-million Jack'. He simply remarked, 'As if the workers hadn't got the deficit in their pockets!'[25]

The battlers on the wheat farms were not impressed. Of four seasons between 1911 and 1914, only 1913 was adequate. To supplement family labour, some farmers hired Aboriginal workers under permit from the Department of Aboriginal Affairs and Fisheries. In those years, Aboriginal people who could no longer travel across the alienated wheatlands were settling in camps of two or three hundred at such towns as Katanning, Moora and Beverley. A minority were working their own farms or finding labouring jobs, and a fortunate few did well. At 'Barnong' station, between Morawa and Yalgoo, an Aboriginal worker was paid £3 a week, more than the standard basic wage. Conditions varied from one country town to another, even in the same district. According to Fred Collard, 'Aborigines cleared fifty per cent of the farm land in the Brookton district and also did fencing and dug wells'. One was a landowner with 320 hectares and 200 sheep, another a member of the Brookton fire brigade who played cricket for the local team.[26] The majority were unemployed, forbidden to mix with white families in the sociability of the pub, and in many cases barred from sending their children to the local state schools. The farmers found difficulty in recruiting a reliable and experienced non-Aboriginal work force, and were displeased when a Rural Workers Union sought to come under the aegis of Commonwealth arbitration. Led by two members of old Avon Valley families, Alex Monger and Maitland Leake, a pressure group calling itself the Farmers and Settlers Association (later the Primary Producers Association) came into being in March 1912.

Within a year, the association mustered enough support to consider endorsing parliamentary candidates for a third party, which, borrowing the old Labor slogan of 'support in return for concessions', might hold the balance between Labor and Liberal. In 1913 the association endorsed the initiative of Walter Harper, from another long-established Western Australian landowning family, in fostering the formation of the Westralian Farmers Co-operative Ltd. In many of the new country towns, stores and agencies came under the umbrella of the cooperative, and the movement promoted a sense of united identity among farming communities of varied origins.[27] At the 1914 state elections, the Country Party returned eight members to the Legislative Assembly but Scaddan's Labor government retained a narrow majority. Desertions eroded this majority by the end of 1915, and the government lost credibility in negotiations with a dubious businessman over the construction of a meatworks at Wyndham; Scaddan's would not be the last Labor ministry to come to grief in this way. In July 1916 the Country Party threw its support behind the Liberals, who returned for a second term of office under Frank Wilson.

By this time, international events were overshadowing domestic politics. Britain and its allies went to war with Germany and Austria-Hungary in August 1914 with the enthusiastic support of most Western Australians. Many, like the locally born Sir Edward Wittenoom, thought of their country as a suburb of the great British Empire.[28] In the South African war of 1899–1902, more than 1,200 volunteers had enlisted from Western Australia. Since then, many professional men soldiered as a hobby with the volunteer militia. Among them were the prominent architect Talbot Hobbs, who was to make a name during World War I on the Western Front as a very competent and level-headed deputy to Sir John Monash, and George Barber, a goldfields doctor and future director-general of the armed forces medical services, who was remembered for observing that the Western Front was nothing compared with a Kalgoorlie dust storm.[29] Most young men since 1911 did a term of compulsory part-time service with the Commonwealth Citizen Military Forces. Many more acquired, in the Western Australian bush, skills that fitted them for armed service.

When the volunteer Australian Imperial Force (AIF) was formed for overseas service in August 1914, Western Australia was allocated a quota of 1,400 recruits; in fact, more than three times that number came forward on the first day. With more single males of military age than the Australian average, more recent British migrants, and more farmers and rural workers experiencing difficulty or unemployment because of the severe 1914 drought, it was not surprising that Western Australia's rate of recruitment was higher than in the rest of Australia. Almost 10 per cent of the total population—32,231 in all—were to enlist during World War I. One observer claimed that the Western Australians were heavier built than recruits from elsewhere in Australia, an impression that might repay further research.[30] Eventually, Western Australia provided the manpower for the 10th Light Horse and the 11th, 16th, 28th, 32nd (part), 44th, 48th (part) and 51st Battalions of the AIF. Late in October 1914, Albany enjoyed its last great moment as a major port when the transport fleet taking the troops to Egypt (and Gallipoli) made its rendezvous in King George Sound.

For many Western Australians, support for participation in the war survived four years of bloodshed, although the loss of life was grievous. Perhaps the worst moment came in August 1915, when 234 men of the 10th Light Horse were killed and 138 wounded in the totally futile charges on the Nek at Gallipoli. The unit survived to form part of the Desert Column advancing into Palestine in 1917–18 and was the first to enter Damascus in September 1918. Suzanne Welborn has calculated that by the end of the war, more than 70 per cent of the men in the 11th and 28th Battalions had been killed or seriously wounded, a rather higher proportion than for the AIF as a whole.[31] On the home front, Western Australians threw themselves into the raising of patriotic funds and the provision of comforts for the troops. Western Australians registered the highest 'Yes' vote of any Australian state in the conscription referenda of 1916 and 1917, but were outvoted by the rest of the Commonwealth. The cartoonist Ben Strange sketched a map of Australia in which the Western Australian coast was transformed into the head of the patriotic British lion while eastern Australia outlined a rabbit with the ears at the Cape York Peninsula.[32] Although the long-awaited completion of the transcontinental railway in 1917 was hailed as marking closer links between the two sides of the Australian continent, the war may have fostered among many Western Australians a tendency to identify more closely with the Mother Country than with the wayward Eastern States.

As in the rest of Australia, however, patriotism led to episodes of xenophobia. After twenty years of respected service among the Fremantle mercantile community, the German consul Richard Strelitz found himself ostracised and interned, and he was not the only citizen of German ancestry to feel the pressure. William Siebenhaar, an impressively scholarly civil servant of Dutch origins, was unfairly suspended in 1917.[33] The most overt violence was displayed against the Greeks, whose homeland remained neutral during the war and was thought pro-German. On a hot Saturday night in December 1916, a gang of more than a hundred youths roved through Kalgoorlie and Boulder, wrecking every Greek or foreign-owned restaurant and greengrocery and some other foreign-owned businesses. About two thousand men, women and children followed them, looting the spoils. The police were powerless to prevent the damage, but arrested fifty young men, most of whom were fined by the local magistrates.[34] Perth and Fremantle also experienced such cases of vandalism, but on a smaller scale. Once again, Western Australians were revealing their mistrust of the outsider at moments of stress.

There were limits to paranoia. After the conscription referendum of 1916, twelve members of the Industrial Workers of the World (IWW), a fringe radical organisation, were accused of distributing seditious propaganda. In New South Wales, such men were sentenced to fifteen years' imprisonment. In Western Australia, Mr Justice Burnside simply deplored the folly of their ideas and released them on bond.[35] Whereas the Eastern States sectors of the Australian Labor Party (ALP) wanted to expel the supporters of conscription in December 1916, the Western Australians fought hard for several months to avoid a split until finally drawn along by federal pressures. David Black suggests that

> the tolerance extended to conscriptionists in the Western Australian Labor movement was a result of the same moderation which enabled the unique integration of its political and industrial wings...in a state where only 17 per cent of the value of production was derived from manufacturing.[36]

Tensions strengthened during the 1917 conscription referendum, with rumours of another IWW plot. Philip Collier, now leader of the Labor Opposition, and John Curtin, the recently arrived editor of the *Westralian Worker*, were both fined for statements judged likely to cause public disaffection. The conscription debate resulted in pushing the Western

Australian labour movement for a few years into an unaccustomed mood of confrontation. Not that the non-Labor parties, despite their possession of the patriotic high ground, showed themselves able to consolidate. Although reinforced by members who had left the Labor Party over conscription and named themselves the National Labor Party, Wilson proved unable to control his restive backbenchers. His ally Mitchell was unpopular with the Country Party because of his misplaced optimism. Both were dropped in June 1917 and replaced by a somewhat unstable coalition of non-Labor interests, with an amiable survivor from Forrest's last cabinet, Sir Henry Lefroy, as Premier.

During 1917 two royal commissions inquired into the state of Western Australia's agriculture, one concentrating on the prospects for a railway serving the 'Mallee belt' north of Esperance, and the other undertaking a general overview of policy. Scientists appearing before the former inquiry drew attention to the rapid increase of salinity in cleared country, and urged caution in opening up more land for settlement. They were ignored. The royal commission, made up of 'practical farmers', strongly urged 'that scientific prejudice against our mallee lands be not permitted to stand in the way of their being opened up'.[37] It was not the last time in Western Australia that the boosters of hasty development swept aside the findings of careful scholarship. The second royal commission echoed the hope 'that every effort to increase production and further development will be amply justified by results'.[38] From the parliamentary back benches, Mitchell scolded the Lefroy government for failing to press forward with plans for soldier settlement and the opening up of new country, in August 1918 moving, with Labor support, an unsuccessful motion of criticism. The stage was set for a push eastward into marginal country and for more rural hardship.

Few saw opportunity elsewhere. With the wartime disruption of markets, mining continued to decline. The local market was too small to attract much investment in manufacturing, and for many years retailers continued to tell their customers, 'You'll have to wait until we can get it in from the Eastern States'. It was becoming apparent, as the war drew towards its close in November 1918, that work and opportunity must be found to reward the returning servicemen who had served their country and to acknowledge the sacrifice of the 7,000 who would not come back.

Sir John Forrest would not be there to welcome the diggers. Having survived to travel by transcontinental railway across the Nullarbor Plain, which he had explored nearly half a century earlier, he had received in 1918 the first English peerage offered to an Australian, only to die at sea on the way to London. He would not have been comfortable in the years immediately following the war's end, for these would be years of unusual disharmony and conflict in Western Australia.

6

A fine country to starve in, 1919–1933

The coming of peace in November 1918 was followed by a period of unusual social disruption. When the 'Spanish' influenza pandemic reached eastern Australia in January 1919, Western Australia unilaterally imposed quarantine measures against the infected Eastern States, but these were eventually unsuccessful, and the nursing profession was strained to the limit as temporary hospitals were created to meet the emergency. Many of the soldiers returning from the war were suffering in mind and body and found it difficult to adjust to civilian life. The trade union movement, split by the conscription debate in 1917, discovered a sharper militancy, especially among the maritime unions, competing for work on the waterfront with 'loyalist' members of the volunteer National Workers. A seamen's strike early in 1919 resulted in shortages of foodstuffs in Perth, and this in turn inspired the waterside workers to declare a strike until the National Workers were removed.

Meanwhile, a party revolt in April 1919 ousted Lefroy from the premiership, replacing him with Hal Colebatch, who was thought more decisive. Colebatch moved to have Fremantle wharf placed under government control and barricaded, and accompanied a party of strike-breakers travelling by river to the waterfront. As their boat passed under the bridges of Fremantle, it was bombarded with large stones, scrap iron and other missiles. Fights broke out between the lumpers and their supporters and the police, and one lumper died of injuries and became a working-class martyr. The crisis was resolved by the withdrawal of the National Workers, but in mid-May 1919 Colebatch resigned as Premier in favour of his ally Mitchell.[1]

Turbulence then shifted to the deeply divided Kalgoorlie goldfields. In June and July 1919 a woodcutters' strike caused fuel shortages that immobilised the mines for several weeks. The last two months of 1919 saw a series of violent confrontations involving two rival unions, returned servicemen and the police, until in January 1920 Mitchell presided over an exhausted truce. A strong fear of public disorder persisted, and in January 1921 Mitchell was inviting Brigadier-General Alfred Bessell-Browne to command a force of special constables 'in the event of organised resistance, actual or probable, to the will of the Government of the State'.[2] In isolated Western Australia, the authorities were seldom confident of their ability to manage dissent. It seemed reassuring when the visit of George V's heir, the Prince of Wales, in 1920 promoted public expressions of loyal sentiment, although embarrassment resulted from the derailment of the royal train on a rain-weakened section of line in the South West.

Mitchell remained Premier for nearly five years, less by good judgment than by good luck in presiding over a return to stability. For a time, industrial unrest continued, even spreading into white-collar professions. In 1920 the state public service and the schoolteachers both went on strike in protest against working conditions and pay that had not kept pace with wartime inflation. The previously unorganised workers in the hospitality industries found leadership in a spirited young woman, Cecilia Shelley. In 1921 Perth's finest hotel, the Esplanade, was the focus of a bitter strike, and in 1925 Albany Bell, master baker and confectioner and owner of a chain of tea-shops, found his reputation as a model employer dented by a prolonged dispute.[3] Some, taking up an idea from the IWW, spoke of a new Workers' Industrial Union unifying all existing workers' organisations. But the solid men of the Australian Workers Union—the railwaymen, the timber workers and others who gained from rural growth in Western Australia—soon had the moderates back in the saddle of the labour movement, thus re-establishing the credentials of the parliamentary Labor Party as an alternative government. This indirectly benefited Mitchell, since although he led a squabbling coalition its members could be disciplined by a realistic fear of losing office.

Beneath the surface, some tensions still remained. The conscription debate had inflamed sectarianism throughout Australia. Although Archbishop Patrick Clune of Perth served during the war as a chaplain-general to the armed forces and strongly dissociated himself from the anti-conscription activities of Archbishop Mannix of Melbourne, Western Australia could not remain unaffected. Nervous authorities banned a St Patrick's Day parade in 1919, but it went ahead anyway, led by a former member of parliament and future president of the Arbitration Court, Walter Dwyer, who ended his days a knight.[4] Catholics came to believe that many firms, including most of the banks and Wesfarmers, discriminated against employing members of their faith. Their suspicions were fuelled by the knowledge that many prominent citizens, among them the Anglican Archbishop Charles Riley, were keen Freemasons and it was thought that this led to favouritism in some professions and branches of the public service. In 1922 a group of Catholic businessmen founded a local chapter of the Order of the Knights of the Southern Cross, to counter this tendency.[5] Sectarian bias was never as overt or as widespread in Western Australia as in some other states, but it set limits to the prevailing wish for social harmony.

Practical tolerance may have been the result of apathy born of long summers. In those decades, critics often referred to WATF, the 'Western Australian Tired Feeling', a habit of easygoing procrastination that left the West dawdling behind the more dynamic Eastern States. With the tourist's trick of generalisation, the English author D. H. Lawrence, on the basis of a two-week visit in 1922 spent largely at a Darlington boarding-house, commented, 'People very friendly, but slow as if unwilling to take the next step: as if everything was a bit too much for them'.[6] To his mother-in-law he described them as 'very nervous, neurotic, as if they don't sleep well, always with a ghost nearby'. He saw the ghosts not as Aboriginal but as environmental:

> The land is here: sky high and blue and new, as if no one had ever taken a breath from it; and the air is new, strong, fresh as silver; and the land is terribly big and empty, still uninhabited. The 'bush' is hoary and unending, no noise, still, and the white trunks of the gum trees are all a bit burnt: a forest, a preforest: not a primeval forest: somewhat like a dream, a twilight-forest that has not yet seen a day...It needs hundreds of years yet before it can live. This is the land where the unborn souls, strange and not to be known, which shall be born in 500 years, live.[7]

Few Western Australians were as impressed by their native timber. In 1916 management of Western Australia's forests became the responsibility of a young and energetic conservator with an international reputation, C. E. Lane-Poole. In his efforts to introduce scientific forestry, especially for the hardwoods of the South West, Lane-Poole was backed by an able minister, R. T. Robinson. Although a party colleague, Robinson clashed with Mitchell's 'predilection for the destruction of trees and the growth in their place of grass or turnips'.[8] Unfortunately, Robinson, an urban lawyer dubbed 'Cocky' because of his temperament, was no match for Mitchell, and after his resignation in 1919 Lane-Poole followed in 1921. 'You are beating the air', wrote his friend Kingsley Fairbridge. 'There will be no forestry in Western Australia until the last mature Jarrah tree has been milled and hewn into sleepers and the last pole and pile cut down and sold.'[9] Lane-Poole's work was carried on effectively during the later 1920s and 1930s by his disciple and successor S. L. Kessell. However, improved policies were unable to avert the destruction of jarrah and karri resulting from Mitchell's second and more disastrous agricultural initiative: the attempt to establish a dairying industry in the South West using inexperienced British migrant families.[10]

Mitchell's tunnel vision about agriculture drew strength from the perception that the soldiers who survived the war deserved 'a land fit for heroes to live in'. In November 1916 he presented Wilson's cabinet with a plan for intensive cultivation on holdings of 100–160 acres (40–65 hectares), part of which would be cleared and fenced by migrants guided by experienced supervisors. Back in office and convinced that Western Australia must become self-supporting in dairy produce, Mitchell concluded an agreement with the British Government providing for 15,000 migrants to work as group settlers. The scheme gained considerable publicity in Britain after Mitchell's one and only visit in 1922. Between 1920 and 1924, a total of 23,622 assisted British migrants arrived in Western Australia. But the migrants and their Australian foremen were often poorly chosen and lacked the skills and resources to clear hardwood timber and succeed as dairy farmers. The scheme was launched without cost–benefit analysis, and without plans for marketing beyond Western Australia. 'An undertaking that required years of methodical preparation was flung together with no book of rules, but only nebulous verbal instructions for the administrators.'[11] Other group settlements set up on the low-lying Peel Estate between Fremantle and Mandurah were no more successful. By the time Mitchell left office in 1924, 42 per cent of the British settlers had already walked off the groups. Private enterprise fared no better. C. J. de Garis, successful developer of the Mildura dried fruits industry in Victoria, bought 20,000 hectares at Kendenup in 1920 and settled 350 families there to grow apples, potatoes and farm produce. By 1924 the scheme had collapsed because of shaky financing, and the settlers were finding their way to join the unemployed in Albany and Perth, leaving de Garis to suicide.[12]

Mitchell's enthusiasm extended to the development of the North West. The Wyndham meatworks was completed under government ownership in 1919, just in time to sustain pastoralists through a twenty-year slump in overseas export prices for beef cattle. The government encouraged the establishment of Western Australian Airlines to serve the northern districts, although its first flight from Carnarvon in December 1921 ended in tragedy. A ministry for the North West was created in 1921, with Colebatch as minister and the engineer Geoffrey Drake-Brockman as resident commissioner at Broome, with a brief to encourage cotton-growing and other tropical agriculture. Without adequate infrastructure, success eluded these efforts, and the ministry was closed five years later. Meanwhile, the extension of the Wheatbelt continued into increasingly marginal rainfall country, though evidence was mounting about the rapid spread of salinity after the clearing of native vegetation. W. E. Wood, the engineer responsible for monitoring water supplies for the railways, published a well-researched paper on this problem in 1924, but it went unregarded.[13]

Mitchell's slapdash methods were also evident in his political management. His most constructive legacy, the admission of women to parliament in 1920, was largely the work of his Attorney-General, Thomas Draper. When Draper lost his seat at the 1921 election to the first woman returned to any Australian parliament, Edith Cowan, Mitchell did nothing to welcome the newcomer and backed the opponent who defeated her in 1924.[14] Impatient with party politics, he did little to court the financial and extra-parliamentary bodies supporting the coalition. Strong-tempered and imperious, he and his senior ministers antagonised conservative businessmen by their pragmatic willingness to maintain state-owned industries and state intervention in price fixing and other industrial activities. The Legislative Council grew mutinous and rejected several measures during 1922 and 1923, including the reform of government hospitals.[15]

Mitchell also failed to push through a redistribution of parliamentary seats, thus giving Labor an advantage in the decaying goldfields constituencies. Several government backbenchers transferred to the Country Party, so that by the end of 1920 its numbers exceeded Mitchell's followers, but its leaders continued to support him and this led to tensions. In 1923 a split occurred between the official Country Party controlled by Alex Monger, who wished to leave the coalition, and a minority who remained. Fragmentation was also fostered by a policy of endorsing several candidates for some Legislative Assembly seats. Not surprisingly, Mitchell lost the 1924 elections to the better disciplined Labor Party led by Philip Collier, who held office until 1930. During their period in Opposition, the non-Labor parties gradually healed their divisions, briefly forming a United Party between 1926 and 1928 and then forming a National–Country Party coalition similar to those elsewhere in Australia.[16]

Collier's advent led to no radical shifts in policy, since his team were scarcely less focused on rural expansion than Mitchell himself. During their six years in office, the ploughs stayed busy. The Agricultural Bank continued to grubstake settlers generously, with the government providing railways, roads and other infrastructure. The seasons were usually good, and 1926 was long remembered as a year of record floods in the South West, when the swollen Swan collapsed the Fremantle traffic bridge and canoeists paddled along South Perth's Suburban Road. The acreage under wheat doubled, and output more than trebled. By 1927 Western Australia was reaping the biggest wheat harvest of any Australian state, and would reach a peak of 53.5 million bushels in 1930 that would not be exceeded for another thirty years. Many years after the other mainland Australian states, Western Australia acknowledged the need for scientific agricultural education when the Collier government opened Muresk College in 1926. Support continued for the dairy industry in the South West. British migrants—more than 20,000 between 1925 and 1929—continued to arrive in search of sunlight and a decent living, and most were encouraged to go on the land.

Although the commissionership for the North West was abolished in 1926, the Collier government continued to speak the rhetoric of northern development and turned a deaf ear to Commonwealth overtures to take over the Kimberley. Frontier life remained harsh. In 1926 a Kimberley cattleman occupying a former Aboriginal reserve at 'Oombulguri' on the Forrest River was fatally speared. Reports spread that the police party seeking his killer shot and cremated a number of unoffending Aborigines. After a royal commission examined the reports, two young policemen were charged with the killings but were discharged by a magistrate for lack of evidence. Exaggerated by some and denied by others, the Forrest River incident remains to this date the subject of intense controversy.[17] For most Western Australians, the far north of their state remained a distant scene of lurid adventure. When two German aviators were lost in the Kimberley in 1932, *The West Australian* seriously surmised that they might have been killed and eaten by bush Aborigines, though eventually they owed their rescue to Aboriginal people.[18]

Despite all the emphasis on rural development, Western Australia's entire population increase between 1921 and 1929 took place in the Perth metropolitan area, growth in the agricultural districts being offset by the continuing decline of the goldfields. The Perth of the 1920s was an overgrown country town with metropolitan ambitions and little sense of heritage values. The Anglican church of St John's and old private residences such as Sir John Forrest's 'The Bungalow' were razed to make room for shops and flats, and even the convict-built Town Hall only just escaped demolition. New motor showrooms and cinemas reflected modern tastes. On the foreshore at the foot of William Street, an entertainment centre and dancehall, White City, gained a raffish reputation—many Perth people were easily shocked—until its closure in 1929. The lure of White City for young Aborigines offered one pretext for the decision in 1928 to debar all Indigenous Australians from entering the central business district without permits.[19]

It was not at White City but at a charity ball in Government House itself that Perth's most sensational murder of that era took place, when a young woman shot her former boyfriend on the dance floor. The jury acquitted her after a trial in which the cut and thrust of opposing barristers was reported in the press at length. Newspaper readers of the

1920s enjoyed detailed accounts of courtroom dramas, especially murder trials. Such stories were the making of the afternoon *Daily News* and a new weekly, the *Mirror*, a great favourite with Saturday afternoon football crowds and a lively chronicler of suburban adulteries.[20]

If the Perth of the 1920s liked to think of itself as moving faster than in the past, this was literally true. The number of licensed motor cars in Western Australia rose from 4,181 in 1921 to 31,130 in 1930 as well as 11,096 vans and utilities. The Royal Automobile Club of Western Australia, a rich man's club at its foundation in 1905, reached out to a wider community in 1926 by establishing a service of roadside assistance mechanics. Motorcycles were popular among the younger set, peaking at nearly 8,000 in 1930. The Claremont Speedway, established in 1927, soon proved its popularity on Friday nights. The price of petrol was nearly halved after Billy Hughes's federal government set up the Commonwealth Oil Refineries (COR) in 1921, and by 1926 COR had its own Western Australian storage facilities near Fremantle. In the suburbs, private motorbus companies threw out a challenge to the established railways and tramlines. The number of tram travellers in Perth reached its peak in 1926 and then slowly declined. Although trams retained their reputation for shifting large crowds after such events as football matches, buses were faster and more versatile, and new bus routes were far cheaper to establish than tramlines. More and more town-dwellers spent their holidays or their weekends enjoying trips and picnics to the ocean beaches or the 'hills' (as the Darling Scarp was known).

For rural Western Australia, cheaper petrol meant that more farmers could be persuaded to invest in mechanisation. Horse-drawn ploughs and sulkies suffered from the drawback that in dry years, hay was scarce and expensive by the harvest weeks of late November and December, whereas for most of the 1920s and 1930s petrol prices remained remarkably stable. After 1923 the number of horses on Western Australian farms began to decline, although for some years bush versifiers found a theme in the unreliability of the new machines.[21] Motor transport had yet to offer the railways a serious challenge. Outside Perth, the roads were still far from perfect. The main road from Fremantle to Mandurah consisted of rubble.[22] Further out, cars travelled in a cloud of dust and gravel chips. It was only with the establishment of the Main Roads Board in 1926 that bitumen was applied to the surface of major highways and, by the mid-1930s, to the main streets of country towns.

As settlement pushed eastward to the 250 millimetre rainfall country, the clamour for railways continued. In 1925 the line serving the group settlers between Busselton and Flinders Bay was opened. In 1927 the railway from Esperance to Kalgoorlie was at last completed, since the trade of the declining goldfields ceased to pose a threat to Fremantle and there were hopes of developing the mallee country north of Esperance. By 1929 the Western Australian railways had extended over 6,000 kilometres and there seemed no end to the optimism. In 1927–28 the Collier government was entertaining a scheme to create 4,500 farms in the marginal country around Forrestania, 200 kilometres north-west of Esperance.

Along the railways, dozens of country towns seemed to be struggling into permanency.[23] All had at least one pub, and a surprising number managed to support a local newspaper. The railway station and the post office and telephone exchange supplemented the local storekeeper, butcher, baker and newsagency in providing employment to those youngsters who could be spared from the farms. Girls before marriage were often encouraged to find work in the shops or on the telephone switchboard, and more rarely as nurses or trainee teachers, as their earnings could be a valuable supplement to family income. Men still outnumbered women in rural Western Australia, but unintentionally the Education Department became a marriage market, as enterprising farmers courted the young city schoolteachers sent to serve their years in the bush.

Contrary to the United States and South Africa, the churches failed to establish themselves as the essential social and cultural centre for country towns. In a society including many first- and second-generation British migrants, religion still followed the ethnic divisions of the British Isles, with the English favouring the Anglican and Methodist churches, the Irish true to their Catholic origins, and the Presbyterians looking back to Scotland. All denominations stretched their resources to the limit in providing manpower and churches (and, in the case of the Catholics, convent schools) to serve the new communities, and tended to absorb themselves in the task of revenue-raising among congregations with little cash to spare. Built with inadequate funds, most country churches were modest replicas of British or Irish prototypes, but in Monsignor John Hawes the Catholic diocese of Geraldton discovered an architect whose distinguished edifices have been described as 'a mixture of Romanesque and Californian Spanish mission style, but with a roughcast simplicity and dignity totally in harmony with the surroundings'.[24] Some customs inherited from the Old Country showed little Christian influence. Many a newly married couple were disturbed on their wedding night by a 'tin-kettling', when the rowdy young bachelors of the district gathered outside their window to serenade them with a great clattering of pots, pans and other noisy utensils.[25]

Instead of the churches, the three mainstays of Western Australian country towns in the 1920s and the 1930s were the Westralian Farmers Co-operative, the Returned Soldiers, Sailors and Airmen's Imperial League of Australia (more conveniently known as the RSL) and the Country Women's Association (CWA). World War I had prompted Westralian Farmers to diversify. Between 1915 and 1922, a compulsory wheat pool, established by the state government, handled the marketing of wheat exports in the unusual conditions of wartime. Competing with established grain merchants, Westralian Farmers, under an energetic general manager, John Thomson, was marketing 60 per cent of Western Australia's total grain production by 1917, and in the next year the state government legislated to make the cooperative the sole acquiring agent. By 1919 Westralian Farmers had established more than ninety cooperative units in country towns, many of them run by storekeepers who combined retail business with the acquisition of wheat. When export sales were deregulated in 1922, Westralian Farmers retained more than two-thirds of the market, either directly or as sole agents for a voluntary pool. Their sources of support were strongest in the older-established wheat-growing districts. Westralian Farmers later organised the cooperative marketing of honey, and, with an imaginative grasp of the needs of farming families and the opportunities they represented, established the state's first radio broadcasting station, 6WF, in 1924.[26]

The RSL was quick to entrench itself in community leadership. Under the inspiration of Padre Arthur White, the Albany branch conducted the first Dawn Service on Anzac Day 1923, initiating a custom that was to spread quickly throughout Australia and entrench itself as a cherished national ritual. The RSL was not merely the focus for reminiscence at Anzac Day parades and socials, where the town drunk and the richest farmer in the district might meet on terms of an absolute equality born of common wartime experience.[27] The RSL also took the initiative in many community activities. As one Kulin farmer remembered it, in the 1920s and 1930s:

> they ran fancy-dress balls, birthday parties, card evenings, socials and picnics at Jilakin Rock with free ice-cream for the kiddies...We had a library in the hall—there were 600 books there by 1939.[28]

The CWA played an equally important role. Founded in 1924, its aims included the improvement of welfare and conditions for women and children in the country. The CWA provided rest rooms in country townships as social meeting places, as well as seaside homes where members and their families could enjoy rare summer holidays. The CWA also aimed 'to raise the standard of home-making', to foster agriculture and 'to promote a wise and kindly spirit'. Like the RSL, its members were to be non-sectarian, non-political and 'loyal citizens of Australia and the Empire'.[29] Among its most durable initiatives was the production of a cookery book to which many members contributed their favourite recipes and household hints. Hitherto Western Australia's main authority on household management was a 1,200-page volume edited by Sir Winthrop Hackett's widow, Deborah, and first published in 1916.[30] For young brides and new arrivals in both country and town, the more convenient *CWA Cookery Book* proved a godsend. First published in 1936, the book had reached its nineteenth edition by 2004. Its tone was practical. On the first page readers were advised, 'When the tape measure cannot be found remember that a kerosene tin measures exactly one yard round the four sides, and a 2 lb golden syrup tin measures 1 foot round'.[31]

By now Western Australia's literary production was extending beyond cookery books. In 1916, when Professor Walter Murdoch edited an anthology of short stories and verse whose proceeds went to the Red Cross, he could claim that it was the first publication of its kind produced in Western Australia. During the 1920s, novels with Western Australian subject matter began to command wider audiences. Befriended by D. H. Lawrence, who collaborated with her, Molly Skinner's *The Boy in the Bush* drew on family history and was published in London in 1924. Although regarded askance by the conservative for her communist and possibly Bohemian sympathies, Katharine Susannah Prichard won national acclaim for her novel *Working Bullocks* (1926), set among the timber workers of the South West karri forests. This was followed by *Coonardoo* (1929), a study of pastoral life in the North West, controversial because of its candid account of the sexuality of white men and Aboriginal women, and *Haxby's Circus* (1930), based on the travelling shows that provided Western Australian country towns with an entertaining break in the year's routine. She was moving towards the subtle exploration of social and gender relationships in her next novel, *Intimate Strangers*, when her creativity was maimed by the trauma of her husband's suicide in 1933.[32]

The University of Western Australia, housed in ramshackle premises in Perth's central business district but destined, through the philanthropy of Sir Winthrop Hackett, to move to a handsome new campus at Crawley in 1931, was also contributing positively to the state's culture. Among its professors, Walter Murdoch was winning a national reputation as essayist and commentator. The physicist Alexander David Ross, together with his wife Euphemia, gave generous and discerning patronage to classical music, encouraging the formation of the Perth Symphony Orchestra in 1928. Younger scholars such as Frank Beasley and Fred Alexander offered well-informed, if at times unpopular, commentaries on international affairs. Edward Shann, an uncommonly elegant and lucid writer, published in 1930 an *Economic History of Australia*, mounting an argument against what he saw as the restrictive effects of arbitration and tariff protection.[33] Although his views were unfashionable at that time, they formed part of a distinctive Western Australian economic tradition linking the anti-federationist writers of 1900 such as Sanderson and Colebatch with the 'dry' politicians of the 1970s and 1980s such as Hyde, Stone and Shack. Shann was also one of the founders in 1926 of the [Royal] Western Australian Historical Society, for, with the passing of the pre–gold rush generation of settlers, the state was ready to recapture its past. It was a somewhat sanitised past: 'The State was founded as a free colony by gentlefolk: the convicts came later, unwanted, and should not be associated with it'.[34]

Nor were Aboriginal people wanted in Western Australian history except as the hostile but unsuccessful resistance to pioneer pastoralists. Many followed Daisy Bates in believing that the impact of European society doomed traditional Aboriginal society to extinction. This view influenced the bureaucrat Auber Octavius Neville, Chief Protector (1915–36) and Commissioner for Native Affairs (1936–40).[35] Despite consistent underfunding, Neville's department interfered increasingly to regulate the lives of a people thought incapable of self-management. He showed no sympathy to the South West Aborigines led by William Harris, who unsuccessfully appealed to the Collier government in 1928 for the same citizenship rights as other Western Australians. Neville favoured the removal of children of Aboriginal parentage to institutions where they might be trained as domestics and farmhands and ultimately merge with the mainstream population. Aboriginal people from every part of the state deemed in need of care and protection were institutionalised in the Moore River (Mogumber) settlement founded in 1918. Neville envisaged the settlement as offering its inmates 'a new life of peace, contentment and usefulness', but conditions deteriorated and discipline hardened at Moore River, and it came to have a bad name in many Aboriginal memories. He had an ambiguous relationship with Christian missions such as the United Aborigines Mission at Mount Margaret run from 1922 by Pastor Rudolph Schenk. Although they were given to interfering with 'heathen' Aboriginal cultural practices, they also educated young people in Western skills in a family environment, without insisting that the Western majority should absorb them.[36]

In September 1929, when Western Australia celebrated the centenary of European settlement, a few Aborigines in traditional garb and body paint led the main procession through the streets of Perth, but the main themes in the parade stressed the contribution of pioneering families and the state's production of wheat, wool and gold. Only a few weeks later, the collapse of the New York stock market heralded the arrival of a worldwide economic depression. Export prices for the wheat and wool on which Western Australia depended for its export income slumped heavily in value. Mitchell, again Premier in 1930, urged the farmers to ride out the crisis by growing more wheat but could not deliver a guaranteed price. Many producers had to resort to the *Farmers' Debts Adjustment Act*, placing their farms into government receivership and devoting nearly all they earned to the repayment of debt. Many more walked off their farms, so that 'by June 1935 the Agricultural Bank had 2,324 properties on its hands, on which £3.96 million was outstanding'.[37] Falling demand created rising unemployment in all industries. In September 1929, 9 per cent of the Western Australian work force were in want of a job. By the end of 1930 the figure had reached 25 per cent, and it peaked at more than 30 per cent in the second quarter of 1932, a little more than the Australian average.

Sudden unemployment on this scale left an indelible mark on the generation who endured it. Even the 70 per cent who remained in employment, while they benefited from a drop in the cost of living, were obliged in many cases to accept reduced wages and lived with the anxiety that they might possibly lose their jobs. The Depression probably entrenched the stereotype that it was a man's role to act as breadwinner and women's part should be played in the home. Interviewing surviving members of that generation forty years later, oral historians found that men who were forced to walk off their farms or had undergone a period of unemployment were reluctant to talk about it, whereas women took pride in the ingenuity with which they had stretched the household resources to provide their families with food, clothing and firewood. Neighbourly cooperation became important; some families threatened with eviction for non-payment of rent found friends who would take care of all their furniture so that the landlord had nothing to seize on taking possession. Small businesses, especially in country towns, stretched their credit to the limit for the benefit of poverty-stricken customers. The Ravensthorpe storekeeper Edgar Daw worked very long hours and extended credit to many marginal farmers but, at the end of thirty-four years, reckoned that he had written off £45,361 in bad debts—at least a million dollars by early twenty-first century values. He in his turn ran the risk that his city suppliers might foreclose on him, but in March 1936 they allowed him time to trade out his deficit. It took six years.[38] It is not easy for modern readers in the credit card era, habituated to debt as the price of an education or a roof over their heads, to appreciate how the Depression taught their grandparents frugality and an aversion to risk.

Depression unemployment created problems of welfare and social control beyond the experience or competence of Western Australia's political leaders. Before the Collier government lost office in April 1930, the Premier was more than once confronted by deputations from the groups of unemployed milling around the streets of Perth, but it was the optimist Mitchell who faced the challenge of justifying his slogan of 'Work for all'. Having written off in 1930 more than £3 million lost on the group settlement scheme, the state government had little revenue for job creation, though sustenance payments were provided for those unemployed who were prepared to work as directed. In 1930 a thousand unemployed were settled in an old army camp at Blackboy Hill, east of Midland, and a second camp was established for several months of 1931 at Hovea, in the Darling Range. Mostly the government concentrated on getting the unemployed out of the politically susceptible environment of the Perth metropolitan area. Until October 1931, farmers were offered a subsidy to take on extra hands, but most of the 'susso' men (as they were called) were directed to labour-intensive public works scheme such as the Harvey irrigation scheme, the clearing of timber in the Frankland River district and later the construction of the Canning Dam in the Darling Range catchment area. Conditions were rough, and many were ill suited to pick-and-shovel work, but there seemed no alternative.[39]

Optimists turned to gambling in hope of a quick lift to their fortunes. Newspapers ran crossword competitions that were thinly disguised games of chance. Many found their way on Saturday afternoons to the illegal starting-price bookmakers who operated near most suburban pubs, with a radio to broadcast the latest results and a couple of lookouts posted to give warning of a raid by the police. Sometimes, either by chance or by prior information, the police succeeded in making arrests, and on Monday morning the magistrates would fine a number of offenders convicted of 'obstructing the passage of pedestrian traffic'—for off-course betting in itself could not have been made illegal without inconvenience to influential members of Perth's business and professional communities. But next Saturday the punters would be back at 'the four-legged lottery', while those in the know meanwhile placed their bets at the local barber's shop—for many barbers were bookies on the side.[40]

Despite legal obstacles, many subscribed by mail to interstate lotteries, Tattersall's in Hobart or the Queensland Golden Casket. Defying misgivings by church groups, the Mitchell government decided in 1932 to compete by setting up a Lotteries Commission to raise money for hospitals, orphanages and similar worthy causes through a series of lotteries. Tickets would be sold through newsagencies and tobacconists—for in an age ignorant of lung cancer, cigarettes were a solace to rich and poor alike, and many older men retained the habit of pipe-smoking. A hundred thousand ticketholders in each lottery (or Charities Consultation, as they were termed) competed for a first prize of £3,000, with numerous minor prizes. 'Charities' soon became immensely popular, public acceptance secured by the knowledge that the proceeds were allocated to deserving causes by a statutory corporation at arm's length from political control.

Protest erupted as month followed month with no apparent end to the misery of the Depression. The authorities readily blamed the communists for stirring up the unemployed, but the bulk of evidence suggests that the relatively few who called themselves communists were radicalised by their Depression experiences. The biggest demonstrations took place on 6 March 1931, when about 2,000 men marched on the Treasury Building. They were driven away by mounted troopers and other police, and their leaders arrested. The authorities stepped up the dispersal of the unemployed to rural projects, but failed to stifle the spirit of protest. In September 1932 a series of grievances provoked more than half the men working at Frankland River to board a train at Mount Barker with the intention of taking their complaints to the government, but they were met by the police, who arrested the leaders and sent the rest back to Frankland River.

The anger revealed in the unemployed demonstrations was not easily channelled into political action, though it must have been widespread. It seems no coincidence that the Australian Rules football season of 1932 is remembered by sporting historians as 'infected with a foulness and viciousness it had not known previously and has not known since...The play among the leading teams was charged with venom'.[41] Like Australians elsewhere, Western Australians groped for unorthodox political solutions. Some urged that parliament should be shut down and replaced by a committee of businessmen. Although a few returned soldiers favoured a military dictatorship, there was no equivalent of the New South Wales 'New Guard'. The populist Labor leader in New South Wales, Jack Lang, found no followers among Western Australian politicians, although between 1936 and 1943 the maverick ex-Labor man Tom Hughes, like Lang a great sniffer-out of corruption in other politicians, held the archetypal working-class seat of East Perth. Prominent citizens such as Walter Murdoch were temporarily beguiled by the easy solutions of the social credit movement, but its appeal was short-lived. Instead, Western Australian frustrations were channelled into the revival of the movement for secession from the Australian Commonwealth.[42]

Since the abortive parliamentary moves in 1906–07, secession had apparently lain dormant as a political issue, but a number of factors kept the possibility alive. Western Australia had rallied to Britain's cause during World War I more strongly than any other part of the Commonwealth, and its population included a higher proportion of recent British migrants. Even for many of the locally born, London seemed no more alien than Sydney. Many of the 'tothersiders' who came during the gold rush of the 1890s had come to identify more strongly with the West than with their state of origin. Wartime centralisation by the federal government was followed by constitutional changes that seemed to leach power from the states. In 1920 the High Court in the *Engineers Case* intervened in an industrial dispute between the State Sawmills and a trade union, thus departing from its previous tendency to uphold state rights in matters of industrial arbitration. The Mitchell government mounted an appeal to the Privy Council in London, retaining the rising young Owen Dixon as counsel, but the appeal failed.[43]

Several events in 1926 pointed to a closer economic integration between Western Australia and the rest of the continent. A Melbourne company connected to the *Herald* acquired *The West Australian* and its associated publications from the estate of Sir Winthrop Hackett, although editorial control remained in Perth. The conservative Western Australian Bank fell to a takeover by the Bank of New South Wales (now Westpac). Following a national referendum, the states handed over authority to raise loans on the overseas money market to the federal government, and so claimant states such as Western Australia had to seek financial support through a Commonwealth Loan Council, set up in 1927–28, acting on agreements hammered out at an annual conference of state premiers with the federal Prime Minister and Treasurer.

These constitutional changes do not seem to have perturbed Western Australian voters greatly; in the first half-century of federation, they said 'Yes' to more referenda to enlarge Commonwealth powers than any other state. But they felt hard hit by the increasing level of tariff protection levied by the Commonwealth, as it benefited manufacturers in Victoria and New South Wales at the expense of the primary producing states such as Western Australia. Also they perceived the new national capital at Canberra, proclaimed in 1927, as a waste of taxpayers' money. When the hard times came with the Depression of the early 1930s, it was not surprising that public anger should direct itself towards the remote and unfeeling Eastern States.

The elderly populists who ran the *Sunday Times* had been preaching the gospel of secession for a long time, without effect, but the movement took wing in 1930 with the formation of the Dominion League agitating for an autonomous Western Australia within the British Empire. Fired by a very able and vehement young spokesman, Keith Watson, the Dominion League fanned Western Australian discontent over the hardships of the Depression by blaming the extravagance and protectionist policies of the Commonwealth Government. In no way mollified when a conservative government replaced Labor in Canberra at the beginning of 1932, the Dominion League persuaded the Mitchell government to submit a referendum to Western Australian voters posing two questions: did they favour secession from the Australian Commonwealth, and would they support a constitutional convention addressing the problems of federation?

The referendum took place on 8 April 1933 concurrently with a state election. By a two to one majority, the voters said 'Yes' to secession, with the goldfields and the Kimberley as the only regions to disagree. By a smaller margin, they also rejected the idea of a constitutional convention. But the Mitchell government also felt the wrath of the voters and was swept from office; Mitchell and several of his cabinet ministers lost their seats. This brought Philip Collier back as Premier of a Labor government opposed to secession but confronted with an unmistakable expression of popular sentiment in favour. Without consulting his party, Collier neutralised Mitchell by making him Lieutenant-Governor, in which office (or as Governor after 1948) he served congenially until just before his death in 1951. Dressed in the three-piece suit of the successful bank manager, ample in jowl and paunch, Mitchell promenaded each morning along St Georges Terrace, handing out tips to schoolboys for ice-cream, an elder statesman who had outlived his shortcomings as a politician. He was another who dreamed grand visions and left it to the rank and file of Western Australians to work out the consequences.

Secession took a little longer to deal with. Collier procrastinated while the enthusiasts of the Dominion League got up a petition to be taken in a jarrah casket to the British Parliament. Meanwhile, the federal government set up the Commonwealth Grants Commission in 1933 as a more formal mechanism to provide financial assistance to claimant states such as Western Australia and Tasmania. Some called it 'an anti-secessionist committee', but it helped to assuage the West's sense of neglect. The British Parliament took its time considering the secession petition, delivering its verdict in May 1935 while loyal Western Australians were celebrating the silver jubilee of King George V. Britain had had no power of intervention since 1931, when the Statute of Westminster defined the self-governing members of the British Commonwealth as autonomous partners. If Western Australia wished to secede peacefully, it would have to win the consent of the federal parliament in Canberra. This was obviously impossible, and interest in the secession movement began to fade fairly quickly. A secessionist weekly established in 1931 under the rather unfortunate name of *The Groper* tried to transform itself into a daily in 1937 but went out of business in ten days.

Discontent was subsiding as the economy improved. Western Australia, having plunged later into the Great Depression, recovered earlier than the rest of Australia. Unemployment among trade union members in Western Australia, having stood at nearly 30 per cent early in 1932, fell to 6 per cent by 1936–37 as against 10 per cent for the whole of Australia. This economic resilience owed little to the developmental policies pursued by Forrest's successors. In the most authoritative assessment of Western Australia's economic performance during the expansion of the Wheatbelt and the South West, the economic historian Graeme Snooks has shown a picture of unbalanced development. Too much emphasis was placed on the rural sector, too much investment was expended on unrewarding infrastructure such as railway construction, and too little attention was paid to mining and manufacturing. In the end, mining was to lead Western Australia's recovery. Snooks also observes that:

> The main, in fact startling, economic consequence of these difficult years of consolidation and adjustment was that the 1913 level of real per capita income was not exceeded until 1950.[44]

But he also finds that in the twenty-five years after 1914, there was an overall reduction in the inequality of incomes. Despite the blundering policies of politicians such as Mitchell, despite seasonal uncertainties and a hostile world economy, Western Australia for most of its ordinary citizens was, in a memorable phrase of Edward Shann's, a fine country to starve in.

7

Recovery and war, 1935–1951

Gold led Western Australia's economic recovery in the later 1930s. Many gave credit to the role of Claude de Bernales, who, from selling second-hand mining machinery, had advanced to the promotion of renovated mining companies and to the cultivation of a notably elegant lifestyle. Between 1933 and 1935, de Bernales, now based in London, floated eight companies with a nominal capital of more £6 million, and in 1936 acquired the Great Boulder Proprietary mine. 'Some of his companies failed', writes a biographer, 'but his proportion of success was better than average for the industry'.[1] International instability stimulated rising gold and minerals prices and justified the development of previously unpayable low-grade deposits of gold ore. In 1937, for the first time in more than twenty years, the state's gold production exceeded one million fine ounces. Kalgoorlie recovered its sense of civic self-confidence, acquiring Western Australia's first Olympic swimming pool in 1938, more than twenty years before Perth followed suit. Builders were busy in other centres such as Wiluna and Big Bell, apparently confident that their works would last longer than the decaying weatherboards of Kanowna and Peak Hill. Hundreds of unemployed and their families found employment; 'Kalgoorlie's gold was *real*', wrote Doll Brooks, whose husband had spent the last two years in Perth living a hand-to-mouth existence as odd-job man and Saturday clerk for a starting-price bookie. He was one of many who found security in a goldfields job. Now in 1935 the family was able to afford the traditional Christmas dinner of roast duck and plum pudding washed down by Hannan's lager, with a tricycle for their 3-year old, the first real toy of his life.[2]

Unfortunately, competition for jobs stirred racial tension. Workers of southern European origin were alleged to offer bribes for jobs and to accept inferior wages and conditions. On a hot night in January 1934, a fatal bar-room brawl in Kalgoorlie inflamed anger against the 'aliens', who were chased from their homes and shops by several thousand rioters in an orgy of looting and arson. Two were killed and many injured. It took three days for police reinforcements to arrive from Perth and restore order.[3] Although this was the last as well as the worst incident of its kind, the riot prompted a number of migrant families to depart for the outskirts of Perth, where they established themselves as market gardeners and vignerons.

None of the state's other staple industries made nearly such a striking contribution to economic recovery, but all contributed, Even before the Depression had run its course, venturesome farmers were testing new ideas. At Carnarvon a young agricultural scientist, Frank Wise, was demonstrating the potential of the Gascoyne River for irrigated banana-growing, and in 1933 the first crops were harvested.[4] In the Manjimup district, one or two survivors from the group settlements noted that the Australian Government wanted to improve its balance of trade with the United States by reducing dependence on American tobacco, and by 1934, 650 hectares had been planted, though much trial and error would be required before the product pleased local smokers. Although the Depression had taught the lesson that Western Australia relied too much on agricultural exports and should diversify its industries, the Labor governments who held office between 1933 and 1947 were at best measured in introducing change. During the 1930s the state's public works program gave most emphasis to water storage for both city and rural use. Several dams were constructed or enlarged, though planning was piecemeal and significantly influenced by the need to find sustenance projects for the unemployed. The engineer Russell Dumas complained of 'no time or money for preparation, and the designs and plans barely a nose ahead of construction if they are so much as that', but his works included Stirling Dam, Australia's highest earthen dam. A Department of Industrial Development created in 1933 did little more than encourage consumers to buy Western Australian local produce; the colonial Legislative Council had done as much eighty years before.[5]

21   Fringe-dwellers: Aborigines with spears and woomera in the 1890s.

22   Local hero: John Forrest, probably around the time he became Premier in 1890.

23   Coolgardie in its infancy, before the railway came in 1896.

24   Prospector A. P. Brophy with his riding camel, 'Misery', Coolgardie 1895.

25   Cobb & Co coaches operated under franchise in Western Australia from the 1890s to the early 1920s.

26   Goldfields picnic; the Byrne family and friends from Menzies at Lake Barlee, 1898.

27   An Afghan guard of honour at Hampton Bungalow, Coolgardie, welcoming Governor Sir Gerard Smith, 1896.

28 Governor Sir Gerard Smith, whose enthuiasm for the goldfields and their speculators eventually landed him in hot water, 1899.

29 Railway trucks with pipes for the Goldfields Water Supply Scheme, 1902.

30 Land clearing at Walgoolan, east of Merredin, 1921.

31 Arrival of wheat at Trayning station, west of Merredin, 1922.

32 How wheat was harvested in bulk, around 1910.

33 Bagged wheat on Victoria Quay, Fremantle, 1910.

34   Crew of the pearling luggers on the beach at Broome, c. 1910.

35   Pearling lugger under full sail, 1910.

36   Chained Aboriginal prisoners on Derby jetty laying railway ballast, probably
     1910–20.

37   Aboriginal women sorting fleeces in shearing shed, Upper Liveringa station, West
     Kimberley, 1916.

38   Wool was brought to Carnarvon by camel team, 1920.

36

37

38

39   Cottesloe Beach in the 1920s.

40   Group Settlement 116: a settler's family dressed up for the photographer.

Gradually, times improved on the land. Pastoralists received better prices for their wool, but the industry was hit by a series of dry seasons from 1935 to 1940, while beef export prices remained low. Technological advance brought some hope to the wheat-growers. In 1931–32 Westralian Farmers pioneered the concept of bulk horizontal storage of wheat by building five experimental bins at Wyalkatchem. Less laborious and expensive than the old system of bagging wheat for export, the scheme met opposition from grain merchants fearful of competition and growers unhappy with low prices. In April 1933 Westralian Farmers and the Western Australian Wheat Pool joined forces to launch Co-operative Bulk Handling Limited (CBH). In its first year of operation, CBH operated bulk-receival equipment at fifty railway sidings. After a royal commission supported these initiatives, CBH was endorsed by legislation in 1935, and expanded rapidly.[6] Despite poor seasons in 1936 and 1940, the wheat farmers were gradually clawing their way out of debt, as export prices inched higher and the bulk handling of harvests extended across the state's entire rail system. Some were able to resume the mechanisation of their properties. The Cunderdin farmer Jim Halbert reported that at harvest time 'in a heavy crop when the horses slowed down the whole machine would choke up but with tractors he had even speed and even power'.[7] South from the Avon Valley, widespread pasture improvement, including the increased sowing of subterranean clover, fostered a renewed growth in sheep farming. Even the dairy farms of the South West gave ground for optimism, thanks partly to a substantial subsidy by the Commonwealth Government. The more fortunate and hard-working settlers bought out their neighbours and consolidated their blocks. Those in debt to the Agricultural Bank complained that their earnings were subject to seizure by the bank in payment of their debts, and this led to some acrimonious confrontations in the winters of 1936 and 1937.[8]

In those years also, the agricultural scientists whose contribution Mitchell had so often belittled made a number of breakthroughs in their research that were to add millions to Western Australia's rural income. In the late 1920s, flocks were losing between 5 and 15 per cent of their sheep from a bacterial toxin known as 'Beverley disease'. The first veterinary pathologist in the Department of Agriculture, H. W. Bennetts, isolated the causal organism and by 1932 had devised a preventive vaccine. Between

1935 and 1937, Eric Underwood and J. F. Filmer published papers showing that a wasting disease in cattle that had been particularly bad among the herds of the group settlers in the South West was due to cobalt deficiencies in the soil and herbage, and could be corrected by the regular dosing of animals. At the same time, Bennetts and F. E. Chapman found that a similar copper deficiency was responsible for a condition known as 'Gingin rickets' in lambs. It would be some years before the long-term benefits of these discoveries were fully realised, but the stimulus of hard times had left farmers with a willingness to apply the findings of science. Leaders in the farming and grazing community played a valuable role in securing this acceptance. Percival Forrest of Dwalganup was noted for pioneering subterranean clover pastures, while in the late 1930s Edward Lefroy of Walebing introduced from South Australia the now controversial practice of mulesing—a surgical operation to prevent fly-strike in sheep—and demonstrated its practical value.[9]

This upsurge of scientific creativity in the later 1930s was matched by a search for new directions among Perth's artistic and cultural circles. Perth Modern School and The University of Western Australia were beginning to pay a social dividend. For the first time, Paul Hasluck observed, 'a young generation of native talent had begun to emerge and bring a new quality into the cultural life of Western Australia'.[10] Among the first was Linley Wilson who, after four years in London in the formative years of the dance teaching profession, returned to Perth in 1926 to bring her rare skills to foster dance and ballet as educational opportunities.[11] For a while it had seemed that the novelists might take the lead, shifting their focus from the bush to find inspiration in the city of Perth. *Money Street* (1933) by (John) Keith Ewers was perhaps too derivative of middlebrow English novels but proved popular among Perth readers who could at last enjoy a work of fiction with a recognisable local setting. In *Upsurge* (1934) John Mewton Harcourt drew on the social realist tradition, but his portrait of a wicked capitalist family who owned a department store was too graphic for a small town like Perth. Having been criticised for its sexual and political radicalism, *Upsurge* was banned by the Commonwealth authorities in November 1934, and Harcourt published no more.[12] Subtler in its witty and perceptive insights, Katharine Susannah Prichard's *Intimate Strangers* (1937) did not appear until several years after its completion, as the suicide of her husband (a Depression victim in both senses) too closely paralleled the novel's original plot. Subsequently, Prichard returned to the bush and the goldfields for her subject matter, and Ewers wrote about the Wheatbelt. Another writer who emerged in this decade, Henrietta Drake-Brockman, set her first novels, *Blue North* (1934) and *Sheba Lane* (1936), in the pearling port of Broome. It would be forty years before serious writers again drew on the urban experience of Perth for their inspiration. Despite their different political leanings, Prichard, Drake-Brockman and Ewers were all active in founding the Western Australian chapter of the Fellowship of Australian Writers in 1938, an influential though sometimes quarrelsome coterie who for the next three decades did a good deal to encourage young talent.[13]

'Modernism first came to Perth through architecture and drama rather than through the visual arts.'[14] To the general public, the impact of the new could be seen most readily in the city's changing public architecture. Young practitioners such as Marshall Clifton, John Fitzhardinge and John Oldham, who had been exposed to the Art Deco movement overseas, found opportunities as a reviving economy created demand for office accommodation. Like up-to-date Kansas City, Perth's central business district acquired 'a skyscraper seven storeys high' in the elegant Gledden Building, and then the ten-storey Colonial Mutual Life (CML) building in St Georges Terrace, which was to remain the city's highest for a quarter of a century. The Emu Brewery (1937) and several hotels in the city and suburbs also exhibited Art Deco character, but Perth's most memorable architectural statement from those years showed no such influence. This was London Court, an arcade commissioned by Claude de Bernales as a pastiche of a sixteenth-century London street.[15] Ironically, this monument to capitalist enterprise and English tradition was to house for several years the headquarters of Western Australia's minuscule Communist Party.

Marxists and the wives of businessmen were to mingle as a younger generation of artists grouped themselves in interlocking coteries. First came the Perth Society of Artists, founded in 1932 by George Pitt Morison and John Brackenreg and confined to professionals. At first few women joined, and this contributed to the establishment of the West Australian Painters and Applied Arts Society, which held its first exhibition in 1936. In the same year, a group of young radicals who had been meeting informally for several years set up the Workers Art Guild, 'to bring the arts to the people with trade union pageants, street theatre, and various classes'. Its motto was 'Art as a Weapon'.[16] Members of the guild included the surrealist Herbert McClintock (Max Ebert); the ex-seaman Harald Vike, who brought a social clarity to his landscapes of inner Perth; and Maurie Lachberg, well known as the standard bearer and marshal on a white horse at Perth's Labor Day processions, though his politics were thought a little extreme for most of his ALP colleagues.[17] All these groups exhibited in Newspaper House, the custom-built quarters into which *The West Australian* had moved its office in 1933.

Perth's flourishing amateur theatre world also included a wide variety of ideologies. The Perth Repertory Club, secure in rented premises after 1933, grew adventurous enough in its repertoire to stage new Australian plays. These included the premieres of Henrietta Drake-Brockman's *Dampier's Ghost* (1936) and *Men Without Wives* (1938), the latter picking up Prichard's controversial theme of liaisons between pastoralists in the North West and Aboriginal women. Perth Repertory cooperated with the Workers Art Guild, which also promoted drama, and a proliferating range of amateur groups to put on a week-long State Drama Festival in October 1937, the first of its kind in Australia, and the precursor of a tradition that lasted until the 1970s. Paul Hasluck, influential drama critic for *The West Australian* during the 1930s, recalled, 'There was a new play almost every week of the year, most of them competently done and a steady audience of about a thousand for each season'.[18] The Workers Art Guild gave Western Australians their first exposure to modern radical playwrights. Katharine Susannah Prichard, increasingly entrenched in Communist orthodoxy, wrote three plays for the guild, but its main value lay in introducing the work of new American and European dramatists. The guild's first production, Clifford Odets's *Till the Day I Die*, was staged in March 1936 only a year after its New York premiere. Others followed, but after 1939 this aspect of the guild's activities was largely taken over by the Patch Theatre, during the 1940s the main source of organised drama instruction in Perth.

Not that radicals made any impact on a state political scene dominated after 1933 by a junta of Labor veterans. Collier gave way as Premier in 1936 to the railwayman John Willcock, but few new faces emerged in cabinet. Meanwhile, it was difficult to ignore the darkening international outlook. After Hitler came to power in 1933, Nazi Germany grew increasingly belligerent, and the Japanese invasion of China in 1937 reminded Western Australians, if they needed reminding, that a potential threat lurked closer to home. Enthusiasm for secession dwindled, though the Commonwealth's upgrading of its coastal military base at Swanbourne worried nearby householders nervous of becoming a target for hostile aircraft.[19] The Kimberley district, Australia's potential front line in a future war, became the subject of fresh attention. At Koolan Island in Yampi Sound, north of Derby, a European firm proposed to mine iron ore for export to Japan, but in 1938 the Commonwealth Government, fearing its potential for military use, imposed a ban on this trade. An exiled Russian politician, Isaac Sternberg, proposed to purchase the Durack properties in the Ord Valley and the Northern Territory as the basis for a community of Jewish refugees fleeing Nazi persecution. His lobbying convinced the state government but Canberra was tardy in making a decision. The scheme died with the outbreak of war, leaving only historians to conjecture how its success might have influenced the future of Aboriginal Australians and Palestinian Arabs.[20]

Few were surprised when eventually, in September 1939, Britain and France went to war against Germany, and Australia automatically followed suit, but the Second World War was not to be a mere replay of the first. Once again, the West contributed more manpower in proportion to population than the rest of Australia. Fewer Western Australian servicemen were killed and wounded, but the 1939–45 conflict was to have a greater impact on the home front. The early phases of the war, between 1939 and 1941—the fall of France, the nightly bombing of Britain, the part played by Australian forces in the struggle for North Africa and the Mediterranean, the German invasion of Soviet Russia—were given greater immediacy through coverage on the radio. The majority of Western Australians still had British family ties or sympathies and could respond to Winston Churchill's defiant rhetoric and to stories of everyday heroism during the Blitz. It was less easy for other ethnic groups. After Mussolini took Italy into the war in June 1940, many Australians of Italian descent were rounded up for internment, leaving their wives and children to work the family market gardens or businesses, although at the same time men from these families were being accepted for enlistment in the armed forces.[21] Later the rural labour shortage was assuaged by the use of Italian prisoners of war captured during the North African campaign, and in general the Italians were seldom treated as mortal enemies. Greek-Australians fared better after an Italian invasion in October 1940 brought Greece in on the anti-fascist side. 'We are an *Allied* shop', some fruitmongers proclaimed, thus countering an Anglo-Australian competitor's racist slogan: 'Shop here before the Day-goes'.[22]

The war brought no great benefit immediately to Western Australia's economy. Gold-mining, the main agent of recovery in the 1930s, was cut back as non-essential industry and would not recover for decades. Problems with transport and marketing checked the potentially limitless demand for food and wool, especially after the introduction of petrol rationing in September 1940. As well, the pastoral industry in the North West was hurt by a series of dry years that would break only in 1942. Graziers and farmers alike were operating in many cases with run-down plant that they had been unable to renew during the Depression years of the 1930s. Despite manpower regulations obliging much of the work force to take jobs as instructed by the Commonwealth authorities, labour was in short supply. Women and children worked long hours, especially on properties where the man of the house had enlisted.[23]

In December 1941 the war suddenly came close. The pride of the Royal Australian Navy, HMAS *Sydney*, vanished without a trace off the Western Australian coast north of Carnarvon after engagement in battle with a German raider.[24] Two days later, Japanese ships bombed Pearl Harbor in Hawaii, and Japan entered the war. It happened that for the first time—and the only time in more than a century of federation—a politician from Western Australia, John Curtin, was Prime Minister of Australia. A Labor man and former journalist respected by many of differing policies, especially in Perth, Curtin had been in office only two months and faced the crisis with an inexperienced ministry. Within two more months, Japanese forces thrust through Southeast Asia to capture Singapore, previously regarded as a sure shield against Asian threats to Australia. By early March 1942, most of the Philippines and Indonesia were in Japanese hands, and Papua New Guinea was invaded. More than 2,000 of the prisoners of war taken at Singapore were Western Australians. Refugees poured into Perth. Bombs dropped on Wyndham, Broome and Port Hedland; at Broome a flying-boat crowded with Dutch refugees was machine-gunned and more than a hundred lives were reported lost. Stories of atrocities committed by conquering Japanese forces gave added sharpness to fears of invasion.[25]

In the critical days of March 1942, the state government sent an emissary to John Curtin to complain that not enough was being done to protect Western Australia. Prompt steps were taken to draw a lesson from the heavy bombing of Darwin in February. Realising that the Treasury Building, the nerve centre of administration, was an easy target, the state government commandeered a modern ten-storey block of flats, with reinforced concrete infrastructure for government offices. Sir James Mitchell was evacuated from Government House in the centre of Perth to safer quarters at Kalamunda. However, no plans were made to rehouse the adjacent Supreme Court or the business offices along St Georges Terrace. Some women and children moved from Perth and the seaports to inland country towns, and plans were discussed for evacuating many more, although it was hard to tell how the underpopulated Wheatbelt could offer resistance to invaders.[26]

Although Perth was to experience only one 'alert' because of unidentified aircraft, the London Blitz suggested the need for air-raid precautions. Schoolchildren dug slit trenches in playgrounds, and retired citizens trained as air-raid wardens. Shops and offices were sandbagged against explosive blasts, and a blackout was imposed at night. Western Australians were understandably nervous, and the rumour flew that they would be abandoned if the Japanese landed. A federal politician who should have known better later elaborated the story. Australian resistance would concentrate on 'the Brisbane line', a perimeter from southern Queensland to Adelaide protecting New South Wales and Victoria and leaving the rest of the continent to its fate. The plan was never official policy, and invasion was never seriously likely, but it probably did not help that the general in charge of Western Command was the controversial Major-General Gordon Bennett, who had left his troops to flee the fall of Singapore.[27]

Help was soon on its way. By June 1942 an estimated 70,000 troops were stationed in Western Australia. A Royal Australian Air Force squadron at Pearce, north-east of Perth, protected the metropolitan area, and the United States Navy set up a submarine base at Garden Island and a Catalina flying-boat base at Crawley. Curtin had aroused some controversy by declaring that Australia must look to the United States in its time of need, but the 'Yanks' were warmly welcomed; several hundred young Western Australian women were to marry Americans and settle in the United States. Sex and alcohol were later to arouse jealousies in Perth, as elsewhere in Australia, between Australian servicemen and the better paid Americans, but despite a number of little-publicised brawls there was less violence in Western Australia than in the Eastern States, except perhaps in the rougher streets of Fremantle. In 1942 the need for unity seemed paramount.[28]

So did the need for social control. Hotels were compelled to close at 6.00 pm instead of the customary hour of 9.00 pm, and nightclubs were prosecuted for illicit dealing in liquor, but public drunkenness was not eliminated. In July 1942 the police formed a special Vice Squad to control the growth of amateur prostitution and the consequent spread of venereal disease.[29] Public concern ran rife; in the Legislative Assembly in 1942, Florence Cardell-Oliver told her incredulous colleagues that 60 per cent of Perth's men had either acquired or inherited the disease. But the war's effects were not all bad. Official statistics suggested that in the 1920s and 1930s more than 12 per cent of Western Australian children were conceived outside wedlock, although in two-thirds of such cases the parents would marry before the child was born. Figures were not kept during the war, but by 1949, although the birthrate was booming, ex-nuptial conceptions had dropped to around 10 per cent. Although many still regarded birth control with disfavour as a threat to national security and family values—in 1939 the Western Australian Parliament legislated to ban the advertising of contraceptives—it seems likely that servicemen and women instructed in basic sexual hygiene during the period in the forces applied their lessons in civilian life.[30]

It was not a good time for dissenters and troublemakers. Although Soviet Russia was a major ally after 1941, the Communist Party of Australia remained an illegal organisation until late 1942. Even after the ban was lifted, its numbers were never significant in under-industrialised Western Australia, and the few prominent communist trade unionists, such as Paddy Troy of the Maritime Workers, supported the war effort. Communists probably attracted most notice by the whitewashed graffiti urging the cause of Russia that would appear overnight on city buildings or the rock face of Kings Park. On the ratbag fringe, an agent provocateur brought about the arrest in March 1942 of three men and a woman for plotting sedition and terrorism. Their leader, Lawrence Bullock, had attempted during the 1930s to politicise the unemployed, without much success. He claimed that instead of fighting Britain's wars, Australia should come to terms with the Japanese. He and another man were now gaoled for five years, and their colleagues interned. The accused claimed links with the Australia First movement, a Sydney republican organisation, many of whose members were also interned through guilt by association.[31]

Although the crisis of war put the secession movement to sleep, Western Australian parochialism could not be stilled. The Labor governments of Western Australia and Queensland joined conservative colleagues in other states to oppose Commonwealth plans to impose uniform income taxation throughout Australia. They took the fight to the High Court but lost—permanently, as it turned out. The state government also disliked Curtin's plans for increased federal powers over social services and other aspects of postwar reconstruction, fearing that if a conservative regime came to office in Canberra, Western Australia would lose its comparatively generous basic wage and workers' compensation legislation. (However, when eventually in 1944 the federal government at a referendum unsuccessfully asked for increased powers over fourteen fields thought necessary for postwar reconstruction, Western Australia was one of only two states to vote 'Yes'—a result startlingly inconsistent with the secession vote of 1933 and less often remembered in subsequent debates on Commonwealth–state relations.) On the other hand, Western Australia supported Curtin in the most embattled decision of his career, the introduction early in 1943 of military conscription for service within Australia and the adjacent region, and this helped to avert the risk of a split in the ALP. It said something for Curtin's prestige in his home state that at the federal election of 1943, every seat went Labor for the first and only time, whereas a little later the state government made only small gains when it faced the polls.[32]

The war brought Western Australian industry a stimulus unknown since federation. Linked to eastern Australia only by inadequate coastal shipping and by a transcontinental railway with four breaks of gauge between Perth and Sydney, Western Australia experienced frequent shortages of imported goods. Suburban householders reverted to backyard production, growing vegetables and keeping fowls for eggs and meat. With Commonwealth support, new local industries were encouraged. Flax and tobacco were cultivated in the South West, and a dried apples plant was set up at Donnybrook, but it was questionable whether the local market was big enough and the quality of the local produce reliable enough to survive the coming of peace.[33] Of greater significance was the decision to establish a munitions factory in the suburb of Welshpool in 1942. The Minister for Industrial Development, A. R. G. (Bert) Hawke, used the Welshpool development as the basis of Western Australia's first dedicated industrial estate. Before the war ended, government subsidies helped to establish a manufacturer of tractors at Welshpool. The Midland Junction railway workshops were expanded in 1943 for the manufacture of shells. At Wundowie, 60 kilometres east of Perth, a charcoal, iron and wood distillation plant made a first modest beginning to Western Australia's quest for new sources of fuel and energy. Some motorists used its product to fuel gas-producers, as a substitute for petrol.[34]

Shortage of petrol was only one of the inconveniences of wartime. Clothes were rationed, but the patching and darning needed to make garments last longer came readily to a generation of housewives schooled by the Depression. Men working in the central business district were still expected to wear suits and ties in all weathers, but rationing gave a pretext for discarding waistcoats. Women were admitted to many jobs from which they had previously been excluded. In the usually masculine area of metalwork and machinery, the numbers of female employees increased more than tenfold between 1939 and 1943. Many went into munitions and engineering; others worked in clothing and food processing factories. In 1942 and 1943 the number of women employed in Western Australian factories rose by 22.7 per cent, more than double the national average. Working conditions were often poor, but most of the women understood that they would be expected to quit the paid work force when the war was over. Very little official pressure was needed, as most looked forward to settling into lives of domesticity.[35] Not that housewives had it easy during the later years of the war. Accommodation was in very short supply, and although government rent controls were meant to stop profiteering, landlords often quietly demanded 'key money' at the start of tenancy. If black marketing never reached the scale of Sydney or Melbourne, grocers, tobacconists and publicans gave priority to regular customers for scarce items, and orchardists and market gardeners did the same. The war relaxed conventional morality. Nevertheless, when peace came in August 1945 and cheering crowds estimated at 30,000 turned out to mill through the streets of Perth, it was noted that the churches were crowded as never before. In a time of thanksgiving as in times of crisis, most Western Australians still turned to the Christian God.[36]

The war had an unexpectedly enlivening influence on the cultural scene in Western Australia. During the 1930s, radio stations proliferated in Perth, some operated by the Australian Broadcasting Commission (ABC) but the rest by locally owned companies supported by advertising (and one established in 1941 by the ALP). By 1941 sixteen broadcasters offered programs to their listeners, nine in the South West and the goldfields and seven in the metropolitan area. Isolation and the limitations of radio technology meant that all stations employed local staff and could use local content. When kindergartens closed in February 1942 because of the threat of Japanese invasion, Margaret Graham prepared a radio program, *Kindergarten of the Air*. 'This was the first program of its type in the world', writes Jean Farrant, 'and was so successful that for many years to come thousands of children throughout Australia, every morning at 9.30, listened to stories, sang songs, and moved to the music'.[37] In the following years, Catherine King at the ABC initiated a women's program reaching beyond the conventional interests of house and garden to discuss books and current affairs. It was an immediate success that would last until King moved to Melbourne twenty years later. Her more radical rival, Irene Greenwood, found sponsorship for several years on 6PM, a commercial station, providing an interesting alternative to 6PR's conservative male commentator, 'The Archer'.[38] Graham, King and Greenwood showed that Western Australia still possessed the capacity to respond innovatively to isolation.

In several respects, it was easier in the 1940s for young Western Australian creative artists to find a local public than it would be fifty or sixty years later. Because many plays and radio productions were broadcast from Perth, the ABC provided a modest source of patronage for actors and scriptwriters. Weekly periodicals the *Western Mail* and *The Broadcaster* published work from poets and short story writers. The postwar cultural scene also gained a quiet stimulus from a few dozen refugees from Germany and Central Europe. Missing the intellectual buzz of urban cafe conversation, such exiles met on Sunday afternoons, originally in the yard behind a Perth fruitmonger with banana crates for seating, creating a discussion group known as 'the Banana Club'. For about a decade after 1945, the 'Bananas' would be an influential cultural ginger group. Their members included Hans and Charlotte Briner, who in 1947 formed the Western Australian Opera Society; the physician Salec Minc, a keen patron of painting; and the artist Elise Blumann, who after 1950 ceased to exhibit in what she considered an unresponsive Perth.[39]

At that time, the arts in Western Australia did not lack enthusiasts, but taste tended to be conservative. A cultivated businessman, Claude Hotchin, opened a private art gallery in 1947 and over a period of twenty-five years presented more than 2,000 works, mainly landscapes, to the Royal Perth Hospital and regional galleries; for most country centres, this was their first systematic exposure to the fine arts. Government backing was minimal. The Art Gallery, the State Library and the Western Australian Museum were all crippled by years of underfunding. Official attitudes meant that when C. Y. O'Connor's daughter Kathleen, for many years a respected if not major figure in Parisian circles, returned to Western Australia in 1948, she was made to pay import duty on her works and had to throw away more than a hundred of them on the Fremantle dockside.[40] A warmer welcome was extended in 1948 to the touring Old Vic Company from London, whose production of *School for Scandal* with Sir Laurence Olivier, Vivien Leigh and Peter Cushing drew large and appreciative audiences. It gave a boost to local drama when Olivier praised the University Dramatic Society's open-air production of *Oedipus Rex*, first of many campus productions directed by the redoubtable Jean Tweedie (Jeana Bradley).

Indigenous Western Australians had gained some benefit from the war. During the 1930s, small but vocal urban middle-class pressure groups such as the Australian Aborigines' Amelioration Association (1932) and the Native Welfare Council (1939) championed reform, but made only modest progress. Despite the recommendations of a royal commission in 1934, the authority of the Chief Protector of Aborigines, A. O. Neville, was, if anything, strengthened. Troublemakers in country towns might still be deported to the Moore River settlement. Although the number of Christian missions increased after 1938, they came under greater departmental control. Neville was not quite unresponsive to shifting federal policies, and before he retired in 1940 was prepared to concede that Aboriginal families who could afford it should not be prevented from renting houses in country towns, provided that their behaviour conformed to their neighbours', but change came slowly.[41] Wartime manpower shortages increased the demand for Aboriginal labour, and hence their pay, especially on the defence installations in the north of the state. Pleased with its own liberality, parliament in 1944 legislated to grant full citizenship rights to Aboriginal people—provided that they were adult, literate, of industrious habits and good behaviour and completely severed from communal or tribal associations. Only a handful of applicants took the opportunity.[42]

Few expected Aborigines to show much aptitude for political organisation, but shortly after the war ended, Aboriginal pastoral workers in the Pilbara district staged a strike in May 1946. A remarkable woman, Daisy Bindi, led 500 men, women and children from the stations south of Nullagine to a camp at Port Hedland. Three of the leaders, Clancy McKenna, Dooley Bin-bin and a white pastoralist worker, Don McLeod, were imprisoned for breaching the laws about Aboriginal employment. A sympathiser, the local Anglican priest, was fined for visiting the Port Hedland camp, but the High Court quashed the conviction. Other clergy and academics were also sympathetic, and the strike gained national publicity. Eventually, many of the strikers went back to work, but more would be heard of McLeod and his 'mob'.[43]

For the Labor state government, the Pilbara affair seemed marginal compared with the challenges of postwar reconstruction. Leadership passed in 1945 to the agricultural scientist Frank Wise. He had consolidated his reputation by rejuvenating the Agricultural Bank in 1944, securing legislation that transformed the bank from 'a moribund collector of debts' to a state bank serving the industrial and community needs of the mid-century, as its new name, the Rural and Industries Bank, suggested.[44] The returning servicemen were easily enough absorbed into employment, aided by Commonwealth schemes enabling them to acquire the skills and education that they could not afford in the 1930s Depression. Many were marrying and starting families, and this placed great strain on the depleted stock of housing and building materials, as well as storing up a heavy demand for health services and schools in the not too distant future. The government responded by establishing the State Housing Commission, setting up estates of low-cost housing in the Perth suburbs and major country towns. Many young couples found themselves obliged to share houses with relatives, and at the 1947 census it emerged that nearly 5 per cent of Western Australians were bedded in sleepouts, mostly partitioned from suburban verandahs. The search for building materials led the Colonial Sugar Refining Company (CSR) to invest in a plant at Wittenoom, in the Pilbara, for processing blue asbestos—for as yet asbestos was not recognised as a health hazard. Local brickworks and building firms had more work than they could handle, their difficulties increased by the old problem of importing materials from the Eastern States.

The tyranny of distance was still impeding Western Australian development. After 1946 passengers had their choice of travelling to and from the Eastern States with two airlines, Australian National Airways and the government Trans Australian Airlines. Both offered daily services to Melbourne and Sydney, usually arriving and departing within a few minutes of each other; the Sydney journey took six and a half hours. Affluent passengers welcomed the saving of time compared to travel by rail or sea. Despite the state's major air disaster in 1950, when a night flight crashed near York shortly after takeoff and twenty-six lives were lost, a certain glamour persisted. It was well into the 1950s before *The West Australian* ended the practice of sending a reporter to meet each incoming flight and greet the passengers in the hope that one might prove worth an interview.[45] But many travellers and most freight had to come by sea or rail, and delays were frequent because of ageing infrastructure, industrial action and the problems of adapting to a civilian economy. Western Australia was still an importing state for much of its household and industry needs. In most years the state spent twice as much on imports from the Eastern States, mostly clothes, spare parts for machinery and electrical goods, as it gained from overseas exports. Inconvenient shortages were not easily tolerated; nor was the persistence of wartime rationing of petrol and some foodstuffs until 1949.

Public discontent fed on a number of grievances in those years. Trade unions saw postwar prosperity as entitling them to claim improved wages and conditions after more than a decade of constraint during the Depression and the war. Several disputes involved industrial safety. In November 1946 railwaymen went on strike over the continued use of the unsuitable Garratt locomotives introduced during the war. The strikers were justified, but that was no consolation for the many who, in the era before widespread car ownership, relied on public transport. Electricity supplies were jeopardised when the Collie coalminers went on strike in 1948 over the use of a recalcitrant pit pony.[46] As the use of horses in a colliery reminds us, it was an age of simpler technology; in many country towns, the electricity supply was unaffected by the strike because the fuel generating their power was local firewood rather than Collie coal. Although the state government purchased the City of Perth's gasworks and set up a State Electricity Commission in 1945, it would not be until the late 1950s and 1960s that a significant part of rural Western Australia was integrated into a state-wide grid. Meanwhile, the Perth metropolitan area was blacked out several times because of breakdowns in the ageing East Perth power station, and reliable supply was guaranteed only by the completion of the first stage of a new facility at South Fremantle in 1951.

These problems may have swayed some voters, but during the 1940s and 1950s the shifts in Western Australian politics were far from seismic in intensity. After fourteen years in office, Labor lost narrowly in 1947 to a coalition between the new Liberal Party (which between 1949 and 1968 called itself the Liberal and Country League) and the Country Party, under the leadership of the Liberal Ross McLarty, a Premier in the rural tradition of Forrest, Moore and Mitchell. He in turn would yield in 1953 to a Labor government under A. R. G. Hawke, but the margins of victory were never great, and the areas of agreement between both sides in politics comparatively broad. Both denounced communism and radicalism. Both sought to improve and diversify Western Australia's economy and to ensure that the resulting benefits were shared among the community with reasonable equity, though the McLarty government was quicker than Labor to dismantle the price controls and other regulations intended to check profiteering. Both drew on the impartially and efficiently given advice of some of Western Australia's finest public servants, among them the under-treasurer (Sir) Alexander Reid (1937–54) and (Sir) Russell Dumas (director and coordinator of works 1941–53).[47]

Wartime consciousness of the underdevelopment of the tropical north had sent Dumas on an investigation of the Kimberley district in 1941. Convinced of the potential for a dam on the Ord River, he encouraged research into sorghum and millet by Kim Durack, son of a pioneering pastoral family whose ideas may have been reinforced by the Sternberg scheme for Jewish closer settlement in the region. In 1945 the Kimberley Research Station was set up near the future site of Kununurra. Dumas became chair of the North-West Development Committee, and in that capacity encouraged the Blythe family and Australian National Airways to develop an imaginative scheme for freighting beef carcases by air from an inland abattoir at 'Glenroy' station to the Wyndham meatworks. Air Beef began operations in 1949, and would last for more than twenty years before yielding to the competition of road transport.[48] Air Beef seemed only the most spectacular of a number of initiatives in northern development in those years. A fifteen-year beef export agreement with the United Kingdom, signed in 1950, spelt security for the cattlemen. Hope of attracting permanent settlement in the north was stimulated by the apparent success of the asbestos community at Wittenoom, where 750 workers and their families lived.[49] A model of a different kind could be found in the Aborigines of 'McLeod's mob', who established the Pindan cooperative in the Marble Bar district in 1950, where they worked deposits of wolfram (tungsten) and tantalite by the traditional technique of 'yandying'. McLeod spoke of founding self-regulating Aboriginal communities who would sustain themselves through their mineral profits. Unfortunately, in 1952 he took into partnership an Adelaide firm, Western Wolfram, and the enterprise ended in a welter of litigation.[50]

In the south of Western Australia, as in the tropics, primary production still seemed the mainstay of the state's economy. Wartime shortages prompted a good deal of diversification, but few of the new products survived the coming of peace and renewed competition from longer-established interstate and overseas suppliers. During the war, the

Commonwealth sponsored flax production at Harvey and Boyup Brook, but although after the war the latter factory passed into the hands of a local cooperative it never grew big enough to command an assured share of the market, and closed in 1966. At Donnybrook a factory processing dried fruits and vegetables for export during the war was converted to cider production. The cider was creditable, but Australian drinking tastes were conservative and the venture was undercapitalised, going into liquidation in 1953. The tobacco industry at Manjimup struggled on for some years, but as import restrictions eased, cigarette smokers returned to the more popular British and American blends. In 1960–61 the tobacco market collapsed, and, soon after, the Michelides interests, the main operators in the industry, were forced into bankruptcy and growers turned to other crops. The opening of a salmon cannery at Hopetoun in 1945 and a crayfishing processing plant at Dongara facilitated a lively export trade. After a lapse of more than twenty years, whaling resumed at Point Cloates in the North West in 1949 and later at Albany. By 1953/54 more than a thousand whales were killed annually, yielding oil to the value of nearly a million pounds. Nobody protested.[51]

Wheat and wool continued to dominate Western Australia's export trade. Markets expanded and prices rose with demand from a wartorn Britain and Europe enduring food rationing into the early 1950s. The farmers prospered as never before. At long last able to shake free from debt, they could invest in mechanisation, beginning with the trucks, bulldozers, four-wheel drive vehicles, earthmoving equipment and other material surplus to the needs of the armed forces in peacetime. The surviving dairy farms in the South West consolidated. Although it would be 1960 before the total Western Australian wheat crop passed the peak figure attained in 1930, the use of trace elements enabled light land previously unworkable to be brought under cultivation. In the North Midlands district, Eric Smart won national recognition and eventually a knighthood for his achievements in using mechanisation in large-scale wheat cultivation, and in showing the feasibility of cultivating lupins in sandplain country. From 1950 until his retirement in 1967, he would be Australia's largest grain grower, producing more than 100,000 tonnes annually.[52] Wool-growers benefited from a spectacular increase in export prices in 1949–50, especially after the outbreak of hostilities in Korea in 1950 brought about massive stockpiling through fears of a third world war.

These fears did not seem unrealistic. Almost immediately after the end of World War II in 1945, the British Empire and the United States had fallen out with their ally, the communist Soviet Union, leading to a 'Cold War' that was to last for more than forty years. Fears that Marxism intended to take over the whole world, including Western Australia, increased after mainland China went communist in 1948–49, and were intensified by the knowledge that atomic weapons would not long remain the monopoly of the United States. In 1951, when the Commonwealth Government held a referendum seeking constitutional power to ban the Communist Party of Australia in peacetime, Western Australia recorded the biggest percentage of 'Yes' votes of any of the states. This response was compatible with the West's long tradition of fear of the alien, but the proposal was narrowly rejected through the votes of the more confident, or perhaps more libertarian, south-eastern states.[53]

Western Australia had to grow, and growth depended on attracting population and investment. Although the birthrate was recovering from the low levels of the Depression period, Western Australia, like the rest of Australia, needed migrants, and federal policy met the need. From 1947 to 1971, 'ten-pound Poms' from the United Kingdom were assured of cheap fares if they stayed for two years or more. They were supplemented by 'New Australians' from continental Europe, at first displaced persons from refugee camps and, later, as a result of agreements with selected European nations. As Fremantle was the first port of call for overseas migrant ships, Western Australia was well situated to receive newcomers. The army camp at Northam was converted into a reception centre. Between 1947 and 1954, the state's population increased from 502,480 to 639,771, nearly half through migration. In 1950 Western Australia attracted more newcomers than in any year since the height of the gold rush in 1896, and its rate of increase was the highest in Australia. More than half the new arrivals were British or Irish, with Dutch, Italian and Greek migrants most prominent among the remainder.[54]

Would there be jobs for them all if the state's economy lost the buoyancy based on wheat and wool? Because of the pegging of world prices, gold was an unattractive investment. It was not yet certain that

Western Australia would find its fortunes in mining. Russell Dumas foresaw that Western Australia must compete more strongly with other states in attracting outside investment in secondary industry. He found an ally in McLarty's only youthful cabinet minister, David Brand. Together in 1951 they succeeded in persuading British Petroleum to establish an oil refinery at Kwinana on Cockburn Sound 20 kilometres south of Fremantle. This development encouraged Broken Hill Proprietary (BHP) to locate a cement works and a steel-rolling mill in the same neighbourhood. The workers would be housed in four Canberra-type suburbs. Environmentalists were later to grumble at the location of industry at a site from which the south-westerly breeze would blow its pollution towards the Perth metropolitan area, but at the time Western Australia's desperation for growth and diversification overrode such considerations. Kwinana was the foundation of Western Australia's first major industrial development and a critically important harbinger of economic takeoff.

8

The coming of the iron age, 1951–1971

In March 1954 the young Queen Elizabeth II and her husband, Philip, Duke of Edinburgh, paid Western Australia its first visit by the monarch and consort. Most of the speeches and editorials in their honour laid stress on the community's deep and continuing loyalty to British traditions. There was predictable rhetoric about the coming of a new Elizabethan age. *The West Australian* expressed confidence that the crowds that turned out to greet the Queen would behave in a more seemly fashion than some over-demonstrative royalists in the Eastern States. Surprisingly, little was said of Western Australia's importance as a member of the British Empire and Commonwealth—if it possessed any importance. It was left to the London *Times*, having declared that the royal couple had seen 'no fairer little city' than Perth, to observe that Western Australia was on the threshold of development.[1] This forecast would be amply justified during the next fifteen years.

For the present, however, Western Australia seemed a land of wide open spaces where British scientists might with impunity conduct experiments with atomic bombs at the Montebello Islands in the North West. The first controlled explosion in October 1952 caused no environmental misgivings. *The West Australian* took pride in contributing to the security of the British Empire during the Cold War, and the inhabitants of the nearby town of Onslow heard the explosion as no more than a break in the torpor of the week following the annual race meeting. Two further nuclear tests in May–June 1956 aroused a little more debate.[2] Controversy intensified later in the year when the Montebellos served as destination for rockets launched from Maralinga in South Australia.

The creation of the Maralinga base deprived the nomadic Aborigines of the Warburton Range of good land and water. An independent member of state parliament, Bill Grayden, assisted by the young Rupert Murdoch, investigated their plight and reported that they seemed close to starvation, and this drew him into dispute with the Department of Native Welfare.[3] The experiments ceased when Britain decided it could no longer afford an independent nuclear deterrent, but left a belief in the potential of nuclear energy in the minds of a number of Western Australians who would come to prominence in the 1960s and 1970s.

For the whole of the state's settled history, Western Australia's growth had been held back by want of cheap energy. Industry needed bigger and better sources of fuel than the sub-bituminous coal of Collie. Postwar governments encouraged the search for oil, and in 1952 West Australian Petroleum, a subsidiary of Caltex and Ampol Exploration, commenced drilling at Rough Range, near Exmouth. In December 1953 Perth and its stock exchange were electrified by the news that oil had been discovered at the first attempt. The euphoria resembled the golden years of the 1890s. But once again the rejoicings were premature. Despite several years of drilling, no further oilwells were found after Rough Range. In the long run, the find gave a stimulus to further mineral exploration, but for the present it still seemed that Western Australia would have to depend on its traditional mainstays of wool and wheat.

All this activity brought an Indian summer of prosperity to the small country towns of the Wheatbelt and the South West. Many had reached their maximum population and would never be more lively with sporting teams and voluntary organisations. Improving transport brought a number of challenges. Once it had been sensible to space country towns at intervals of 15–20 kilometres, accessible within a few hours' trot by horse and buggy. Now farmers and their families travelled in utilities and station wagons at greater speed to larger centres further apart. The state government decided in 1956 to close 20 per cent of the rural railway lines, as the cost of maintenance made them no longer payable in the face of competition from motor transport. Other lines were maintained only for the carriage of freight, and were replaced by passenger bus services. This meant there were fewer jobs for country lads as railway station staff. Their sisters who had found employment before marriage operating local telephone exchanges were also displaced as automation came to the national system. Small rural schools closed as improved roads made it easier to bring students by bus to larger and better-resourced centres. Almost imperceptibly, the process was beginning that would convert many of the country towns founded with high hopes in the early years of the century into deserted villages.[4]

Perth, meanwhile, after half a century of development within the limits chalked out by the real estate developers of the gold rush era, was once again beginning to expand. The state government in 1952 invited an internationally renowned town planner, Professor Gordon Stephenson, to draw up plans for the future development of the metropolitan area in the age of the automobile. Together with the local planner J. A. Hepburn, Stephenson put together a blueprint that was to shape city planning for the rest of the century. He called for a system of freeways and major highways enabling commuters to cross the city easily from far-flung suburbs, but also generously provided for open spaces dividing the built-up areas.[5] As if to emphasise the priority of private transport over public transport, the last tram services in Perth were closed in 1958. Rough Range may not have guaranteed oil in commercial quantities, but Western Australia's decision-makers took it for granted that petrol for the private motorist as for industry would always be cheap and plentiful. As a first step in the freeway system, it was essential to grapple with the problem of bridging the Swan River at the Narrows, often discussed but never previously carried into effect. The Hawke government grasped the nettle, and the Narrows Bridge—the notion of calling it the Golden West Bridge was abandoned as somehow too pretentious—was opened in 1958. For several years more, the construction of the bridge and the associated freeways called for the reclamation of land along the river banks on a scale that dismayed many. The veteran feminist Bessie Rischbieth cut an iconic figure as she stood, umbrella aloft, ankle-deep in the river, defying the bulldozers; but the work continued, and landscape architects such as the respected John Oldham softened the consequences. It was only in 1965 that mounting public concern discouraged schemes for further reclamation.[6]

Modest but significant cultural advances matched Perth's growth during the 1950s. After many years of government parsimony, the state's leading cultural institutions began to rejuvenate. In 1953 the Western

Australian Art Gallery curated a travelling exhibition of modern French paintings that gave strong stimulus to local artists. The creation of the Library Board of Western Australia in 1954 initiated a major reform that in two and a half decades saw the establishment of a public library in every local authority in Western Australia, spelling an end to the small, privately owned lending libraries that until then had served public taste. In 1953 The University of Western Australia, under the inspiration of Professor Fred Alexander and John Birman, established the annual Festival of Perth, the first of its kind in Australia, with a professionally directed production of *Richard III*. The festival gave a stimulus to the screening of foreign films. The same year saw classical music gain a canny and powerful champion with the arrival at the university of Professor Frank Callaway.[7] Perth still lacked adequate venues for performances, and so a recital by the Griller Quartet in the RSL's Anzac House had to compete with the rumble of kegs for a nearby party. In 1957 the Playhouse Theatre provided a modest facility for drama, and in 1960 a new ABC building included the Basil Kirke studio, with excellent acoustics for orchestra rehearsals. From 1958 artists from all over Australia found a new outlet in the Skinner Galleries, where the entrepreneurial Rose Skinner promoted the works of Guy Grey-Smith, Robert Juniper and other rising artists who had been exposed to contemporary influences overseas. And the traffic went two ways: in 1959 Elizabeth Blair Barber organised an exhibition in London of six Western Australian artists.[8]

Although *The Broadcaster* and the *Western Mail* both ceased publication in the 1950s, new writers were still emerging, and some gained recognition beyond Western Australia. Several found subject matter in experiences of World War II. Among them Tom Hungerford's *The Ridge and the River*, set in the New Guinea campaign, attracted national attention, as did Jack Harvey's study of navy life, *Salt in Our Wounds*. In 1958 a dazzling young talent emerged in Randolph Stow, with the publication of *The Merry-Go-Round in the Sea*, an evocation of the home front in wartime that heralded the publication of a rapid succession of novels during the 1960s, among them a delightful children's story based on the myths of Western Australia's colonial history, *Midnite*.[9]

Higher professional standards in the writings of Western Australian history were attainable after the appointment in 1945 of Mollie Lukis as State Archivist, with the task of collecting and preserving the state's public records and private collections in what became known after 1954 as the Battye Library, within the State Library of Western Australia. She found an ally in Frank Crowley, lecturer in Australian history at The University of Western Australia from 1952 to 1964 (only the second appointment of its kind anywhere in Australia), who compiled a comprehensive bibliography and, in 1960, a history of the state, *Australia's Western Third*. Outside the academy, Alexandra Hasluck produced a perceptive biography of the botanist Georgiana Molloy, *Portrait with Background* (1954). Mary Durack won acclaim for her family history *Kings in Grass Castles* (1959), providing an evocation of the pastoral outback that offered a different perspective from the New South Wales–based Russel Ward's *The Australian Legend*. In Western Australia as elsewhere in Australia, historians, like creative writers such as Prichard and Drake-Brockman, still tended to avoid the urban environment in seeking their subject matter.[10] Those who yearned for wider horizons, like the versatile artist and entertainer Rolf Harris and the novelist Randolph Stow, settled in England.

Developmentally, the 1950s were a time of hope deferred. The Hawke government was not backward in searching for new and diversified investment, but its luck was poor. In 1949 the Department of Agriculture set up a research station in the Esperance district to demonstrate the area's potential for grazing, 'with emphasis on the removal of as much as possible of the original vegetation by burning before ploughing with heavy disc machines', followed by liberal dressings of superphosphate supplemented by trace elements. By 1956 the Esperance district was deemed ready for subdivision into farms. In that year another dreamer of great dreams backed by little research appeared in the person of an American, Allan Chase, already promoting a large-scale rice-growing project in the Northern Territory. His syndicate purchased about 600,000 hectares of Crown land, with a commitment to sell half the developed farms to settlers. Within two years the scheme was clearly floundering from want of preparation. In 1960 Chase withdrew from all his Australian projects. His Esperance lands were taken over in 1962 by another company with American and Australian interests who were more prepared to listen to the agricultural scientists, and by 1965

Esperance was supporting 436 farms totalling nearly 700,000 hectares, carrying half a million sheep and a significant number of cattle.[11]

The Hawke government's attitude towards mineral development was governed largely by policies that had served its predecessors since recovery from the Depression of the 1930s. Lenore Layman has identified them as

> support for individual prospectors and for a great number of small-scale mining ventures rather than a concern to attract large private capital; secondly, only limited, piecemeal and sometimes delayed support for the larger companies operating in the resource area...[12]

This suited the battling prospectors and mine workers in the Labor-dominated electorates of the goldfields and North West, but the apparent success of Wittenoom as a company town suggested the possibility of an approach on a larger scale by private investment backed by a planned and coordinated provision of extensive government assistance. Dumas had been urging this approach at least since 1947, but it was only in the 1950s that increasing demand on world markets stimulated potential investors to send their geologists to re-examine mineral deposits previously thought unworkable or unprofitable. In 1958 Western Mining began to examine the bauxite resource in the Darling escarpment south of Perth, while other explorers tested the mineral sands deposits south of Bunbury.[13]

Attention also turned to the prospects of iron ore. It had long been known that the Pilbara region held promising iron-ore deposits, but it was only after World War II that improvement of transport technology and an unprecedented period of sustained industrial growth in North America, Europe and especially Japan made it possible to justify the major investment required for large-scale enterprise. Hitherto Western Australia's iron-ore industry had been confined to a small government-owned project at Koolyanobbing, north-west of Coolgardie, serving the Wundowie charcoal iron works. During the 1950s BHP undertook development of the Yampi Sound deposits for the domestic market. Further expansion was strongly discouraged by a Commonwealth Government embargo on the export of iron ore imposed for strategic reasons in 1938 and maintained long after the war's end by successive federal governments who seriously underestimated Australia's iron-ore reserves. In 1958 the Hawke government tried to persuade the federal authorities to abandon this policy, but was rebuffed.

Hawke was defeated at the 1959 election and the Liberal David Brand took over.[14] The last of the rural Western Australian premiers, Brand had the diplomatic skills needed to manage an often uneasy relationship with his coalition partners, the Country and Democratic League (formerly the Country Party), as well as appealing to the wider public. In its early years, his government's policies blended change with continuity. For Brand, as for most conservative governments since Forrest, privatisation was not a dogma. Although the state's building and sawmills operations were sold to a British company, Stateships continued to ply between Fremantle and the North West and Kimberley ports. A Metropolitan Transport Trust was formed to buy out Perth's private bus companies and unify the public transport system under one management. In 1960 a Totalisator Agency Board (TAB) was set up to replace the starting-price bookmakers, who had been allowed to operate lawfully since 1955 under the eye of the Betting Control Board. This followed a royal commission suggesting evidence of malpractice, and although a second inquiry in 1967 found some fault with the TAB, it had by then become entrenched in public acceptance.[15] The Brand government even showed some taste for constitutional reform, abolishing the property qualification for voters for the Legislative Council in 1963. Although this meant that the upper house would henceforth be elected by adult franchise, the constituencies were still weighted against the metropolitan area, so that the non-Labor parties could be sure of keeping control.

The Brand government proved more of a new broom in industrial relations. In 1963, following similar changes in the Commonwealth and Queensland, a four-man Industrial Commission was created to replace the Arbitration Court. Protest was parried by the appointment as chief commissioner of the pragmatic and experienced Fred Schnaars, a former employees representative.[16] Earlier, in 1960–61, the government had faced down a prolonged strike of Collie coalminers resisting the retrenchment of more than half the work force and the development of open-cut mining in preference to underground collieries. This kept coal in the picture as a source of fuel and energy, but when new power stations were built during the 1960s for the generation of electricity, oil was the preferred fuel.[17]

In matters of Aboriginal policy, the Brand government was capable of surprising some of its critics. During the 1950s the Hawke government, tutored by Commissioner Middleton, had tried to remove many restrictions, in 1957 introducing legislation to grant full citizenship to all Aboriginal people except those specifically deemed to need departmental protection, but the Liberal–Country Party majority in the Legislative Council rejected this and most other proposals for change. Meanwhile, living conditions in the South West improved during the 1950s as rural expansion created job opportunities, and state schools no longer banned Aboriginal children but in fact made some attempt to meet their special needs and cultural interests. Aboriginal families became eligible for State Housing Commission housing in the more progressive country towns such as Quairading and Bruce Rock. For urban Aborigines, a housing community, Allawah Grove, was established at South Guildford in 1957 under the management of an active Aboriginal social organisation, the New Coolbaroo League.[18] After Brand came to office, most of his rural colleagues, products of the hard-won respectability of small country towns, still mistrusted change, but in 1961 the largely urban state executive of the Liberal Party came out in favour of full citizenship rights. In 1963, partly in response to federal pressure, many restrictions on Aboriginal people were swept away including the bans on alcohol consumption and sexual intercourse with non-Aborigines. In 1964 the Liberal Party endorsed the first Aboriginal candidate for a seat in state parliament, but he was unsuccessful.

All these reforms were compatible with the prevailing goal of assimilation that would see Australians of Aboriginal ancestry conforming to the same way of life as the majority, but awkward issues remained to trouble later decades. There has been much debate in recent years about a 'stolen generation' of Aboriginal children removed from their mothers to institutional care and in many cases growing up without the skills to nurture their children and grandchildren, but there was more than one generation involved. It was only in 1960 that the Department of Native Welfare came to accept that it was preferable for Aboriginal children under 12 to remain with their parents. In the North West and Kimberley districts, there was also the question raised by Don McLeod: how much pay did Aboriginal pastoral workers deserve? By 1959 some properties were reported to be paying full wages to efficient workers in preference to the old system of handouts, but the practice was by no means widespread when a federal court judgment in 1965 ruled that Aboriginal workers should receive equal pay.[19] Pastoralists felt that this was more than they could afford, and discharged many of their work force to find a future in the towns. With little demand for their skills, limited job prospects, and legal access to alcohol, these displaced Aboriginal communities faced daunting social problems beyond the imaginative grasp of most Western Australians. In 1967 a Commonwealth referendum proposing the removal from the Australian Constitution of clauses discriminating against Aborigines received a 78.7 per cent 'Yes' vote in Western Australia, but this was the lowest percentage among the states. And it would not be long before issues of Aboriginal entitlement were swept into the side effects of a mineral boom transforming much of the Western Australian outback.

This transformation was to make the reputation of the Minister for Industrial Development, Charles Court, whose skills as an accountant were to serve him in the development of bold government policies, as Forrest in his time had been served by his experience as a surveyor. Wartime service had given him valuable experience in negotiating with Americans and Japanese. Brand and Court made a good team. With a loyalty uncommon in politics, Court was to serve twelve years under Brand, concentrating on a dynamic and aggressive resource policy. Although the Brand government suffered an unexpected rebuff in 1960 when the Legislative Council rejected a proposal to create a three-man Industrial Development Authority, it could draw on some capable officials: Dumas, although in semi-retirement, was still consulted, while (Sir) Kenneth Townsing, under-treasurer (1954–77), was probably the ablest public servant to hold that office.[20]

Brand and Court also had their share of luck. Labor's inability to mount a successful challenge was sometimes blamed on the Democratic Labor Party (DLP), formed at the federal level in 1955 when right-wing members of the ALP, with support from sections of the Catholic Church, broke away to form a new party based on family values and a strong affirmation of anti-communism. Although most of the DLP's preferences went regularly to the Liberals, the party was never as influential in Western Australia as in Victoria and Queensland, and was probably significant only at the 1959 election.[21] A more lasting cause of weakness was the growing tension between the political and industrial wings of the Labor Party in Western Australia after the election as state secretary of F. E. (Joe) Chamberlain in 1949. An uncompromising survivor of the Depression, Chamberlain worked to strengthen the trade union influence within the party at the expense of the long-entrenched parliamentary leadership, whom he saw as too given to compromise. The tension increased after 1963 when Western Australia, after a long delay, followed the other states in setting up a Trades and Labour Council, and boiled over in 1965 when Chamberlain, one of the most virulent critics of the DLP, denounced Hawke for suggesting the merits of a rapprochement between the two parties. Relations improved after 1966, when Hawke yielded the leadership to another veteran, John Tonkin, but by that time the Brand government was riding the crest of a mineral boom such as Western Australia had not known since the 1890s.[22]

Like Forrest before them, Brand and Court were fortunate in the timing of their mineral boom, and like Forrest also they used their luck well. Supported by recent research into transport costs, Brand tried again in 1960, in a more auspicious political climate, to persuade the Commonwealth to end the embargo on iron-ore exports. This time Canberra consented, though for a while some restrictions still applied. In 1961 the Commonwealth also agreed to contribute substantially to the standardisation of the railway from Kalgoorlie to Perth and Kwinana, with a branch line to the iron-ore leases at Koolyanobbing. These were acquired by BHP, which undertook to establish an integrated iron and steel industry at Kwinana. Canberra's shift in policy was enough to stimulate the pegging of a large number of claims, on the basis of which Court addressed himself to securing multinational capital on a scale never before attempted.[23] Within six years, four major iron-ore projects were in progress: the Goldsworthy mining corporation, Hamersley Iron, Cliffs (WA) and Mount Newman. Each was a joint venture involving British, American, Japanese and Australian investors, although except for Mount Newman (where BHP and CSR were major partners) the overseas interests dominated.

The companies had to pledge themselves that within two years, they would begin to export not less than a million tons of iron ore annually, and would each commit themselves to between £20 million and £40 million in development expenditure, building railways and port facilities and company towns to house the workers. Overseas investors sometimes blinked at these demands, 'but Court just smiled'.[24] Unlike Wittenoom (its own future under a cloud as the profits from asbestos dwindled and doubt began to surface about its long-term effects on workers' health), the new towns would not receive infrastructure from the state government beyond the usual public services such as hospitals, schools and police. Before long, new names dotted the Pilbara map—Tom Price and Newman, Karratha and Dampier—each with a young population. In these towns, despite refrigeration and air-conditioning, wives and mothers eagerly awaited the coming of the winter and the arrival of supportive grandparents visiting from south.[25]

Still a claimant state receiving federal support from the Commonwealth Grants Commission, Western Australia was limited in its ability to raise finance, and was troubled during 1965–66 by Commonwealth attempts to regulate the export trade, but by providing a secure environment for investors, with twenty-one year renewable contracts, the Brand government was able to make advantageous terms. The investors responded promptly. Within eighteen months, Hamersley Iron laid Australia's heaviest standard-gauge railway track, traversing 400 kilometres, and constructed the towns of Tom Price and Dampier. The first shipment of 52,000 tonnes of iron left Dampier for Japan in August 1966. By 1969 Western Australia's annual iron ore exports were valued at $132 million.

There were critics. Australian nationalists worried about the power that might be wielded by international capitalists controlling a major export and its infrastructure. Lang Hancock, who registered many of the earliest claims for iron-ore mineral leases, and his astute partner, Peter Wright, believed in 'the almost divine right of the prospector to develop his finds as he thinks fit' and loudly resented the state government's orchestration of mineral policy.[26] But in seeking to control the ground rules for investment and development, Brand and Court were working in the established tradition of Western Australian governments since Forrest. Hancock, a member of an old Pilbara pastoral family, was the maverick. He was to reveal a penchant for grand concepts: an artificial port created by nuclear explosion, a transcontinental railway linking the Pilbara with the coalfields of Queensland, a Western Australia seceding from the baleful influence of Canberra to an autonomy where his influence might prevail. He was especially beguiled by the potential of controlled nuclear engineering and the creation of energy using tidal power.[27] He and Court became sworn foes, but it was as well for the state that policymaking lay with the experienced accountant rather than the visionary amateur.

Not that Court's initiatives all prospered at first. In the tradition of Forrest, he saw mineral development as going hand in hand with agriculture. In the north of Western Australia, the regular summer rainfall of the Kimberley district offered the greatest promise. Fifteen years of experimentation at a research station on the Ord River justified the opening of a diversion dam in 1963 and the arrival of the first farmers around what became the township of Kununurra. Despite bitter disagreement among academics about the viability of Ord agriculture, from 1965 to 1967 the state government lobbied the Commonwealth for funding for a second and larger dam. Canberra yielded in 1967, leading by 1972 to the creation of Lake Argyle, a small inland sea holding nine times the volume of water in Sydney Harbour in normal times and perhaps seven times that volume in times of flood. It was an impressive piece of engineering and offered potential for hydro-electric generation, although some questioned its environmental impact.[28] Unfortunately, the Ord River farmers could not find a major crop capable of succeeding in the face of established competitors and predatory wildlife. Cotton, sugar and sorghum were all tried, unsuccessfully, and it would be two decades before the project started to achieve stable productivity.

For the mining industry, it seemed success all the way. The bauxite deposits in the Darling escarpment were proved commercially viable. Alcoa of Australia, a subsidiary of a powerful United States aluminium corporation, joined with Western Mining in its development, eventually building refineries at Kwinana and Pinjarra.[29] Oil was found in moderately commercial quantities at Barrow Island in 1964, and came into production in 1967. In 1966 significant nickel discoveries south of Kalgoorlie led to the development of Kambalda by the Western Mining Corporation. In 1970 it began refining at Kwinana, not far from BHP's blast furnace opened two years earlier. Another significant nickel discovery was made at Leinster, north of Leonora, and when a third find was reported at Windarra in the same district in 1969 the stock market went crazy. Shares in the fortunate discoverers, the Poseidon company, soared relentlessly, reaching $259 in February 1970. Then the reaction set in, and many punters took losses. Windarra achieved a modest productivity some years later, but Poseidon stood as a warning that even the stupendous mineral discoveries of the 1960s were not enough to justify a stampede on the stock market. It was a lesson that many would forget.[30]

By 1968 Western Australia felt strong enough to end its status as a claimant state for federal subsidising, and Brand negotiated withdrawal from the Commonwealth Grants Commission. Self-sufficiency in fuel and energy remained a major priority. Between 1968 and 1971 the state government took an alert interest when John Gorton as Prime Minister showed signs of fostering the use of nuclear power, until deflected by the economic and political risks. Imported oil and local coal were still the uncertain engines of Western Australia's economic growth. The discovery of natural gas in the Dongara region, brought into production in 1971, promised a viable alternative, but output could not yet meet the state's needs. These considerations were not enough to diminish optimism. Economically, the 1960s were a coming of age.

And change came irrevocably for the comfortable Western Australia of the 1950s and early 1960s. For many households, the index of change was no more dramatic than the acquisition of the family's first car or of one of the new black-and-white television sets first marketed in 1958. A few progressive businesses were hesitantly considering the uses of computer technology, and an increasing number of those who had to travel were weighing the convenience of flying against the lesser expense of rail or sea journeys. But Perth was still a bland, easygoing community where everyone had acquaintances in common, and its major function was still as a service centre for primary producers. The Royal Agricultural Show at the beginning of October remained a centrepiece of the social calendar. The office buildings and hotels of St Georges Terrace, spruced up for the Empire Games of 1962, presented an array of late-Victorian and Edwardian frontages of modest height, harmoniously integrating the two mementos of the 1930s, the Art Deco CML office block and the mock-Tudor London Court. Until well into the 1950s, strollers along the terrace might set their watches by a one o'clock gun fired at the Perth Observatory, just as they had fifty years previously. Young men in respectable businesses such as banks and jeweller's shops were expected to wear suits and ties, no matter how hot the summer day. Young women were not supposed to wear trousers to work. Married women could not hold permanent jobs in the public service or the university. More families went to church than would be the case at any time in the future, their numbers increased by recent migrants seeking the assurance of the familiar. Taste was exemplified in Lord Mayor Howard's remark that neat rose gardens were more attractive than tall native trees. Rebellion went little further than Randolph Stow's satirical rejoinder:

> His delicate fingers moving among the roses
> Became a symbol. His words a battle-cry:
> 'Nothing shall be taller than Lord Mayor Howard
> but insurance buildings.'[31]

Sir Harry Howard could claim credit for initiating the bid that won the Empire Games for Perth in 1962. This was apt because since the war Western Australia had produced several athletes who distinguished themselves in the Olympic and Commonwealth games: John Winter, Shirley Strickland and Herb Elliott foremost among them. Swimmers were handicapped by Perth's lack of adequate training facilities, and Howard stirred controversy by his persistence in urging the alienation of part of Kings Park as an aquatic centre. But since the turn of the century, Kings Park had entrenched itself as the pride of Western Australians, who rebuffed all attempts, however well intentioned, to threaten its inviolability. Howard's scheme was twice defeated in state parliament, and from that time Kings Park has remained intact. Instead, the games went successfully enough, with swimming at Beatty Park and the main stadium at Perry Lakes.[32]

Earlier in 1962, Perth assumed the title of 'City of Light', a name that blended civic pride uneasily with a continuing sense of isolation. When the astronaut John Glenn became the first American to circle the earth in a space capsule, Perth's streetlights shone all night as a landmark for the space travellers. Howard revelled in his invitation to join the New York street parade honouring the astronauts, though at first he had cast cold water on the idea.[33] Perth was a clear beacon because it was so far from any town of similar size, though it was not yet so large and sophisticated a city that its citizens were expected to be out of doors in the small hours of the morning. Only the milkmen, a few of them still delivering by horse and cart, and later the newspaper deliverymen flinging copies of *The West Australian* on the suburban nature strips, had any business to be up and about at such times.

Danger could still lurk in the dark, and between 1959 and 1963 suburban householders were kept on edge by the activities of a night-walking murderer who chose his victims at random, at one time shooting a student in his sleepout, at another knocking on a front door and gunning down the babysitter when she answered. The culprit, Eric Cooke, was at length arrested and in October 1964 became the last Western Australian to be executed by hanging. (The death sentence was retained in Western Australia for another twenty years, longer than in any other Australian state, but was never carried into effect.) Cooke's story has stirred the imagination of several novelists, among them Tim Winton, Robert Drewe and Randolph Stow, but his impact on the collective imagination of the people of Perth was apparently profound. Until Cooke's rampage, many will say, Perth was a safe, trusting city where it had been unnecessary to lock doors and windows at night, but it was never the same afterwards.[34] Too many strangers were coming into the state. Nobody was surprised when police pursuing a petty criminal shot the man dead in a suburban backyard, and the inspector in charge sought to put the startled householder at ease by telling him 'it was only a young fellow from the Eastern States'.[35]

Young people from the Eastern States and newcomers from overseas (still overwhelmingly British and European, but including a few from South and Southeast Asia as the White Australia Policy eased) poured into the land of promise that was Western Australia in the 1960s. From that time onward, its population grew more rapidly, its intake of migrants was proportionately greater, and the rise in income per head higher than in Australia as a whole. The figures told the story. It had taken more than a century—from 1829 to 1946—for Western Australia's population to increase to half a million; it took less than quarter of a century to pass the million mark, in 1970. Most population was concentrated in the Perth metropolitan area, pushing the trend that by 2008 would see Western Australia the most urbanised of Australian states, with three-quarters of the population living within an hour's drive of the Perth central business district.[36] The suburbs sprawled across the coastal sandplain and reached into the Darling Scarp. It was fortunate that a Metropolitan Region Scheme based on the Stephenson–Hepburn plan was in place from 1963 to keep some order in the process of development.

These thriving times founded the fortunes of a number of real-estate developers who would come to prominence in the 1980s, such as the young Alan Bond. In the 1960s, however, Western Australia's foremost entrepreneur was 'Tom the Cheap Grocer'. Starting as an ex-serviceman in a conventional corner shop, Tom Wardle returned from a visit to Europe in 1955 with an innovative concept: self-service stores where customers took their purchases off the shelf and paid at a checkout counter. Within twenty years this concept, soon taken up by nationwide competitors such as Woolworths and Coles, would drive most of the independent grocers out of business. Because Wardle's profit margins were less than half those of his competitors, wholesalers black-banned him, but he found other suppliers, demanded big credit, ran tight budgets and survived. Unusually at that time, his managers were all married women: they were cheaper. 'Tom the Cheap Grocer' expanded interstate until, at his zenith, he owned 245 stores, with a national turnover of $78 million. Lord Mayor of Perth from 1967 to 1972, a knight, a philanthropist and the chair of many public charitable corporations, he was responsible for Perth's inclusion in the itinerary of Test cricket matches against England, and was a strong supporter of Perth's much-needed new concert hall, opened in 1972. From 1971, as Australia's relations with China thawed, he was one of the first importers to tap that low-cost supplier, but was brought low by a credit squeeze in 1974–75 and forced to liquidate his empire. He could be seen as a role model for later entrepreneurs who wanted to show that Western Australia need no longer be a mere branch office for outside investors but could take on the rest of the world, even if at the end downfall awaited.[37]

Wardle and his successors at the Perth City Council seemed powerless to prevent the destruction of many of the office blocks that had graced

St Georges Terrace since early in the century, although at the same time their colleagues in Fremantle were proving able to preserve the port's old buildings, or at least their facades, in what many visitors praised as an unusually well preserved Australian streetscape. Of course Perth needed high-rise air-conditioned office blocks, but demand for a St Georges Terrace address overwhelmed all alternatives. The result would be that Perth's main thoroughfare became what Jenny Gregory has described as 'a windswept canyon of concrete, steel and glass' and George Seddon as a 'Potemkin village'.[38]

These developments did not pass unnoticed by what was becoming an increasingly vocal conservation movement. By establishing the Western Australian chapter of the National Trust in 1962, the Brand government provided a focus for champions of the state's built heritage, but official policy did not always seem mindful of heritage values. The construction of the Mitchell Freeway serving Perth's northern suburbs called for the demolition of the colonial Pensioner Guard Barracks building at the head of St Georges Terrace. This was favoured by the state government, as it was in the process of completing long-delayed extensions to Parliament House, which would replace the Barracks as the focal point at the west end of the terrace. Despite sustained protest, the two wings of the Barracks were knocked down in 1966. The arch was also scheduled for destruction, but to the government's surprise and vexation a conscience vote in the Legislative Assembly later in 1966 produced a good majority in favour of retention. The Barracks Arch was to survive as a reminder to future parliamentarians of the power of public opinion.[39]

Heritage and environment were coming increasingly to the fore during the 1960s as proper concerns for the state government. Confronted with the challenge of protecting four seventeenth- and eighteenth-century Dutch wreck sites located off the coast between Fremantle and Shark Bay, the government passed legislation in 1964 vesting the historic wrecks in the Western Australian Museum and supporting a program of maritime archaeology with few parallels anywhere in the world. A treaty signed in 1973 between the government of the Netherlands and the Commonwealth Government reinforced this protection so that when the High Court ruled in 1976 that the state's jurisdiction did not extend offshore, this internationally significant research could continue undisturbed.[40] In 1964 the state government also set up a council to monitor air pollution, for industrialisation came at a cost to the pristine atmosphere on which even urban Western Australians prided themselves. In common with most of the Australian states and in response to growing public concern, Western Australia thought it desirable to create an Environmental Protection Authority, and this came into being in 1971.

Concern for the environment reflected a realisation that Western Australians could travel to remote corners of their state and leave their imprint much more easily than at any time in the past. The number of licensed motor vehicles grew from 220,000 in 1960 to 415,000 in 1970, and they could be driven on an excellent system of main roads, including the Eyre Highway, which from 1969 connected the West to the rest of Australia by an unbroken line of bitumen inviting high speeds. With the arrival of Malibu surfboards in the early 1960s, young people began to find their way in increasing numbers to uncrowded surf beaches, particularly on the coast between Cape Naturaliste and Cape Leeuwin. In that region where Mitchell's dairy farmers had struggled for a living a generation earlier, an agricultural scientist, John Gladstones, declared in 1964 that the Margaret River area offered great promise for winegrowing. His advice was soon followed, and it was not long before an older generation of tourists began to follow the surfies south.[41] After more than a hundred years when most Western Australians had had to practise frugality, the boom of the 1960s promised that a time was coming for relaxation and enjoyment.

Enjoyment did not preclude a continuing commitment to education. Government high schools doubled in number from 1960 to 1970. In 1958, in an ill-judged moment of egalitarianism, the state government decided that an intellectually elite school like Perth Modern was no longer required, as bright youngsters should be shared among all the junior high schools. In consequence, talented students whose parents could afford it tended to shift to the specialised facilities offered by private colleges. At the tertiary level, the most significant developments included the mobilisation of public support leading to a medical school for The University of Western Australia in 1958; the establishment in 1964 of the Western Australian Institute of Technology (after 1987 the Curtin University of Technology); and the decision in 1970 to create

Murdoch University. Post-secondary students now had an ample range of choice, but an unexpected result of improved higher education was an increase in articulate protest movements. As elsewhere in Australia, the compulsory recruitment of national servicemen to fight the Vietnam War provoked demonstrations in Perth between 1966 and 1971 in which university students were conspicuous.[42] Women's issues also came to the fore. Although in 1967 the Brand government lifted the ban on permanent employment of married women in the public service, and The University of Western Australia followed suit next year, there were still inequalities in opportunity and pay needing redress.[43] But in an era of full employment and buoyant economic growth, reformers could afford optimism.

Amid all the exciting progress, it was sometimes easy to forget the disruptive power of natural disasters, but during the 1960s Western Australia had experienced several reminders. In January 1961 a destructive series of bushfires swept parts of the South West, obliterating the small town of Dwellingup, less than 100 kilometres from Perth. In 1964 the Pilbara coast around Onslow was struck by what would prove the strongest cyclone in forty years, leaving widespread devastation. In October 1968, after a prolonged period of seismic inactivity, an earthquake shook buildings in Perth's centre and left in ruins the small Wheatbelt town of Meckering, 130 kilometres to the east. But the most potentially serious long-term threat to Western Australia's prosperity came unnoticed. From about 1970, a shift in climate meant that the annual average rainfall for Perth and most of the South West would be about 20 per cent lower than it had been earlier in the century. Vehement argument persists as to whether this shift is a temporary phenomenon, part of a longer cyclical change, or the result of carbon emissions, but the outcome raised two questions. To what extent would it be possible to sustain the Wheatbelt east of the Avon Valley, whose establishment had been the pride of the state in the early twentieth century but where effects of erosion and salinity could no longer be ignored? And how much would the growth of Western Australia as a whole be constrained by its limited water resources?

9

The gilded age, 1971–1992

In 1971 it might have seemed that the economic boom was fading. Poor seasons and falling export revenues beset the farmers and graziers; between 1968/69 and 1971/72 the area under wheat fell by more than a million hectares. The Poseidon fiasco cast a shadow over mining investment. The Brand government suffered a somewhat unexpected defeat at the state elections in that year, and John Tonkin, at 69 the oldest man to become Premier, formed a Labor government with the slenderest of majorities. The new government was able to make some reforms, in 1972 securing the appointment of a state ombudsman and lowering the minimum voting age to 18, but it was more often frustrated by financial constraints and a hostile Legislative Council. There was, however, bipartisan support for a plan to replace the Perth–Fremantle railway with a busway and an underground electric railway through the central business district. A proposal for daylight saving was rejected, although supported by business interests inconvenienced by a three-hour lag in communication with the Eastern States during the summer. It emerged that the sceptics had the majority of Western Australians on their side, as daylight saving was rejected by no fewer than three subsequent referenda, in 1975, 1984 and 1992. Another experiment introduced for the summers of 2006–08 was widely expected to leave public opinion unchanged. The strongest resistance was in the country, but it was clear that many city-dwellers had no wish to change their habits just because Sydney and Melbourne started earlier.[1]

Tonkin met considerable trouble from Hanwright, the company formed by Lang Hancock and Peter Wright. The Brand government had refused to admit Hanwright's claim to rights of occupancy for a group of mining leases. Although the Tonkin government awarded several of them to Hanwright, it planned to allocate others to an American company. Hanwright threatened litigation but the government legislated to overrule it and was supported by most of the Opposition. Hancock lashed out at both major parties and thereafter busied himself with supporting minor parties that might hold the balance of power in a tightly contested election and in financing a newspaper sympathetic to his views.[2] Hanwright was also part of the Pacminex consortium that sought to build a third alumina refinery in Western Australia. The Tonkin government was keen for the project to go ahead, but the site chosen in the Swan Valley was less than 25 kilometres from the city centre and close to long-established vineyards. The Environmental Protection Authority would not grant approval. Reluctantly, its verdict was accepted, thus feeding further Hancock's already furious detestation of the environmental movement.[3]

In December 1972, however, the first federal Labor government since 1949 came to power, under the leadership of Gough Whitlam. This was a mixed blessing for the Tonkin government, as although Whitlam was an energising force for reform, his government took a cavalier attitude to state rights and its interventions ignored local feeling. Aboriginal policy was one example. During 1971 and 1972 the Tonkin government had been dismantling the remaining legislation that treated Aboriginal people differently from other members of the community, forming a 'colour-blind' Department of Community Welfare and creating an Aboriginal Affairs Planning Authority in 1972 to carry on those cultural and economic functions that fell outside existing government departments. The Whitlam government was to increase federal expenditure on Aboriginal affairs from $6.9 million in 1972–73 to $16.9 million in 1974–75, buying some pastoral properties for Aboriginal use. Canberra wanted to take over Aboriginal policy from the states, but in the end a compromise was worked out under which, from mid-1974, the same officer, Middleton's successor Frank Gare, administered Aboriginal planning under both federal and state jurisdiction. Gare worked in the light of a royal commission appointed by the state government in 1973–74 whose recommendations included an acknowledgment of the right of Aboriginal people to choose either the path of assimilation or a communal and traditional lifestyle.[4] These years also saw the creation of an Aboriginal Legal Service, originally staffed by rising young Perth lawyers but eventually to find staff from qualified Aboriginal practitioners such as Rob Riley and Dennis Eggington.

Such was the reaction to what were seen as the Whitlam government's centralising tendencies that in August 1973 Governor Sir Douglas Kendrew seriously contemplated encouraging the Legislative Council to refuse supply to the Tonkin government, expecting that its defeat at the subsequent election would ensure Court's return as the only state premier capable of confronting Canberra.[5] (Court, now Sir Charles, had become leader of the Opposition after Brand's retirement for health reasons in 1972.) When Tonkin lost the state elections in March 1974, he was widely seen as the victim of association with federal Labor. A few weeks later, when Whitlam came to Perth to address a meeting in Forrest Place, he was pelted with soft-drink cans and other missiles, mostly thrown by incensed farmers. Until the dismissal of the Whitlam government in November 1975, relations between state and Commonwealth were often stormy, though not so stormy as to prevent practical cooperation. Court was the first of the non-Labor premiers to come to terms with implementing the Commonwealth's Medibank scheme in 1975.[6] But he was implacably hostile to Rex Connor, Whitlam's Minister for Minerals and Energy, whose forceful intervention in overseas marketing and energy policy muscled in on Court's territory.

Even after the Whitlam government's dismissal, relations with Canberra remained uneasy. The resource-rich states of Western Australia and Queensland wanted freedom to attract foreign investment without federal interference, but were apt to protest if their perceived prosperity cut their share of Commonwealth funding. Court welcomed the 'new federalism' promised by the Liberal Prime Minister Malcolm Fraser, with its goal of restoring authority to the states, but was soon chafing at federal restrictions on Western Australia's capacity to borrow for public works. To a Sydney observer in 1981, it seemed a breathtaking arrogance to assert that 'mineral resources do not belong to the Commonwealth but to the individual States which, by accidents of history, geology and map-drawing, happen to be able to claim them'.[7]

Western Australians would argue that after the Whitlam interlude, it took some time to restore investor confidence, and with it the hope of new developments. Exploration around Barrow Island and adjacent parts of the North West Shelf during the mid-1970s revealed unexpectedly huge reserves of natural gas, sufficient to overcome at last Western Australia's energy deficiencies. In order to secure the viability of a pipeline from Dampier to Perth and the South West, Court brokered a deal in 1978 with Alcoa of Australia, permitting it to build a third alumina refinery at Wagerup, on the Darling Scarp, provided the firm took a guaranteed quota of North West gas. When another company in 1980 planned a refinery further south at Worsley, it drew on North West gas as well as Collie coal. Once again, private enterprise and the state worked to mutual advantage. Meanwhile, in the Kimberley district, the Ashton syndicate, in which Conzinc Riotinto of Australia was a major shareholder, located low-grade diamonds in 1979 in quantities large enough to make a significant impact on the world market.[8]

The Court government and the developers now had to operate in the view of an increasingly articulate environmental movement. Particular concern was felt about the native forests of the South West. For some years, jarrah and other native trees had been seen to lose their foliage and die, and in the 1960s the forester Frank Podger identified the cause of 'jarrah dieback' in a fungus that might be transported by human activity. By the mid-1970s, critics were ready to blame Alcoa's mining operations for spreading dieback. In 1981 the Western Australian Conservation Council unsuccessfully tried to launch an action against Alcoa in the United States District Court. The state government made the Wagerup refinery the subject of strict environmental control, and the company itself invested substantially in rehabilitating worked-out land, but its activities remained a source of controversy.[9]

Campaigners to save the native forests were dismayed in 1971 when state parliament authorised a trade to market woodchips to Japan for paper manufacture. The woodchip trade was intended to find a use for waste timber, especially marri, useless for any other purpose. Critics of the trade came to suspect that good jarrah and karri also found its way into the woodchip shipments. They pointed to the devastated appearance of forest country clear-felled for woodchipping and complained that replanting might at worst replace the native timber with commercial exotics such as pines and at best could not restore the original biodiversity of fauna and flora. Forestry workers in the timber towns around Manjimup saw the 'greenies' as threatening their jobs, and angry confrontations followed. Two young men were gaoled in 1977 for attempting to blow up a stack of woodchips awaiting shipment at Bunbury. For many years, woodchipping was to divide communities in the South West and provide stimulus to the advocates of greater environmental responsibility by business and government.[10]

Such controversies, following the protests over national service for Vietnam, suggested that if the ideal of community consensus had ever had validity in Western Australia, it was now on the wane. Court, who seems sincerely to have believed that much of the protest against developmental policies was stirred up by outside influences wishing ill, if not evil, to the state's prosperity, advocated facing down opposition by confrontation. Hardworking and masterful, he dominated Western Australian politics as completely as Forrest and Mitchell had done in their later years, winning elections in 1977 and 1980. In 1978 his methods led his National Party colleagues to quit the cabinet, but their party split and two of their members, Dick Old and Peter Jones, after a short period in a separate National Country Party, joined the Liberals and were readmitted to the ministry. Until 1993 the National Party, ably led by Hendy Cowan, remained outside the coalition, usually though not invariably siding with the Liberals against Labor.

As a new minister, Court had been advised by the veteran South Australian Premier Tom Playford, 'You know, young Charles, this country, and especially the individual States, are still at a stage when they need a benevolent despot'—adding with a chuckle, 'The difficult thing for the people and the dictator is to decide when he ceases to be benevolent'.[11] It was an apt forecast for Court's premiership. Irked by occasional hostile public demonstrations, in 1976 his government passed an amendment to the *Police Act*, section 54B, that made it illegal to convene public meetings of more than three people without securing a police permit. During the next six years, section 54B was used against the government's critics on several occasions, notably the lengthy Hamersley Iron strike of 1979. Court expressed disappointment when, after ten weeks, the company came to terms with the unions. Frequent industrial unrest continued.[12]

Court's enjoyment of confrontation was never more evident than in 1980 when the drilling company Amax applied for the right to seek oil at 'Noonkanbah' station, south-east of Derby. The owners of 'Noonkanbah', the Yungngora community, complained that sacred sites would be disturbed. This was not a new issue. As early as 1955, Aboriginal people had complained about a monitoring base for atomic tests at Talgarno, on the coast between Broome and Port Hedland. In 1969 there was a more widely publicised controversy about the threatened removal of stones from 'Weebo' station in the Mount Margaret district. In 1972 the government had legislated for the protection of Aboriginal sites of major religious and cultural significance, entrusting its administration to the Western Australian Museum, but retaining the right to excise portions of Aboriginal reserves for mining. Amax, accustomed to such negotiations in North America, might have parleyed, but the Court government insisted on upholding the right of mineral exploration on pastoral holdings. In a striking display of force, convoys of drilling rigs with strong police escorts were despatched to 'Noonkanbah' amid vigorous public protests. The exploration proceeded, but no oil was found. It has been argued that if the Court government in Western Australia and Bjelke-Petersen in Queensland had been more conciliatory about Aboriginal land rights, the High Court would never have been invited to pronounce the judgment that overturned the doctrine of terra nullius twenty years later. The Ashton diamond syndicate at Argyle displeased the state government by taking pains to reach a satisfactory agreement with representatives of local Aboriginal groups before commencing operations, although some complained that they had not consulted all the traditional stakeholders.[13]

The benevolent side of Court expressed itself in improving the city of Perth's cultural infrastructure on a generous scale. Work continued on the completion of the Perth Cultural Centre, with the opening of new buildings for the Art Gallery in 1979 and the State Library in 1982. In Fremantle the colonial Commissariat Building became an internationally acclaimed museum for historic shipwrecks. His Majesty's Theatre, one of the two remaining Edwardian theatres anywhere in the British Commonwealth, was rescued from the threat of destruction and renovated to provide a venue for drama, opera and ballet. Members of the public whose tastes differed from those of the audiences at His

Majesty's were served by the Perth Entertainment Centre, part-owned by TVW Channel 7. No Premier could boast a more impressive record of patronage.[14]

During Court's term of office, Western Australia celebrated the sesquicentenary of its foundation by Captain Stirling in 1829. In 1979 the celebrations started with a New Year concert at which Ken Colbung, having played his didgeridoo as scheduled, presented the State Governor, Sir Wallace Kyle, with a petition requesting recognition of prior Aboriginal occupancy of the land. As Colbung was one of the most moderate of Nyungar elders, this was a telling reminder of unfinished business. Although it was hoped that the celebrations would publicise Western Australia to a wider world, the main events of 1979 to make headlines overseas were fortuitous. The Miss World contest ended in confusion with the collapse of the platform on which the finalists paraded, fortunately without causing injury. The remains of an American space station, Skylab, were programmed to fall in the vicinity of Western Australia, arousing some anxiety in residents of Perth, but it broke up and landed in the open spaces east of Kalgoorlie. Otherwise there were sanitised re-enactments of the arrival of pioneers, and a great number of street parties at which neighbours enjoyed themselves, but no defining statement of what it meant to be Western Australian. Official rhetoric went little further than extolling the productivity resulting from 150 years of hard work and investment.[15]

Sir Charles Court retired in January 1982, leaving his successor as Premier, Ray O'Connor, to face a rejuvenated Labor Opposition. Their leader, Brian Burke, a master of media presentation, was yet another leading Western Australian who dreamed great visions without having a sufficient strategic grasp to sustain them. He promised a modernised Labor with the zeal of one who bore family grudges against the ineffective old guard of the state ALP. Social reform would not be neglected, but Labor would outdo Court in efficient government and bold entrepreneurial activity, as well as securing harmony in the workplace. The message attracted voters who thought it time for a change, and in February 1983 Labor was returned to power, followed a few weeks later by the return of a like-minded federal Labor government under the former Western Australian Bob Hawke. Brian Burke formed a youthful ministry, most of them university-educated, who gave an impression of vigour and imagination. They owed no allegiance to the conservative businessmen who had supported Court or to the equally old-fashioned trade unionists of the Chamberlain type. Unfortunately, they nearly all lacked administrative or business acumen, and, like Sir James Mitchell's before them, their leaping enthusiasms were not tempered by experience outside Western Australia.[16]

Nor would they take advice from the seasoned public servants who, since World War II, had guided Liberal and Labor governments alike. Instead, Burke embarked immediately on a major makeover of the state public service. Government departments were streamlined and amalgamated; thus the old office of Surveyor-General was abolished, and a new Department of Conservation and Land Management (CALM) united somewhat uneasily the old portfolios of Lands, Forests and Agriculture. Treasury lost ground to a new Department of Premier and Cabinet, whose Policy Secretariat 'effectively became the most powerful decision-making body in Western Australia'.[17] Scorning the tradition that a civil service should provide politicians with an independent voice of experience, the Burke government filled the leading positions in its bureaucracy with pliable nonentities and obedient ministerial advisers appointed on contract, thus setting a bad example for their opponents to follow when their turn in office arrived. They were not the first Western democracy to tread this path, but they must have been one of the least convincing.

In order to dodge the tedious necessity of reporting to a parliament with a hostile Legislative Council, power was vested in a number of statutory corporations. Some, such as the Water Corporation, proved their value and survived later changes of government. The South West Development Authority was entrusted with the promotion of development in the Bunbury hinterland, a useful model for regional authorities elsewhere in the state. Others were more contentious. The Western Australian Development Corporation (WADC) was established to conduct profit-making business activities on behalf of the state government. It was competently managed but operated outside the customary norms of ministerial accountability, and some of its subsidiaries such as the Export-Import (Exim) Corporation showed an appetite for risk. Headstrong despite its inexperience, the Burke

41 A Depression demonstration: a thousand unemployed march to the Treasury building to see Premier Sir James Mitchell, March 1931.

42 Christmas Eve, 1931: cases of mutton are distributed to the unemployed.

43 Unemployed workers mending their clothes in Stirling Gardens, December 1930.

44 Volunteers enlisting ten days after the Second World War was declared.

45 Ration books were required for tea, sugar, meat and clothing for much of the war.

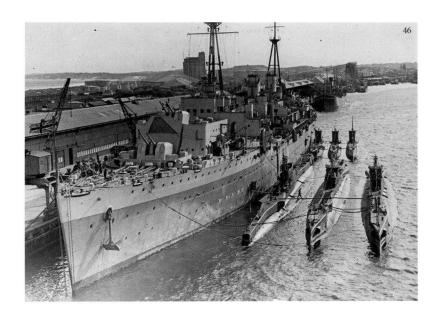

46 HMS *Adamant* and six submarines berthed at Fremantle, 1945.

47 St Georges Terrace, Perth looking west towards the Old Barracks, 1952.

48 Decorations for the visit of Queen Elizabeth II and Philip, Duke of Edinburgh, 1954.

49 Government House garden party: Queen Elizabeth II and Governor Sir Charles Gairdner with pastoralist (Sir) Ernest Lee Steere and Jackie Lee Steere.

50 Aerial view of the Rough Range oil well and drilling site, 1954.

51 Technology comes to the wheat belt: harvesting, 1961.

52 You can't stop progress: the Narrows Bridge and interchange, 1960.

50

51

52

53   Narrows Bridge and city skyline, 1959.

54   Opening ceremony of the British
     Empire Games at Perry Lakes
     Stadium, 1962.

55   Charles Court enters Parliament, 1953.

56   The Ord River Diversion Dam under
     construction, 1961.

57   Cotton harvesting on the Ord at
     Kununurra, 1961.

58   Iron ore dump trucks parked at Mount
     Newman, late 1960s.

59   Iron ore freight train at Mount Tom
     Price, late 1960s.

60   The iron ore carrier *Barbo* takes on a
     cargo of iron ore at Port Hedland, 1967.

56

57

58

59

60

government was venturing into new enterprises on a scale not seen since 'Gone-a-million' Jack Scaddan seventy years previously.

Energetic and innovative in its first three years of office, the Burke government made several overdue social reforms. Capital punishment, although still supported by most Western Australians, was abolished.[18] Section 54B, restricting the right of political assembly, was repealed. The establishment of an Occupational Health and Safety Commission in 1984 was an overdue reform improved by further legislation in 1986. An Equal Opportunity Commission aimed to prevent discrimination based on race or gender. The right to vote at local government elections was extended to all adults. Labor would have liked to introduce a 'one-vote-one-value' system of parliamentary elections, under which the weighting given to rural and regional voters disappeared, but this was seen as leading to domination by the Perth metropolitan area. In 1987 a more modest reform equalised city and country seats in the Legislative Council and introduced proportional representation. It was now possible for independents and minor parties to gain seats and, by holding the balance of power, to reduce the grip of the non-Labor parties in the upper house, although it was to be ten years before this came about.

Following its Labor predecessor, the Court government had tended to run down the public transport system, closing the Perth–Fremantle passenger railway in 1979. Under Burke, this trend was reversed. The Fremantle line was reopened, the suburban services renovated, and a new line commissioned stretching beyond the satellite city of Joondalup. The state's first purpose-built suburban railway, it was completed in 1989. An upgraded and electrified service from Perth to Bunbury was promised but never delivered, overtaken by less useful but more exciting schemes. Here the Burke government's reforming zeal ended. In 1983 Paul Seaman was given a commission to recommend appropriate forms of land title for Aboriginal communities, but the majority of Western Australians were not ready for the idea that past dispossession called for compensation. After one ineffectual attempt at an Aboriginal land bill, the Burke government was easily scared into inaction by the opposition of mining companies. When the Commonwealth Government showed signs of reform-mindedness in 1986, Western Australia, thumping the old drum of state rights, threatened to challenge any federal initiatives on land rights in the High Court. So it was that nothing happened until the High Court's decision in the *Mabo* case in 1992 overturned the old doctrine of terra nullius and forced governments to rethink their policies on Aboriginal land rights.[19]

The Burke government's sensitivity to lobbying surprised few. Eager to prove that a Labor government was not hostile to business, Burke and his colleagues tended to bypass the old Perth establishment. Instead, they looked for alliances with a set of youngish businessmen who had done well out of the mineral and property booms of the 1970s. Burke described them as

> *a new breed of entrepreneurs who are somehow regarded as not quite right by the establishment, excluded because they did not go to the right schools. These are the people who do things and get things done and create the wealth.*[20]

Events were to show that these men were regarded as 'not quite right' for reasons that had nothing to do with their background or schooling.

In 1984 Burke set up the John Curtin Foundation, an advisory 'think-tank' bringing together Labor veterans and leading businessmen of the new breed. Prominent among them was Laurie Connell, whose apparently limitless capacity for mobilising venture capital, mostly through his merchant bank, Rothwells, brought him into demand as a lender of last resort. Most flamboyant of all was an English migrant, Alan Bond, enriched by a series of property deals and undismayed by a troubled foray into an iron-ore investment at Robe River during the 1970s. Bond's most successful gamble came when he financed the syndicate contesting the world's premier yacht race, the America's Cup, at Newport in the United States, with a revolutionary fixed-keel yacht, *Australia II*, designed by Ben Lexcen and built near Fremantle. In September 1983, after a disappointing start, *Australia II* snatched a dramatic last-minute victory over its United States rival, thus ending more than a century of American supremacy. Bond became a national hero. He and his wife were accorded a parade through the main streets of Perth, lined with roaring crowds. For the time being, he could do no wrong, and his advice weighed strongly with the Burke government as it ventured into new deals.[21]

The cosy alliance between the Burke government and such entrepreneurs as Bond and Connell was dubbed 'WA Inc'. It paid to be among
the state government's mates. In 1984–85, building on hopes that the
defence of the America's Cup in Fremantle would bring many visitors to
the city, Perth's first casino, together with an extensive tourist complex,
was built at Burswood, on the eastern edge of the central business district.
(Moralists who feared the social evils of gambling could take comfort
that Western Australia, alone of all the states, had consistently banned
poker machines from pubs and clubs; the casino was aimed at the wealthy,
particularly wealthy Asians. Western Australians seemed satisfied with
patronising the state lottery system, whose profits supported an increasing
number of charitable, sporting and cultural causes.) After Connell had
been paid a consultancy fee of $2 million, the franchise went to the local
entrepreneur Dallas Dempster, acting with a Malaysian consortium and
the Perth-based Australia-wide construction firm Multiplex. Access to
government contracts and commercial opportunities seemed easier for
some members of the business community who contributed to Burke's
secret Leader's Fund.[22]

Burke and his senior colleagues thought it right to operate without
questioning, scrutiny, or accountability to either their party or the public
service, and they made several poor decisions after making a few good ones.
The WADC made its first major purchase in 1984 by acquiring Bond's 5 per
cent stake in the Argyle Diamond Mine for $42 million. The funds were
provided by the owners of the mine, in return for which the government
exempted them from a commitment to build a town at the project site. A
year later, the government sold its shareholding for a profit of $3 million, thus
answering critics who claimed that the price it had paid was higher than
the value of the shares on the open stock exchange. No such justification
could be made in 1986 when the government compelled the State Electricity
Commission to pay too high a price for the purchase of the Fremantle Gas
and Coke Company, the last privately owned business of its kind, from
Yosse Goldberg. Goldberg had recently obliged the government by selling
it the Swan Brewery building on the Swan River foreshore at a very small
profit, and Connell was paid $225,000 for brokering the deal.

Unperturbed, the voters returned the Burke government for a second
term in 1986. Its credentials as youthful social reformers still stood

high with the public. Apart from Patrick O'Brien, almost a lone voice in the academic community, few criticised Burke's cavalier methods of governance.[23] The pace was too good, as the West seemed destined to outdo the rest of Australia as a powerhouse of the economy, with only Queensland to match it. Economic performance went with sporting prowess. Laurie Connell was Australia's biggest racehorse owner, although questions were asked when his horse Rocket Racer won the Perth Cup by nine lengths in January 1987 and died shortly after. If Australia lost the America's Cup at its re-run in 1987, Fremantle had a moment of international glory and a decade of gentrification to show for it. Business support was also mobilised for the first state-wide Australian Rules football team, the West Coast Eagles, who entered the Australian Football League competition in 1988. Only the 1890s had seen such euphoria, and that had been on a smaller scale. Meanwhile, Bond, Connell and the like seemed able to conjure up an unceasing stream of investment into Western Australia. Electronic transfer could now shift capital quickly, and following deregulation Australia's leading banks scrambled to compete for borrowers. The new breed of Western Australian entrepreneurs showed great dexterity in shifting capital between interlocking companies and in involving influential stakeholders in the success of their enterprises. Their ambitions grew.

Robert Holmes à Court had the knack of buying substantial minority shareholdings in national companies such as BHP and the Fairfax media group and allowing himself to be bought out at a profit. Alan Bond was the leviathan of them all. '"WA" used to mean "Wait Awhile"', said Bond: 'I wanted to change all that'.[24] He bought breweries: Swan, which he hoped to make Australia's dominant beer, Tooheys and Castlemaine in the Eastern States, and Heileman in the United States. He took over *The West Australian*; because of media regulations, he could not acquire its stablemate, the *Daily News*, which ceased publication in 1990. As Lang Hancock and Holmes à Court had both failed to establish rival newspapers, this left *The West Australian* as Perth's monopoly daily newspaper. Bond owned much of Kalgoorlie's Golden Mile and amalgamated its workings into a super-pit reputedly visible from the Moon. In 1987 he acquired a half-share in Chile's telephone network and Kerry Packer's Channel 9 network. At over $1 billion, the price was too high. Bond was overextending dangerously.[25]

Such men entertained opulently. Between 1985 and 1987 Connell drew nearly $500 million from Rothwells for his own private expenditure. The marriage of Alan Bond's daughter allegedly cost her father $300,000. Asked by a journalist for comment, one 18-year-old woman exclaimed: 'These people are our royalty'.[26] Such men also planned and built expensive houses. Lang Hancock spent $30 million providing a roof over his and his wife's head; the flamboyant Rose (by then Rose Porteous) subsequently had it demolished. Bond gave his name and support to a private university, not in Western Australia but on Queensland's Gold Coast where he had property interests. At least he had his creditable monument; so had Denis Horgan, whose enthusiasm stimulated the founding of Australia's first private Catholic university, University of Notre Dame Australia, in Fremantle. In 1986 the site of the Midland abattoirs was sold cheaply to a businessman who said he would start a brickworks in competition with the industry's main provider, a staunch opponent of the Labor Party.[27] The government pressured the State Superannuation Board and the State Government Insurance Office into partnerships in city real-estate investments with Bond and Connell, with the government agencies providing most of the capital for no more than half the equity. Bond's last hurrah marked the opening of Observation City, a multi-storey beachside hotel at Scarborough defying a common understanding that there should be no Gold Coast–style high-rise buildings overshadowing the Indian Ocean beaches. Matt Price, covering the event for Channel 7, recalled that

> French champagne flooded the foyer, mountains of food were served from each of the restaurants in the hotel complex, entertainment cranked through the night...While an amazing beachside fireworks display reminded those who couldn't attend what they were missing out on.[28]

That was early in October 1987. Three weeks later, the fun came to an end with a major international stock market slump. Some feared a repeat of the 1930s Depression and were ready to take desperate measures. Connell, fresh from intervening in the Fairfax family's feud over control of the *Sydney Morning Herald*, was immediately in trouble. The state government, working with Bond, who drew a $16 million commission for his trouble, at once put together a package to bail out Connell's companies, compelling several state government instrumentalities and the state-owned Rural and Industries Bank to contribute generously in covering Rothwells's debts. Burke retired in February 1988, soon to become Australia's ambassador to Ireland and the Vatican, and so he was out of the way when 'WA Inc.' started to unravel—but his successors continued in his tradition. In April the State Government Insurance Corporation, in tandem with Bond, saved Holmes à Court's bacon by buying his large stake in the Bell Group of companies by tactics that strained the takeover laws to their utmost. Later in 1988 the state government purchased an environmentally controversial project for a petrochemical plant at Kwinana, paying Connell $500 million for his half-share and his partner Dallas Dempster a mere $50 million. The petrochemical plant never came into being. It was widely believed that such largesse afforded a breathing space for the many investors in Rothwells, among them the Catholic and Anglican churches, to withdraw without excessive loss. Bond meanwhile continued to spend, fulfilling the successful migrant's dream by buying a manor house in England. He invested heavily in real estate near Rome and made a raid on the British conglomerate Lonrho. He was out of his league. Lonrho counter-attacked, fatally damaging Bond's credit in the fracas.[29]

The new Premier, Peter Dowding, began the process of damage control. In January 1989 a commission on accountability, headed by a retired Chief Justice, Sir Francis Burt, recommended that the WADC and its subsidiaries should be brought under ministerial control and lose their authority to invest Treasury funds. Unexpectedly, the voters of Western Australia in February 1989 returned the Labor government for a third time, though still with a hostile Legislative Council threatening to bring down the government by blocking supply. In this they were encouraged by an ungrateful Bond, irked at Dowding's refusal to release him from some of his obligations. A constitutional crisis was averted, but the post-mortems continued. Investigating Rothwells, Malcolm McCusker, QC, reported in October 1989 that the state government stood to lose $144 million on its support for the now liquidated bank. This support, he suggested, resulted from ignorant optimism rather than corrupt or criminal behaviour.[30]

In February 1990 Dowding's colleagues turned on him. In two years preoccupied with damage control, there was little legislative achievement to boast of beyond the repeal of the laws making homosexuality between consenting adults a crime. Dowding was replaced by Carmen Lawrence, psychologist by training and the first woman and the first PhD to become an Australian state Premier.[31] Although three members of parliament left the party, her government managed to survive till the next election in 1993, but at the cost of a virtual paralysis of creative initiative. The legislative record of those years produced little beyond tough laws against those who caused death or grievous bodily harm by driving cars at high speed (Aboriginal juveniles were sometimes offenders) and the compulsory wearing of helmets by bicycle riders. Environmentalists complained because the government permitted mining in several national parks and commissioned a coal-fired power station in the marginal seat of Collie, rejecting the report of an inquiry recommending the use of Western Australia's copious reserves of gas.

Carmen Lawrence's government was nevertheless contaminated by the fallout from 'WA Inc.', and the ill luck continued. Its reputation for financial acumen was not improved by its patronage of Western Women, a financial advisory group designed, as its name suggested, to cater for the particular needs of women investors. Western Women collapsed after a career of amateurish malpractice earning its principal an excessively long prison sentence. The government's energies were further distracted by debate over the future of the Swan Brewery site on the Swan River foreshore. Ignoring Aboriginal claims that the site had sacred significance and Burke's early commitment to adapt the building for a museum, the government during 1990 had to confront a High Court decision that the site came under Aboriginal heritage legislation. Eventually, the old brewery was sold to private enterprise for development as a restaurant and high-priced residential apartments. As so often in modern Western Australia, money talked; the deal enabled the government to recoup much of the $14.7 million of public money outlaid on the brewery.[32]

The government was equally luckless in planning an orderly and coherent system of advanced education. The state's two universities, Western Australia and Murdoch, were joined by a third in 1987 when the Western Australian Institute of Technology was upgraded to become

Curtin University of Technology. This made Perth consistent with cities of similar size such as Brisbane and Adelaide, and conformed to the unified tertiary education system favoured by the Commonwealth Government. In 1988 Canberra also brought an end to a long-established Western Australian tradition by charging fees for tertiary education. The Higher Education Contribution Scheme, which established the orthodoxy that debt was a necessary result of a university education, was the work of John Dawkins, himself a graduate of The University of Western Australia in an era without fees. With the consent of both institutions, the Dowding government then legislated for a merger between The University of Western Australia and Murdoch University, but opponents of the scheme easily persuaded the conservative majority in the Legislative Council to throw out the proposal.

Defeated in this attempt at consolidation, the government then fragmented the system further in 1990 by elevating the Western Australian College of Advanced Education into a fourth university, Edith Cowan, named at Lawrence's suggestion after the first woman member of parliament. Meanwhile, the Catholic University of Notre Dame Australia was establishing itself among the colonial buildings at the west end of Fremantle. The Lawrence government welcomed the newcomer in 1992 with the offer of a 150-hectare grant of land north of Perth. This caused resentment, as no state government had given any such endowment to Murdoch, Curtin or Edith Cowan, despite the encouraging precedent of The University of Western Australia.[33] Belatedly, the government offered to find similar grants for the other universities, but it was defeated soon afterwards and its successor called off all offers.

Hampered by the hostile Legislative Council, Lawrence had to concentrate on cleaning up the financial mess. The WADC and its subsidiaries were abolished and their functions returned to orthodox government instrumentalities. A debt of $230 million arising from the failed petrochemical project was amortised through cuts in government spending and special taxes. Corporate control was vested in the Commonwealth Government's new Australian Securities Commission, though only after the Opposition majority in the Legislative Council, blinkered by the local patriot's obsession with state rights, tried to block the legislation until persuaded by the federal Liberals. In November 1990

Lawrence reluctantly authorised a full-scale royal commission of three senior judges to examine the state government's investment decisions during the 1980s. It took them nearly two years to disentangle the complex dealings of 'WA Inc.', not least because during the hearing the witnesses suffered loss of memory at an estimated rate of once every eight minutes. The commission's findings suggested little evidence of illegal corruption but a good deal of malpractice due to party advantage rather than the public interest.[34]

Most of the heroes of the 1980s emerged with damaged reputations. Even Carmen Lawrence, after losing office, became the subject of a royal commission investigating claims that she had misled parliament over her knowledge of the suicide of a woman on the fringe of 'WA Inc.', but survived to pursue a career in federal politics, including a brief spell as a cabinet minister.[35] Bond was ousted from the directorship of his companies late in 1989, by which time Bond Corporation carried debts of $9.3 billion. Bond himself was put on trial and suffered a convenient amnesia, but served a term of imprisonment for improperly disposing of assets. On release, he resumed business as a moneylender and an investor in mining in Third World countries. Connell died in 1996 while facing legal proceedings. Among the politicians, Burke, his cabinet colleague David Parker, and his predecessor as Premier, the Liberal Ray O'Connor, all served terms of imprisonment, but they were convicted for comparatively minor peccadilloes and not for the stunning misjudgments of 'WA Inc'. Unable to resist the political ambience, Burke then set up as a lobbyist, and during 2006 and 2007 was still seen as so controversial in his methods that state and federal cabinet ministers were obliged to resign when their dealings with him were revealed.

These misjudgments should be seen in perspective. Following Sir Charles Court, who although sometimes high-handed operated within the Westminster conventions of government, Burke and his colleagues wanted to use the powers of government to outdo Court's performance in economic management. Arguably, Western Australia was still too dependent on mineral and agricultural exports and needed to diversify. The petrochemical plant, for instance, had been contemplated by the Court government as a logical follow-up to the state's mining and energy growth. Unfortunately, the Burke government's innovations too often involved cutting corners and underestimating risk. It was not alone. Other Labor state governments during the 1980s ventured out of their depth in economic management, and the conservative regime of Sir Joh Bjelke-Petersen in Queensland blatantly defied standards of good governance. Perhaps for the Burke government and the businessmen such as Bond, there was also a peculiarly Western Australian factor, that persistent dream motivating Stirling, Mitchell and other leaders, who believed that bold policies disregarding cautious advice would unlock the West's potential and advance Cinderella to pre-eminence among her sisters.

Retired from an eminent career as federal cabinet minister and Governor-General, Sir Paul Hasluck noted that 1829, the year of Western Australia's foundation, also saw the composer Felix Mendelssohn's first season in London. He wrote a verse imagining Mendelssohn and Stirling giving accounts of themselves in the Hereafter:

> And tell me, Felix, what did you achieve?
> 'I tossed some semiquavers in a pond.'
> And you—young Jamie Stirling, I believe?
> 'I helped to pave the way for Alan Bond.'[36]

10

Happily ever after? 1993–

From 1993 Western Australian public life eased back to normality. In that year, the Liberal–National Party coalition returned to power under the leadership of Richard Court, son of Sir Charles but by no means a carbon copy of his father. His government continued the task of cleaning up the debris left by 'WA Inc.', gradually removing the taxes imposed to cover its losses and in 1994 appointing a commission on government to recommend reforms in Western Australia's governance.[1] The commission's recommendations, following other reforms by the Lawrence and Court governments, improved the state's systems of financial accountability, introduced procedures governing the destruction or preservation of public records, and included freedom of information legislation.

In Opposition the Liberals had seemed to include some of the most conservative elements in Australian politics—they had resisted the largely bipartisan decision to scrap the award of British honours such as knighthoods to Australian citizens—and some of their early priorities in office appeared to confirm this impression. They strenuously fought the High Court decision of 1992 that recognised, for the first time, the concept of Aboriginal rights of native title arising from their occupancy of the country before British settlement. It was understandable that Richard Court's government disliked the uncertainty that native title might bring to the allocation of mining rights at a time when investor confidence needed rebuilding, but its public statements at times suggested a fear that nobody's property would be safe from dispossession. Late in 1993 the government pushed through legislation extinguishing native title, although allowing Aboriginal people traditional usage if it did not conflict with the rights of others.[2] Commonwealth legislation overrode the Western Australian formula, and when the state government brought a legal challenge before the High Court it was unanimously rejected in 1995. In the result, native title made very little difference to the onward progress of Western Australia's mining industry. By setting up its headquarters in Perth, the National Native Title Tribunal facilitated mediation between Aboriginal groups, mining interests and the state government. This helped to soothe Western Australian perceptions that policies were imposed by Canberra without awareness of local needs and conditions.

His strong stand on native title, while popular in Western Australia, gained Richard Court a misleading reputation in matters of Aboriginal policy. At the height of the native title controversy, he commissioned a social justice report identifying Aboriginal needs in health and education. His sympathies, as well as his unwillingness to follow the lead of Canberra, came to the fore in 1997 when the *Bringing Them Home* report, coauthored by the Western Australian jurist Sir Ronald Wilson, documented the damage done to Aboriginal families and communities by the policy, pursued over many years in the past, of forcibly removing children from their parents. When the Labor Opposition proposed that the state parliament should make a formal apology for these events, Court immediately welcomed the motion, which passed with unanimous support. This contrasted with the unwillingness of the federal Prime Minister, John Howard, to make a similar conciliatory gesture.

In other respects, the (Richard) Court government was a good example of the business-oriented governments prevalent in the English-speaking world during the 1990s. More enthusiastically than any of its predecessors, it embraced the ruling fashion for privatising government instrumentalities. After the unorthodox use made by the Burke government of such bodies as the Rural and Industries Bank (renamed BankWest in 1994) and the State Government Insurance Office, it was easy to accept recommendations that they would be better run by private enterprise, and they were sold off in 1995. The Dampier to Bunbury natural gas pipeline was sold to a private purchaser. In 1995 the government also disposed of the State Shipping Service, no longer required now that blacktop highways traversed the length of Western

Australia, and sold the metropolitan transport system to a number of private operators, retaining an overall supervisory role.

There was no strong tradition of local government enterprise to complicate this process. The Court government attempted to improve municipal efficiency by redrawing the boundary lines of local authorities. Accepting that there would never be a Greater Perth administering the entire metropolitan area Brisbane-fashion, the government restricted the city of Perth to the central business district, creating three medium-sized 'towns', Cambridge, Vincent and Victoria Park, out of its suburban appendages. Elsewhere, entrenched local loyalties made it too difficult to enforce major change, though the Court government and its successors urged amalgamations.[3] Peppermint Grove, serving one small but prosperous suburb, enjoyed equality of status with sprawling outer-suburban municipalities covering many thousands of ratepayers. Unlike parts of the Eastern States, Western Australia did not follow the custom that major political parties endorsed candidates at the local government level (though behind the scenes there was a good deal of ill-concealed lobbying); however, aspirants to state or federal politics sometimes served apprenticeship on a local council. Occasionally, the state government had to intervene by suspending a council whose members behaved with outstanding incompetence, sending in an outsider as manager. But as the Commonwealth Government gradually leached away some of the powers exercised by the states, state governments, Western Australia among them, looked after many of the functions that once might have been handled by local authorities.

Believing that trade union militancy hindered productivity and discouraged potential investors, the Court government made several attempts to change the industrial relations laws. In 1995 and again in 1997, legislation was introduced providing for the conduct of secret ballots before a strike could be declared and imposing various other curbs on the powers of trade unions over their members. On both occasions, the changes were strenuously resisted by the union movement, which staged demonstrations at Parliament House; in 1996 the unionists, following Aboriginal precedent, set up an 'embassy' outside Parliament House for several months. The secret-ballot legislation was pushed through parliament, but some of the more contentious proposals were abandoned, including the idea of cancelling a union's state award rights if it sought federal cover. By 2006 the position would be reversed, and Western Australia, as one of eight Labor state governments, would be seen as offering the trade unions a better deal than a federal government determined to impose market-determined workplace agreements.

Whether because of its legislation or simply because of favourable markets, Western Australia under Richard Court recovered its international credit rating as determined by the influential but anonymous authorities in such matters, Moody's and Standard and Poor's. Western Australian businessmen continued to play on the national scene, but they were more measured in their judgment than the high-flyers of the 1980s. Among them, Michael Chaney gained a national reputation through prudent and energetic management of the state's largest locally based company, Wesfarmers, completing the transformation of the old farmers' cooperative into a diversified investor in agribusiness and energy.[4] Kerry Stokes came to control TVW Channel 7 and the *Canberra Times*, and Bill Wyllie played an important role in attracting East and Southeast Asian investment into Western Australian property. Essentially, however, Perth was now a branch office city, although the multinationals investing in Western Australian minerals and energy and purchasing privatised entities such as BankWest maintained active local offices with considerable responsibility. Minerals and energy continued to dominate the export economy. For some years in the mid-1990s, gold overtook iron ore as leader among Western Australia's exports, stimulating the reworking of many old mines and the development of a new field at Boddington in the South West. If Japan seemed to falter momentarily as a market for iron ore in the wake of the Asian economic recession of 1998, new opportunities were presenting themselves in China and South Korea. The North West Shelf continued to reveal apparently limitless new reserves of natural gas, and the natural gas pipeline was extended to Kalgoorlie.

Western Australia retained its ambitions to be more than a quarry for East Asia, but it was disappointingly difficult to establish new secondary industries based on the state's mineral wealth. For some years, hopes rose and fell for a steelworks backed by Chinese finance at Oakajee, with potential for supplementing the limited facilities of the nearby port of

Geraldton, but it did not materialise.[5] The logic of globalisation insisted that Western Australians should not aspire to a strong manufacturing sector when they could draw on imports made by cheaper labour, paying for them with the dividends from mining, energy and the older but less spectacular agricultural and pastoral industries. This applied to the whole of Australia, but with especial force to the frontier states, Western Australia and Queensland, who between them provided more than half the nation's export income. In every year since 1993, Western Australia sent away 25 per cent, and sometimes almost 30 per cent, of Australia's exports. Western Australian politicians were fond of emphasising these statistics.

This might have fostered a strong developmental ethos among Western Australians, but it was tempered by an increasingly vocal environmental movement that lost little of its effect from drawing support from the urban middle class as well as from the 'greenies' of the South West. On coming to power, Richard Court drew some criticism for remodelling the Environmental Protection Authority in a way that some thought diminished its authority, and the same critics complained in 1994 when Western Australia, mistrustful of outside intervention, refused to join the Commonwealth's national Environmental Council. On the other hand, in 1994 the state government banned petroleum exploration around Ningaloo Reef, and in 1995 reserved the Beeliar wetlands when they were threatened by metropolitan expansion south.

At the 1997 state elections, Richard Court's government, though returned with a comfortable majority in the Legislative Assembly, lost control of the Legislative Council. This was a belated result of the Burke government's reforms, and meant that the balance of power in the upper house rested with three Greens members and two sympathetically minded Democrats. Environmental issues came to the fore. Alcoa's alumina refinery at Wagerup was targeted, not only because of its role in the spread of jarrah dieback (despite the company's sustained efforts to control the problem, which earned it a United Nations award in 1990), but also because neighbouring townships complained of emissions borne by the easterly winds. The Greens directed the brunt of their energies against the woodchip industry, mobilising support for the campaign to save native forests and a number of urban and rural pressure groups but meeting staunch resistance from timber workers and their families. The Court government during 1997–98 negotiated a federally initiated Regional Forests Agreement. Some of the most prized sections of the karri and jarrah forests were quarantined from exploitation, and Western Australia went well beyond most of the other states in a commitment to replace timber from old-growth forests with plantation hardwood. These were constructive policies but could not satisfy the critics.[6]

This campaign had an unexpected effect on the 2001 state elections. It might have been expected that Richard Court would be returned for a third term. As the state's fortunes improved, his government commissioned several public monuments and buildings, among them a somewhat controversial belltower on Perth's riverside and a new maritime museum at the entrance to Fremantle's Victoria Quay. In January 2000 lavish public celebrations heralded the opening of the twenty-first century. They were a year too early, perhaps reflecting a widespread wish to get out of the turbulent twentieth century as soon as possible. Dissatisfaction with both major political parties nevertheless led a significant number of voters to turn to alternatives, since as well as the Greens and the declining Democrats, Western Australia now contained the populist One Nation Party, whose anti-multicultural policies reflected a deeper uneasiness about the economic effect of globalisation, especially in country districts. Its candidates secured three seats in the Legislative Council in 2001, though they proved unable to stay united for long. The Greens increased their number to five, thus holding the balance of power. In addition, a new urban group, Liberals for Forests, took one Legislative Assembly seat from a cabinet minister. The drift of preferences from Greens and One Nation candidates enabled Labor to pick up enough seats to form a government in its own right, with Dr Geoffrey Gallop as Premier.[7]

Gallop, a political scientist by profession, had become a friend of the British Prime Minister, Tony Blair, while both were at Oxford, and shared his ethos of a modernised but just society. Having gained experience as a cabinet minister while the previous Labor government tried to undo the misadventures of the Burke government, he was well aware that his ministry's credibility depended on sound governance. The change of government made little impact on overseas investment or on the local business community, and the privatisations of the Court government were not reversed, though some of its industrial relations legislation was repealed. Perhaps taken by surprise by its victory, Labor under Gallop concentrated immediately on trying to satisfy the environmentalists. Existing woodchip contracts were honoured, but large areas of the South West native forests were quarantined from further exploitation, and encouragement was given to the cultivation of commercial timbers such as Tasmanian bluegum in plantations. In the Pilbara, the demands of the natural gas industry endangered the unique collection of ancient Aboriginal petroglyphs on the Burrup Peninsula, and although a Commonwealth decision in 2007 quarantined all but 1 per cent of the area from development, more would be heard of the conflict between the preservation of wilderness and the priorities of resource development. Many of the mining companies were learning to accept ecological responsibility, and so environmental protests came gradually to loom less large in state politics. But major problems remained.[8]

Of concern to town and country alike was the long-term supply of water. The dams in the Darling Scarp had been enlarged several times to cope with increasing population, but in most years since 1970 rainfall failed to reach the average, with no obvious indication that the trend might be reversed. Suburban householders were encouraged to cultivate native plants rather than thirsty exotics, and regulations restricted the use of sprinklers in gardens, but stronger measures were needed. Three major options were canvassed. One was the increased use of water from the aquifers stored beneath the coastal plain, already exploited as a supplementary source of supply. If Perth was to be served on a larger scale it would be necessary to withdraw groundwater from the Yarragadee aquifer underlying much of the South West. As nobody was quite sure of its extent—though it was known to be considerable—this gave rise to anxiety among residents and landowners in the South West who feared the environmental consequences. The Gallop government preferred to move more immediately to desalination, commissioning a plant in the Kwinana region, but this was also subjected to environmental criticism as well as raising issues of cost.

A bolder solution appealed to some, who evoked the memory of C. Y. O'Connor and his unprecedented goldfields pipeline, as well as the Ord River Dam. Since the 1980s, Ernest Bridge, his credentials established as Western Australia's first Aboriginal member of parliament and cabinet minister, had proclaimed that his Kimberley constituency's regular summer rainfall was a wasted asset, calling for a pipeline three times as long as O'Connor's to bring water to Perth. Those who disagreed with him included Aborigines such as his successor as Member for Kimberley, Carol Martin, who argued that the water would be required locally, but his message convinced some. Colin Barnett, leader of the Liberal Party at the 2005 elections and a senior cabinet minister under Richard Court, made it a central plank of his policy, and private investors were thought to be interested. The Commonwealth Government was noncommittal. After the election, Gallop set up a committee of inquiry, which reported that the cost of bringing Kimberley water to Perth would be prohibitive, whether by pipeline, open canal or shipment in large tankers. This left desalination or the use of the Yarragadee aquifer as the likeliest hopes for ensuring an adequate water supply for Perth and its environs. In 2007 the government decided to leave the Yarragadee alone, at least for the time being, but committed to a second desalination plant at Binningup, north of Bunbury. It remained feasible that at some point in the twenty-first century the community would arrive at a limit to sustainable growth and thus would call for some tough political decisions.[9]

The continued spread of salinity in the farmlands east of the Avon Valley raised problems of no less substance. Some scientists thought that a solution lay in restoring the ancient rivers and creeks tributary to the Avon–Swan system. Almost permanently dry except after rare and exceptional rains, these channels might be replenished as watercourses capable of flushing out the excess salt to be carried eventually out to sea, though there was some uncertainty about the ecological effects. The Swan River in its lower reaches was frequently subject to outbreaks of algal bloom, and any further disturbance looked problematical. Others called for large-scale reafforestation, replacing the canopy of salmon gum and York gum that had held salt creep in control before the clearance of the pioneer farmers. This had the disadvantage of taking land out of agricultural use and might require generous compensation for the farmers whose livelihoods were at stake. In 1995 the Environmental Protection Authority issued a report cogently calling for remedial action, but, as one of Richard Court's cabinet candidly admitted, it was not an issue to which city voters gave high priority. The agricultural districts were diminishing in their political importance, and their produce now took second place among Western Australia's exports, below minerals and energy; therefore, governments lacked incentive to tackle the problem on the large scale required. Without remedial action, salinity threatened to bring a lingering and unhappy end to the high hopes with which settlers of the inland South West had arrived a hundred years previously.[10]

The families on the land in Western Australia responded resourcefully to change. The number of beef and dairy cattle pastured in the state continued to fall, from a peak of 2.6 million in 1978 to 1.7 million in 2005. In an unprotected marketing environment, the times were also hard for wool-growers. Sheep numbers fell, to stabilise after 2001 at around 23 million, about 22 per cent of the Australian total, although pastoralists showed versatility in trying new breeds to meet specialised markets. In the early 1990s, some wheat-growers went in for the cultivation of new crops such as canola and barley, while others turned to varieties of wheat appealing to the East Asian market; by 1998 Western Australia could claim to be Japan's largest source of wheat for noodles. The growing reputation of wines from the Margaret River and Frankland River districts attracted many investors, ranging from large Australia-wide companies to professional families wanting a hobby farm, but by 2005 a glut was threatening. Other small farmers made olive oil or grazed alpacas. No longer monocultural, the South West presented a pleasing variety of rural landscapes. Though the fortunes of farming were as fickle as ever, country towns were still capable of asserting their individual character. At Kulin, site of a long-established spring race meeting, the road from the town to the racecourse was lined with homemade replicas of horses fashioned from such materials as fencing wire, concrete pipes and palings. The entrance to Wagin was dominated by the statue of a ram of formidable masculinity. At Balingup, scarecrows provided the dominant theme, while 50 kilometres away at a crossroads in the Ferguson Valley a colony of garden gnomes flourished and increased. Times might be uncertain for the country townships, but spirit and humour persisted. However, many of the Wheatbelt towns were stagnating and some disappearing, while the health of most mining centres depended on a single industry, and often on a single employer. Once an agrarian society with agrarian habits of thought, Western Australia was dominated by its metropolis.

Perth was growing faster than the rural districts, and this had its political dimension. 'One-vote-one-value' was a mantra of Western democracies, but in Western Australia, since the beginning of parliamentary government in 1890, it had been customary to give a weight of advantage to the North West, goldfields and rural South West over the Perth metropolitan area. This was justified by the need to protect the interests of the rural minority against Perth's concentration of population, which by 2001 exceeded 70 per cent of the whole. It suited Labor to urge one-vote-one-value, just as it suited its opponents, now stronger in rural Western Australia, to maintain the status quo, but even on the Labor side the maverick Member for Pilbara, Larry Graham, claimed that the North West and Kimberley would secede if such a measure was passed.[11] In 1995, while in Opposition, Labor unsuccessfully appealed to the High Court to declare in favour of one-vote-one-value. In office, and with the opportunity of negotiating with the minor parties, Labor was at last able to push through its reform in 2005. Opponents complained that by increasing the proportion of suburban seats, Labor was entrenching itself in office, and the dwindling National Party faced an uncertain future after the next redistribution of seats, but the wider public seemed unconcerned. At the state elections of 2005, fought under the old system, Labor was returned with a scarcely diminished majority, although the minor parties suffered losses.

Debate over the voting system reflected broader social and environmental issues arising from the relentless spread of the Perth metropolitan area over the coastal sandplain between Yanchep and Dawesville. Though some growth would spill over into the Avon Valley and the South West, with small rural properties and beaches and vineyards attracting the retired as the Darling Range had done formerly, the city far outweighed the provincial centres. Most of the Australian states were centralising in this way, but none more so than Western Australia. Perth in the first decade of the twenty-first century held fifty times more people than Bunbury or Kalgoorlie, a hundred times more than Esperance or Albany. Forecasts suggested that by 2030 the population of Perth would exceed more than two million, with no realistic prospect of securing a more balanced distribution. In 1973 a visiting journalist (male, of course) had personified Perth as 'a pert and pretty girl—enlivened by a faint undercurrent of aggression'.[12] Since that time, the pretty girl had stuffed herself with the chocolates of progress, to the detriment of her waistline and complexion.

The Court and Gallop governments both sought to address the challenges of Perth's growth. Traffic was an obvious problem. It was possible to build on the foresight of the 1950s by extending the north–south freeways more than 70 kilometres, with scope for more, and Richard Court's government eased east–west communication across the city with a tunnel serving the Graham Farmer Freeway. (Its name commemorated an accomplished Aboriginal footballer, and began a practice of naming bridges and other public works after notable Indigenous people.) The Gallop government preferred to extend the suburban rail system to Mandurah, a project whose mounting costs drew criticism, but which seemed increasingly justified as the price of petrol soared. None of these palliatives appeared to solve entirely the road congestion in a city with as many motor vehicles as adult inhabitants. It was no consolation that much of rural Western Australia was served by an admirably uncrowded road system, since foolish drivers were tempted to excessive speed, and the country produced more than its share of fatal accidents.[13]

As Perth became a big city, the social problems of a big city followed. Once almost unknown, beggars appeared in the streets. The ethnically diverse square kilometre north of the railway line, remodelled as 'Northbridge' in 1979, became as planned a lively scene of restaurants, nightclubs and town houses but also generated enough rowdiness and violence late at nights to gain an unsafe reputation in some eyes. Young people supplemented the traditional substances of addiction, alcohol and tobacco with a spectrum of drugs ranging from marijuana through cocaine and heroin to imported designer drugs such as 'ecstasy'. From the northern and eastern suburbs came frequent reports of elderly citizens victimised by burglars, and of teenagers driving stolen cars at dangerously high speeds, attracting police pursuit and sometimes ending in fatality. One such case resulted in the deaths of a mother and baby whose car was struck by a young driver fleeing the police, and this was followed by a well-attended candlelight vigil and the passage of tougher legislation. Delinquency among Aboriginal youths caused the Gallop government to set up a 'Nyungar patrol' and later to impose a curfew prohibiting those under 18 years of age from wandering the Northbridge streets unsupervised after 10 pm.[14]

Yet many still found the environment almost excessively comfortable. Western Australians who had lived elsewhere sometimes shook their heads at the complacency. In 1976 Alexandra Hasluck wrote: 'this may be a peaceful lotus land, but it is none the less a backwater'. Of a younger generation, the journalist Paul Toohey in 2003 found the blandness pervasive: 'Nobody wants to rock the boat. Nobody wants to change'. He quoted a visiting English backpacker, who wrote: 'Perth lacks the substance and charisma and the tension of diverse wealth and ethnicity, that makes a really great city more than just a group of skyscrapers'. He was wrong about the diverse wealth and ethnicity, but Toohey noted how *The West Australian* jumped to publicise this comment on its front page under the headline 'DULLSVILLE'.[15] In an environment with a largely benign Mediterranean climate, clean and accessible beaches, low unemployment and an apparently broad spread of good living, it was easy to question the need for change. Probing a little further, Toohey noted that 13 per cent of Perth's population were British-born, the biggest ethnic concentration in the country, reinforced by South Africans and New Zealanders, and wondered if it had become 'a natural sanctuary for whites', with consequent bias in racial attitudes. Yet in 1989, when Asian restaurants were firebombed, the responsibility lay with a fringe movement, the Australian Nationalists Movement, whose leader, Jack van Tongeren, proved to be of Dutch-Indonesian origins.[16]

Many Western Australian attitudes were still the product of isolation. From time to time, an incident such as the prolonged airline pilots' strike of 1989 or the collapse of Ansett airlines in 2001 reminded Western Australians of this isolation. Even in normal circumstances, in comparison to residents of the south-eastern states, it took longer and it cost more for Western Australians to fly to Canberra, Melbourne or Sydney. This meant that, even with all the modern advantages of email and telecommunications, it was troublesome for Western Australians to participate fully in the national decision-making processes of politics, business and culture. Australia's elite were concentrated in New South Wales and Victoria, and this had its effect on politics and the judiciary. From 1945 to 2007 these two states monopolised the Australian prime ministership, although two Western Australians, Sir Paul Hasluck (1969–74) and Major-General Michael Jeffery (2002–), became governors-general. In more than a century of its existence, only two Western Australians (Sir Ronald Wilson 1979–89 and John Toohey 1987–98) were nominated to the High Court bench, and if this was two more than South Australia or Tasmania achieved it showed some lack of balance in a tribunal responsible for making authoritative decisions in the vexed field of Commonwealth–state relations.

It probably said something about community priorities that sport was the only activity in which Western Australians seemed able to overcome the tyranny of distance. Following their victories in the Australian Football League in 1992 and 1994 (after which a drought followed until 2006), the West Coast Eagles were joined by a second team, the Fremantle Dockers, and neither they nor their opponents seemed to begrudge the frequent air travel involved in a season's competition. Cultural activities, on the other hand, were restricted. The Australian Chamber Orchestra visited Perth less frequently than other state capitals. At a conference on popular music in Perth in 2003, the visiting Sydney and Melbourne experts left an impression of assuming that through two annual visits 'they can hoover up the talent and move the bands to Sydney'.[17] Visiting art exhibitions displayed in Canberra or Melbourne seldom found their way across the Nullarbor. However, Sydney and Melbourne media complained when an enterprising director secured a Monet exhibition shown only at the Art Gallery of Western Australia and in Canberra.

As in the past, some Western Australians responded by striving to compete, but the results were uneven. Despite signs of promise in the 1970s, Western Australia never developed a significant film industry. The Western Australian Academy of Performing Arts, located at Edith Cowan University, built up a sound reputation as a nursery of talent, but most of its graduates had to leave the state to follow their careers. Attempts to build up a state-supported theatre ended in failure, although the Black Swan Theatre, founded in 1991 with support from Janet Holmes à Court, was nominated as the resident company when the state government planned a new theatre in Northbridge for completion in 2011. In proportion to population, drama was probably in a less flourishing condition in the early twenty-first century than it had been in the 1940s and 1950s.

This was disappointing, as Western Australia was capable of producing playwrights of stature. Irreverent and lively-minded, Dorothy Hewett blended autobiography and fantasy in a number of well-received plays, among them *The Man from Mukinupin* and *Bon-Bons and Roses for Dolly*. Jack Davis brought Aboriginal Australia into mainstream drama with *No Sugar*. A musical set among the Broome Aboriginal community, *Bran Nue Dae*, received national acclaim. But it was not easy for aspiring writers to find audiences habituated to passing intelligent judgment on the new.[18]

Western Australia was home to at least one novelist of international stature, Tim Winton, and some considerable poets, among them Fay Zwicky. Classical music still produced good performers and commanded good audiences. Perth's pubs and clubs fostered a popular music scene so vibrant that the city between 1987 and 1994 was claimed to be 'the dance capital of the world', 'the Liverpool of the South Seas'.[19] Patrons such as Janet Holmes à Court and Kerry Stokes and businesses such as Wesfarmers and (until its sale) BankWest built up impressive collections of paintings, and their patronage extended to both established artists, such as the belatedly recognised Howard Taylor, and the new school of Aboriginal artists coming forward in the Kimberley and Pilbara districts, of whom perhaps the most distinguished was Rover Thomas. Of a younger generation, Julie Dowling adapted Western artistic conventions to depict powerful statements of Aboriginality.[20] Western Australia was in no sense a cultural desert, but could not always be sure of the appreciation, provocation and stimulus that came of traffic with a wider world.

Isolation could also produce a habit of consciously refusing to comply with the orthodoxies of the rest of Australia, but persisting, sometimes from principle and sometimes perversity, in Western Australia's idiosyncratic ways. One example was the continued refusal to follow the Eastern States into daylight saving. Shopping hours were another point of difference. Possibly spurred by a wish to protect smaller local businesses from being overwhelmed by nationwide supermarket chains, the voters at a referendum in 2005 rejected the extension of Sunday trading, defying the editorial scorn of the national newspaper the *Australian*.[21] It seemed that the gambling instincts of Western Australians were sufficiently met by Lotterywest. Evolving out of the state-authorised Lotteries Commission, Lotterywest ran a variety of games of chance, channelling the profits to the support of deserving charities, hospitals, sporting activities and the arts. This relieved the state government of the need to find taxation revenue for these purposes, as well as providing welcome support for the suburban and country newsagents who might otherwise have been hard-pressed in an era when print culture faced electronic competition.[22] More contentiously, in 2008 Western Australia seemed steadfast in its refusal to allow uranium mining, despite mounting pressure from business interests and federal politicians, and was one of the states declining to authorise the planting of genetically modified crops. Also it was still uncertain in 2008 whether the Western Australian economy would be subordinated to an Eastern States–dominated federal government and multinational investors or whether Perth might advance to become the headquarters of national business enterprise. If some applauded the panache with which Wesfarmers bid for the Coles retailing giant, others noted that, although it had been stipulated that after privatisation the State's gas provider, Alinta, should remain domiciled in Western Australia, there seemed no way of preventing its takeover by outside interests.

Collectively, these issues suggested an ongoing tension between Western Australian aspirations to control the state's own destinies and a steady tendency in Canberra towards centralisation. In the 1960s and 1970s, state governments under Brand and Court resented the attempts of federal ministers to intervene in mineral export policy, and though disagreement reached its greatest intensity during the period of the Whitlam Labor government, it was at times not much better when the coalition was in office. In the 1980s Burke and the federal Labor Prime Minister Bob Hawke had a comparatively smooth relationship. After 1991 two Sydney-based prime ministers, Labor's Paul Keating and the Liberal John Howard, showed an increasing readiness to overrule the states when they could. Although the introduction of the goods and services tax was expected to provide the states with a steady flow of federally collected funding, disputes still occurred between the Commonwealth and Western Australia, threatening to intensify when the Commonwealth Government passed industrial relations legislation in 2006 reducing the role of trade unions and increasing the power of employers.[23]

These grievances fed an ongoing mindset. Western Australians still felt that politicians anchored in Sydney and Canberra were 'tothersiders', lacking in empathy with their own needs and hopes. Mistrust of the centralising potential of an Australian republic helped to make Western Australia one of the strongest supporters of retaining the monarchy when the issue was put to a federal referendum in 1999, though the vote may have owed something to the state's high number of British-born migrants. An opinion poll in 2006 showed 37 per cent of the respondents as favouring secession, probably an increase over the numbers when Lang Hancock promoted the idea thirty years previously.[24] Yet at the same time Western Australians participated enthusiastically in the renewed trend to celebrate Anzac Day as Australia's most significant national ceremony; no sense of separatism there. If there was minimal risk of invasion by a hostile power, Western Australians still backed the Commonwealth Government in repelling illegal immigrants. The first federal detention centre for such arrivals was set up in 1992 at Port Hedland, with another subsequently at the Curtin air base near Derby.[25] And when in the early years of the twenty-first century there was an increase in the number of Indonesian fishermen poaching in Western Australian waters, the state government and the Perth media were quick to attack Canberra for what they saw as tardy and ineffectual intervention. Secession would never be a practical proposition in the face of the defence argument.

The same poll that in 2006 surveyed attitudes towards secession also found that Western Australians were mostly contented people, pleased with their environment and their living conditions and mildly optimistic for the future. They were not a profoundly religious people. By 1996 Catholics had overtaken Anglicans as the most numerous faith, but not all who claimed a religion on the census form were regular worshippers. Attendances at most churches were declining, and the remaining faithful were elderly. When young people were drawn to attend church, they often chose a Christian congregation without traditional links, attracted by bright contemporary music and informality. By 2001 nearly 20 per cent of Western Australians had no religious affiliation, and in some districts in the far South West the figure was 30 per cent. It has been surmised that many living among the forests and beaches of that region were 'greenies', for whom environmentalism provided a substitute religion.[26] Some religious sense might be seen in folk rituals. At roadsides, carefully tended wayside crosses marked the spot where someone had fallen victim to a fatal traffic accident. And nowhere in Australia, or perhaps in the English-speaking world, was the practice more widespread of inserting notices in the morning newspaper, in this case *The West Australian*, often spontaneous and without artificial literary graces, to mourn the death of a friend or relation. Among some ethnic groups, including Aboriginal Western Australians, it seemed that respect for the deceased might be measured by the number of death notices she or he attracted.[27]

Death may not often have preoccupied the thoughts of hedonistic Western Australians except on the rare occasions when a swimmer was taken by a shark, but the shadow fell sometimes. Accustomed for decades to holidaying on Rottnest in a relaxed atmosphere of fishing, swimming, beer and amorous flirtation, Western Australians took easily to Bali as a tourist destination during the 1980s and 1990s. Bali offered all the attractions of Rottnest in an exotic environment accessible in less flying time than the Great Barrier Reef or Surfers Paradise. In October 2002 terrorist bombs wiped out a large number of Australian holidaymakers, including many Western Australians, at nightclubs in Kuta. The obituaries for those who died at Bali often described them as ordinary, fun-loving people who enjoyed going to parties. The historian James Froude more than a hundred years ago had written of Australians: 'It is hard to quarrel with men [and women, he might have added] who only wish to be innocently happy'. It was a shock to be reminded of a world where fanatics could see evil in the love of pleasure.[28]

The first generations of nineteenth-century pioneers who strove to wrest a living from what they saw as the alien land of Western Australia would have been amazed at the ease with which their descendants enjoyed the pleasures of the natural environment, but they would not have been so surprised at the connection with Bali. Captain Stirling and the founders of Australind always envisaged that trade with India and Southeast Asia would be a vital factor in Western Australia's growth. Until the middle of the twentieth century, Colombo or Singapore were the most usual first ports of call for travellers departing from Fremantle. Where geography suggested that most Australians would see themselves as members of a Pacific nation, Western Australians knew that their shores faced the Indian Ocean. If there was any merit in maintaining a separate Western Australian perspective, it would be shown in taking care to understand the nations bordering the Indian Ocean: Indonesia, Singapore, Malaysia, India and, beyond them, Africa and the Islamic world of the Middle East. Intermittently, the universities tried to promote this understanding, but it was not obvious that the message was getting through to the wider public.

Not that Western Australians were unaware of the importance of applying intellect to social and scientific problems. Community support had come readily to Fiona Stanley's researches on cerebral palsy and more generally on child and Aboriginal health, leading to the establishment in 1989 of the Telethon Institute for Child Health Research and to her appointment in 2004 as executive director of the Australian Research Alliance for Children and Youth. Fiona Wood gained national recognition after the Bali bombings for her work in the burns unit of Royal Perth Hospital. Both Stanley and Wood were honoured as Australian of the Year. Another distinguished product of the medical school at The University of Western Australia was Barry Marshall, who won the 2005 Nobel Prize in medicine with Robin Warren of Royal Perth Hospital for identifying the cause of peptic ulcers. Outside medical research, it was harder to muster philanthropic support, and yet so many of the questions confronting Western Australia during the twentieth century required research and analysis. Water resources and salinity were recognised as two major environmental issues, but there seemed to be less attention given to the preservation of Western Australia as a humane and adaptable society. Perhaps life was too pleasant for the long-term problems to secure recognition.

It was at least hopeful that the old tradition of entering into grand visionary schemes without careful research was at last on the wane; the decision to submit the proposal for a Kimberley pipeline to an inquiry suggested this. In each generation, the visionaries had been seduced by Western Australia's size and potential into big projects hastily planned and executed. Stirling with 'Hesperia', Hordern and the advocates of desert railways, Mitchell with his agricultural enthusiasms, de Garis and Chase the developers, Bond and Connell the bold riders of the 1980s—all allowed their dreams to outreach reality, and all left predicaments for others to make good. The most lasting results were achieved by premiers such as Sir John Forrest and Sir Charles Court, who at their best buttressed bold concepts with appropriate professional experience and a willingness to take professional advice.

Possibly the issue deserving the most incisive thought was the status of the sixty thousand Aborigines among Western Australia's two million inhabitants. Since the middle of the twentieth century, two distinguished Western Australians had helped to shape Commonwealth policy. Sir Paul Hasluck, federal Minister for Territories from 1951 to 1963, had seen the goal as education towards assimilation, hoping to provide opportunities to bring Aboriginal people into the same schooling, work force and living standards as other Australians. Herbert (Nugget) Coombs, addressing the needs of the later 1960s and 1970s, saw most hope in enabling Aboriginal Australians to establish communities in their traditional country, but by that time 'the grog had come in', and so by the turn of the twenty-first century some of these communities were severely dysfunctional. In Perth and the larger country towns, inadequately schooled and parented young Aborigines fell foul of the law, apparently part of a cycle of marginalisation that left them without the skills and attitudes that would enable them to thrive in modern Western Australia. All was not hopeless. Some Aboriginal people won through to tertiary education and entered the professions. Some mining companies created programs to promote the employment of Indigenous labour—an example of enlightened self-interest, because Aborigines brought up in the locality were more likely to stay with the company than outsiders flown from Perth. But Halls Creek in the Kimberley district was the fourth most impoverished community in the whole of Australia, and the life expectancy in such communities was more than fifteen years beneath the national average. In Western Australia's gaols, 42 per cent of all prisoners and 90 per cent of those north of the Tropic of Capricorn were Aboriginal. Anywhere else in the world, commented John Sanderson, 'such figures would be seen to constitute a state of civil war—such is the alienation they represent'.[29] Western Australia could never call itself a contented society while these problems remained.

In January 2006 Geoff Gallop resigned as Premier and was replaced by Alan Carpenter. One of Gallop's last official decisions involved the appointment of a new state Governor. Two respected senior military officers, Michael Jeffery and John Sanderson, had brought a new prestige to the office, and their successor was to be Ken Michael, a former Commissioner of Main Roads and member of a family of Greek origin who had played a prominent role in the community. It was decided that his induction ceremony should include a welcome on behalf of the Aboriginal community by a senior Nyungar, Kim Collard. This had considerable symbolic importance, and Collard spoke well. He pointed out that Western Australia might have been saved a good deal of trouble if Captain Stirling had thought to make some similar gesture on arriving in Western Australia. It was a reminder that consultation and forethought were essential qualities in making Western Australia a good society.

Abbreviations used in Notes and Select Bibliography

ADB	*Australian Dictionary of Biography*
BDWA	*Biographical Dictionary of Western Australians*
CUP	Cambridge University Press
FACP	Fremantle Arts Centre Press
HS	*Historical Studies*
JAS	*Journal of Australian Studies*
JHSWA	*Journal of the Historical Society of Western Australia*
JPWAHS	*Journal and Proceedings of the Western Australian Historical Society*
MUP	Melbourne University Press
NLA	National Library of Australia
OUP	Oxford University Press
RWAHS	Royal Western Australian Historical Society
SWAH	*Studies in Western Australian History*
UNSW	University of New South Wales
USH	*University Studies in History*
UWAP	University of Western Australia Press
VPLC	*Votes and Proceedings of the Legislative Council*
WAPD	*Western Australian Parliamentary Debates*
WAPP	*Western Australian Parliamentary Papers*

Notes

Introduction

1   *London Review of Books*, 23 August 2001.

2   F. Dunn, 'Brave new words', *The West Australian Magazine*, 2–3 April 1994, p. 36; J. Ritchie & M. Brooks, *Words from the West: A Glossary of Western Australian Terms*, MUP, Melbourne, 1994.

3   W. B. Kimberly, *History of West Australia: A Narrative of Her Past Together with Biographies of Her Leading Men*, F. W. Niven, Melbourne, 1897.

4   J. S. Battye, *Western Australia: A History from Its Discovery to the Inauguration of the Commonwealth*, Clarendon Press, Oxford, 1924.

5   F. K. Crowley, *Australia's Western Third: A History of Western Australia from the First Settlement to Modern Times*, Heinemann Press, Melbourne, 1960.

6   C. T. Stannage (ed.), *A New History of Western Australia*, UWAP, Nedlands, 1981. At ch. 22 (pp. 677–91), 'Western Australia reflects on its past', I offer a more ample account of the state's historiography as at 1979.

Chapter 1: A shabby-genteel society, 1826–1850

1   D. S. Garden, *Albany: A Panorama of the Sound from 1827*, Thomas Nelson, West Melbourne, 1977; L. Johnson, *It Was the Amity Brig*, Albany Town Council, Albany, 1977.

2   S. Hallam, *Fire and Hearth: A Study of Aboriginal Usage and European Usurpation in South Western Australia*, Australian Institute of Aboriginal Studies, Canberra, 1975, p. 111. Beban's details are in *BDWA*, vol. viii, UWAP, Nedlands, 1990, pp. 3, 88.

3   L. R. Marchant, *France Australe*, Artlook Books, Perth, 1982—the standard reference for early nineteenth-century activities in Western Australian waters.

4   P. Statham-Drew, *James Stirling: Admiral and Governor of Western Australia*, UWAP, Nedlands, 2003; R. T. Appleyard & T. Manford, *The Beginning*, UWAP, Nedlands, 1980, ch. 2; F. K. Crowley, 'Sir James Stirling', in *ADB*, vol. 2, pp. 484–8; D. Markey, *More a Symbol than a Success: The Foundation Years of the Swan River Colony*, Westbooks, Bayswater, 1977; G. Seddon & D. Ravine, *A City and Its Setting*, FACP, Fremantle, 1986, ch. 4, esp. pp. 65–6; J. M. R. Cameron, *Ambition's Fire: The Agricultural Colonization of Pre-Convict Western Australia*, UWAP, Nedlands, 1981; 'The foundation of Western Australia reconsidered', *SWAH*, vol. 3, 1978, pp. 1–17.

5   M. Bassett, *The Hentys: An Australian Colonial Tapestry*, OUP, London, 1954, p. 35.

6   ibid., p. 53.

7   A. Hasluck, *Thomas Peel of Swan River*, OUP, Melbourne, 1965.

8   W. L. Milligan, 'Four year report on the climate and diseases of the new colony of Western Australia', *Calcutta Courier*, 14 May 1835, quoted in *Perth Gazette*, 5 September 1835.

9   F. R. Mercer, *Amazing Career: The Story of Western Australia's First Surveyor General*, Paterson Brokensha, Perth, 1962; J. L. Burton Jackson, *Not an Idle Man: A Biography of John Septimus Roe*, FACP, Fremantle, 1982; W. L. Brockman's lifelong resentment, *Herald*, 9 April 1870.

10   A. Hasluck, *Thomas Peel*, chs 6–8.

11   Eliza Shaw, quoted in M. Durack, *To Be Heirs Forever*, Constable & Constable, London, 1976, p. 41; Henry Trigg to Amelia Trigg, 16 February 1830, quoted in B. Devenish, *Man of Energy and Compassion*, Wongaburra Enterprises, South Perth, 1996, p. 87.

12   R. M. Lyon to Secretary of State for Colonies, 11 February 1831, quoted in Battye, *Western Australia*, p. 95; G. F. Moore, *Diary of Ten Years Eventful Life of an Early Settler in Western Australia*, London, 1884; facsimile edn with introduction by C. T. Stannage, UWAP, Nedlands, 1978, pp. 59–60 (a new edition by J. M. R. Cameron, *The Millendon Diaries: George Fletcher Moore's Western Australian Diaries and Letters, 1830–1841*, Hesperian Press, Carlisle, 2007, appeared as this book was going to press); P. Hetherington, *Settlers, Servants and Slaves*, UWAP, Nedlands, 2002, p. 202; T. Mazzarol, 'Tradition and environment: The indentured labourer in early Western Australia', *SWAH*, vol. 3, 1978, pp. 30–7.

13   J. Fall, 'Crime and criminal records in Western Australia 1830–1835', *SWAH*, vol. 3, 1978, pp. 18–29.

14   A. Burton, 'The diary of Joseph Hardey', *JHSWA*, vol. 1, no. 6, pp. 7–28; R. Johnston, *The Tranby Hardeys*, Parmelia, Serpentine, 1988; V. F. Epton, *The Story of the Hardey Family*, V. F. Epton, Perth, 1964; R. Erickson, *Old Toodyay and Newcastle*, Toodyay Shire Council, 1974.

15   Moore, *Diary*, p. 100; S. Le Soeuf, 'Albany Nyoongars', in B. de Garis (ed.), *Portraits of the South-West*, UWAP, Nedlands, 1993, p. 1.

16   P. B. Edwards & R. B. Joyce (eds), *Anthony Trollope in Australia*, University of Queensland Press, St Lucia, 1967, p. 561; also Moore, *Diary*, p. 200; M. Durack, *The Courteous Savage*, Nelson, Melbourne, 1964; Appleyard & Manford, *The Beginning*, chs 5–6.

17   A good summary of the historiography of the Battle of Pinjarra is P. Statham, 'James Stirling and Pinjarra: A battle in more ways than one', *SWAH*, vol. 23, 2003, pp. 167–94. See also Pinjarra Massacre Site Research and Development Project, Report for Stage 1, Pinjarra, c. 1998; K. Bell & W. P. Morrell (eds), *Early Days in Western Australia*, OUP, London, 1930, p. 174; R. Richards, *The Murray District of Western Australia*, Shire of Murray, [Pinjarra], 1978, p. 98; C. Fletcher, 'The battle for Pinjarra: A revisionist view', *SWAH*, vol. 8, 1984, pp. 1–6; *Subiaco Post*, 7, 21 June 2003.

18   *Perth Gazette*, 15 June 1837; also 30 July 1836; P. Hasluck, *Black Australians*, MUP, Melbourne, 1942, pp. 74–6; B. Pope, 'Aboriginal message and mail carriers in Western Australia in the early and mid 19th century', in de Garis, *Portraits*, pp. 57–77; C. Collins, 'Matters of social conscience: Western Australia 1829–1890', *USH*, vol. 3, no. 3, 1969, pp. 3–4.

19   The Bonny Dutton episode is treated in Durack, *To Be Heirs Forever*, p. 534; also
        A. Burton, 'The diary of Anne Whatley', *JHSWA*, vol. 3, no. vii, 1930, pp. 24–5;
        W. S. Cooper & G. McDonald, *A City for All Seasons: The Story of Melville*, City of
        Melville, Ardross, 1989, p. 22. For other 'stolen children' stories, Moore, *Diary*, p. 200;
        Ted Lewington as reported by Sir Paul Hasluck, cited in G. Bolton, 'Oral historian', in
        T. Stannage, K. Saunders & R. Nile, *Paul Hasluck in Australian History: Civic Personality
        and Public Life*, University of Queensland Press, St Lucia, 1998, p. 41.

20   P. M. C. Statham-Drew, 'The Economic Development of the Swan River Colony', PhD
        thesis, The University of Western Australia, 1980.

21   Cameron, *Ambition's Fire*, p. 198.

22   G. Grey, *Journals of Two Expeditions of Discovery to North-West and Western Australia
        1837–39*, T. & W. Boone, London, 1841; facsimile edn London, 1969; D. Hutchison,
        'The First Agriculturalists of the Victoria District', unpublished paper prepared for the
        Geraldton Museum, 2001; Hallam, *Fire and Hearth*, pp. 12–13.

23   Moore, *Diary*, p. 300; G. Chessell, *Richard Spencer: Napoleonic War Naval Hero and
        Australian Pioneer*, UWAP, Nedlands, 2005.

24   I. D. Heppingstone, 'American whalers in Western Australian waters', *Early Days*, vol. 7,
        no. 1, 1969, pp. 35–52; 'A whaling family', ibid., vol. 10, no. 5, 1993, pp. 461–72.

25   James Stephen annotation on Stirling to Glenelg, 25 September 1839 (CO 18/24; f461),
        quoted in Statham-Drew, *James Stirling*, p. 383.

26   E. Shann, *Cattle Chosen*, OUP, London, 1926; R. Pascoe, 'Professor Shann meets the
        gentry', *SWAH*, vol. 6, 1983, pp. 70–7; I. G. Heppingstone, 'Alfred and Ellen Bussell:
        Pioneers of the Margaret River', *JPWAHS*, vol. 6, no. 3, 1964, pp. 33–45.

27   A. Hasluck, *Portrait with Background*, OUP, Melbourne, 1955; W. J. Lines, *An All
        Consuming Passion: Origins, Modernity and the Australian Life of Georgiana Molloy*, Allen
        & Unwin, St Leonards, 1994.

28   G. C. Bolton & H. Vose (eds), *The Wollaston Journals*, 2 vols, UWAP, Nedlands,
        1991–92, vol. 1, p. 232.

29   For the Anglican Church, A. Burton, *Church Beginnings in the West*, A. Burton,
        Perth, 1941; C. L. M. Hawtrey, *The Availing Struggle*, C. L. M. Hawtrey, Perth, 1949;
        J. Tonkin, *Cathedral and Community*, UWAP, Nedlands, 2001. For the Catholic
        Church, D. F. Bourke, *The History of the Catholic Church in Western Australia 1829–1979*,
        Archdiocese of Perth, 1979; G. Byrne, *Valiant Women: Letters from the Sisters of Mercy in
        Western Australia 1845–1849*, Polding Press, Melbourne, 1981. For Wesleyan Methodism,
        W. E. McNair, 'A second look at the early years of Methodism in Western Australia
        1830–1855', *Early Days*, vol. 7, no. 1, 1979, pp. 79–87. For an overview, M. Aveling, 'Western
        Australian society: The religious aspect', in Stannage, *A New History*, pp. 575–98.

30   D. Markey, 'Common meals as cultural spoor: Food in the Swan River Colony,
        1829–1950', *Early Days*, vol. 9, no. 6, 1988, pp. 39–51; D. Hough, 'The playmakers', in
        G. Bolton, R. Rossiter & J. Ryan, *Farewell Cinderella*, UWAP, Nedlands, 2003, pp. 9 ff.,
        esp. pp. 10–16.

31   Eliza Brown to William Bussey, 3 July [1841], quoted by P. Cowan (ed.), *A Faithful
        Picture*, FACP, Fremantle, 1977, p. 21. The Logue anecdote is from M. A. Bain, *Ancient
        Landmarks*, UWAP, Nedlands, 1971, p. 58.

32   G. Dutton, *The Hero As Murderer*, Collins, London, 1967, chs 7–8; W. T. Graham,
        'Edward John Eyre, explorer—150 years later', *Early Days*, vol. 10, no. 2, 1990,
        pp. 194–200.

33   Cameron, *Ambition's Fire*, chs 7–9; W. Cooper, G. Moore & M. White, *Adversity and Achievement: A History of the Royal Agricultural Society of Western Australia*, Royal Agricultural Society, Claremont, 2004, pp. 21 ff.

34   P. E. C. De Mouncey, 'Whaling in the early days', *JHSWA*, vol. 1, no. 8, pp. 58–60; M. Gibbs, 'Nebinyan's songs: An Aboriginal whaler of Western Australia', *Aboriginal History*, vol. 27, 2003, pp. 1–14; 'The Historical Archaeology of Shore Based Whaling in Western Australia', PhD thesis, The University of Western Australia, 1996.

35   A. J. Barker & M. Laurie, *Excellent Connections*, City of Bunbury, 1992, pp. 13–27; A. C. Staples, *They Made Their Destiny*, Shire of Harvey, 1979, chs 5–7.

36   P. Hasluck, *Mucking About*, MUP, Melbourne, 1977, p. 145; A. Gill, *Forced Labour for the West: Parkhurst Convicts 'Apprenticed' in Western Australia 1842–1851*, A. Gill, Maylands, 1997; D. Hutchison, 'Many years a thief', *Tirra Lirra*, vol. 14, no. 3, 2005, pp. 22–8.

37   Charles Bussell, 'Diary', Bussell papers, WASA 337A, Battye Library, Perth.

38   E. Braid, 'John Septimus Roe, first explorer of the wheatlands: The search for an inland sea', *Early Days*, vol. 7, no. 7, 1975, pp. 81–97.

39   F. W. Birman, *Gregory of Rainworth: A Man in His Time*, UWAP, Nedlands, 1979.

40   J. Nairn, *Walter Padbury: His Life and Times*, North Stirling Press, Padbury, 1985, chs 4–11.

41   Garden, *Albany*, p. 84; *Perth Gazette*, 8 January 1848.

42   R. Glover, *Plantagenet*, UWAP, Nedlands, 1979, pp. 49–51.

43   *BDWA*, vol. 2, p. 1014.

44   A. Hasluck, *Portrait with Background*, pp. 54–5; Durack, *To Be Heirs Forever*, pp. 66–8.

45   Hetherington, *Settlers*, p. 16; M. Grellier (Anderson), 'The family: Some aspects of the demography and ideology of mid-19th century Western Australia', in Stannage, *A New History*, pp. 475–510.

46   Moore, *Diary*, p. 400.

47   B. Buchanan (ed.), *The Journal of Gerald de Courcy Lefroy*, B. & A. Buchanan, Perth, 2003, p. 204.

Chapter 2: Convictism and its legacy, 1850–1879

1   H. Willoughby, *The British Convict in Western Australia*, Harrison, London, 1865, ch. 6; A. Hasluck, *Unwilling Emigrants*, OUP, Melbourne, 1959; FACP, Fremantle, 1991; Erickson, *Old Toodyay and Newcastle*, pp. 102–3; *The Brand on His Coat*, UWAP, Nedlands, 1983; T. Stannage (ed.), 'Convictism in Western Australia', *SWAH*, vol. 4, 1981; J. Sherriff & A. Brake (eds), 'Building a colony: The convict legacy', *SWAH*, vol. 24, 2006; P. Statham, 'Origins and achievement: Convicts and the Western Australian economy', *Westerly*, vol. 30, no. 3, 1985, pp. 37–44; N. Reeves, 'This is his mark: Convicts and literacy in Western Australia', ibid., pp. 50–6.

2   Garden, *Albany*, pp. 138–9; P. Hasluck, *Mucking About*, pp. 148–9.

3   *Perth Gazette*, 21 June 1861; Richards, *The Murray District*, p. 349; F. A. Hansford-Miller, *A History of Medicine in Western Australia 1829–1870*, vol. II, *Hospital Services in Early Colonial Western Australia*, Abcado, Willetton, 1997; V. Hobbs, *But Westward Look: Nursing in Western Australia 1829–1979*, UWAP, Nedlands, 1980; G. C. Bolton & P. Joske, *History of the Royal Perth Hospital*, UWAP, Nedlands, 1982.

4   Willoughby, *British Convict*, p. 18; Crowley, *Australia's Western Third*, pp. 30–1; M. Gibbs, 'The convict places of Western Australia', *SWAH*, vol. 24, p. 89; a graphic account of the journey and its difficulties is given by Marianne North in *A Vision of Eden: The Life and Work of Marianne North*, Webb & Bower, Exeter, 1980, pp. 171–4.

5   J. R. Robertson, 'The Western Australian timber industry', *USH*, vol. 3, no. 1, 1957.

6   Erickson, *Old Toodyay and Newcastle*, pp. 168, 224–8, 315–18, 322; *ADB*, vol. 3, pp. 90–1,
        suppresses his convict origins. For another example of an ex-convict who made good, see
        S. Potter, 'Alfred Daniel Letch: A white collar convict', *SWAH*, vol. 24, 2006, pp. 37–47.

7   For an example of a Resident Magistrate's duties (George Eliot at Bunbury), see Barker
        & Laurie, *Excellent Connections*, chs 2–3. For the origins of the police, see P. Conole,
        Protect and Serve: A History of Policing in Western Australia, Western Australian Police
        Service, Perth, 2002, pp. 17–27.

8   *Perth Gazette*, 24 March 1863; *Inquirer* (editorial), 12 June 1865; Willoughby, *British
        Convict*, ch. 6; G. Bolton & J. Gregory, *Claremont: A History*, UWAP, Nedlands, 1999, p. 9.

9   Crowley, *Australia's Western Third*, p. 34.

10   I. Elliott, *Moondyne Joe: The Man and the Myth*, UWAP, Nedlands, 1978; Kimberly,
        History of West Australia, p. 202; Margaret Hamersley to Capel Brockman, 14 March
        1867, ACC2181A, MS477, item 2/8, 1A/43, Battye Library, Perth (I owe this reference to
        Dr Amanda Curtin).

11   Lewington quoted in Bolton, 'Oral historian', p. 40; G. C. Bolton, 'The Fenians are
        coming, the Fenians are coming', *SWAH*, vol. 4, 1981, pp. 62–7.

12   A. G. Evans, *Fanatic Heart: A Life of John Boyle O'Reilly*, UWAP, Nedlands, 1997;
        V. Brady, 'The return of the repressed: J. B. O'Reilly and the politics of desire', *Westerly*,
        vol. 33, no. 21, 1985, pp. 105–13.

13   T. Stannage, 'Bishop Salvado: A review of memoirs', *SWAH*, vol. 8, 1984, pp. 33, 35;
        M. Berman, 'Bishop Salvado, a reappraisal', ibid., pp. 36–46; G. Russo, *Lord Abbot of
        the Wilderness: The Life and Times of Bishop Salvado*, Polding Press, Melbourne, 1980;
        E. J. Stormon (ed.), *The Salvado Memoirs*, UWAP, Nedlands, 1972; Byrne, *Valiant Women*,
        A. Ride, *The Grand Experiment*, Hachette, Sydney, 2007.

14   · B. Pope, 'Postal Services in Western Australia: The Growth of an Organisation', MPhil
        thesis, Murdoch University, 1988.

15   R. Strong, 'The Reverend John Wollaston and colonial Christianity in Western
        Australia, 1840–1863', *Journal of Religious History*, vol. 25, no. 3, 2001.

16   P. Hasluck, *Black Australians*, pp. 93–6.

17   A. de Q. Robin, *Matthew Blagden Hale: The Life of an Australian Pioneer Bishop*,
        Hawthorn Press, Melbourne, 1976.

18   Quotation from Edward Withers in Bolton, 'Oral historian', p. 42; F. Crowley, *Big John
        Forrest*, UWAP, Nedlands, 2001, pp. 1–5; G. C. Bolton, *Alexander Forrest: His Life and
        Times*, MUP, Carlton, 1958, ch. 1; P. Hasluck, 'The early years of John Forrest', *Early Days*,
        vol. 8, no. 1, 1977, pp. 69–97.

19   G. Blainey, *Gold and Paper*, Georgian House, Melbourne, 1958, pp. 81–3; C. Greenhill,
        'The Western Australian Bank 1841–1927: An Historic Economic Research of Western
        Australia's Only Private Banking Institution', MA thesis, The University of Western
        Australia, 1959.

20   C. Fyfe, *The Bale Fillers: Australian Wool 1826–1916*, UWAP, Nedlands, 1983; also 'The
        early days of wool in Western Australia', *Early Days*, vol. 10, no. 1, 1991, pp. 265–78.

21   J. Clydesdale, *Pioneer of the Road: The Story of Australia's First Self-powered Road Vehicle*,
        J. Clydesdale, Yokine, 2002.

22   R. Erickson, 'Alfred Carson: An exceedingly clever and learned man', *Early Days*, vol. 10,
        pt 5, pp. 549–60; G. Kutching, 'Solomon Cook 1813–1871: Blacksmith, shipwright,
        engineer and entrepreneur', *Early Days*, vol. 9, no. 3, 1985, pp. 123–36.

23   *Western Mail*, 28 October 1911, p. 14; Erickson, *The Brand on His Coat*, pp. 247–9;
      G. P. Stevens, 'The east–west telegraph, 1875–77', *Early Days*, vol. 2, no. 13, 1932,
      pp. 16–35; 'Inauguration of the electric telegraph in Western Australia', *Early Days*, vol. 2,
      no. 20, 1933, pp. 26–30.

24   R. Erickson, *The Dempsters*, UWAP, Nedlands, 1978.

25   K. Forrest, *The Challenge and the Chance: The Colonisation and Settlement of North
      West Australia 1861–1914*, Hesperian Press, Carlisle, 1996, ch. x; N. Withnell Taylor,
      Yeera-Muk-a-Doo, FACP, Fremantle, 1980; M. McCarthy, 'The Denison Plains Pastoral
      Company and its people re-assessed', *Early Days*, vol. 11, no. 6, 2000, pp. 657–75;
      C. Richards, *There Were Three Ships: The Story of the Camden Harbour Expedition
      1864–1865*, UWAP, Nedlands, 1990.

26   Ashworth quoted in Bolton, 'Oral historian', pp. 41–2.

27   P. Cowan, *Maitland Brown: A View of 19th Century Western Australia*, FACP, Fremantle,
      1988; B. Scates, 'A monument of murder: Celebrating the conquest of Aboriginal
      Australia', *SWAH*, vol. 10, 1989, pp. 21–31; I. Crawford, *We Won the Victory: Aborigines
      and Outsiders on the North-West Coast of the Kimberley*, FACP, Fremantle, 2001, ch. 7;
      Conole, *Protect and Serve*, pp. 53–6, 67, 69.

28   *VPLC*, 1880/A6: Report by the Government Resident at Roebourne on the Pearl
      Fisheries of the North West Coast; *Inquirer*, 1 March 1876; K. de la Rue, *Pearl
      Shell and Pastures*, Cossack Project Committees, 1979; Forrest, *The Challenge
      and the Chance*, pt 2; S. Kwaymullina, 'For marbles: Aboriginal people in the
      early pearling industry of the North-West', *SWAH*, no. 22, 2002, pp. 53–61;
      B. Shepherd, 'A History of the Pearling Industry off the North-West Coast
      of Australia from Its Origin until 1916', MA thesis, The University of Western
      Australia, 1975.

29   M. Love, *The Sherwood Papers: a Swan River Story*, M. Love, Dalkeith, 1996,
      pp. 161–2.

30   P. de Serville, *3 Barrack Street*, Helicon Press, Wahroonga, 2003; T. S. Louch, *The
      History of the Weld Club 1871–1950*, Weld Club, Perth, 1980.

31   Cowan, *Maitland Brown*, pp. 137–9; D. Hutchison, 'An Early Landcare Scheme',
      unpublished paper prepared for the Geraldton Museum, 2001.

32   C. T. Stannage, *The People of Perth*, Perth City Council, Perth, 1979, pp. 166–8;
      S-J. Hunt & G. Bolton, 'Cleansing the dunghill', *SWAH*, vol. 2, 1977, pp. 1–17;
      C. W. Collins, 'Matters of social conscience in Western Australia, 1829–1890', *USH*,
      vol. 5, pt 2, 1968, pp. 1–22.

33   P. Tannock, 'Sir James George Lee Steere', unpublished manuscript, Perth, 1975;
      C. Murray, 'Sir James George Lee Steere', *Early Days*, vol. 3, no. 7, 1943, pp. 12–18;
      B. Hicks, 'Sir Alexander and Sir Thomas Cockburn-Campbell', *Early Days*, vol. 6, no. 6,
      1967, pp. 71–84.

34   H. M. Wilson & I. D. Heppingstone, 'Mrs John: The letters of Charlotte Bussell of
      Cattle Chosen', *Early Days*, vol. 7, no. 4, 1972, p. 1028, and vol. 7, no. 5, 1973, pp. 41–78;
      the quotation cited is at p. 55.

35   Edwards & Joyce, *Anthony Trollope in Australia*, pp. 569–70; Mrs E. Millett, *An
      Australian Parsonage: or, The Settler and the Savage in Western Australia*, E. Stanford,
      London, 1872; facsimile edn UWAP, Nedlands, 1981, p. 332; M. Aveling (ed.), *Westralian
      Voices*, UWAP, Nedlands, 1979, pp. 36–7; W. Matthews, 'A Means of Punishment: The
      Mount Eliza Depot, 1878–1905', *SWAH*, vol. 25, 2007, pp. 8–23.

36   *Inquirer*, 5 June 1879.

37   *West Australian*, 9 July 1898; *Eastern Districts Chronicle*, 9 July 1898.

38   P. Bolger, *Hobart Town*, Australian National University Press, Canberra, 1973, p. 151.

39   J. M. Bennett, *Sir Archibald Burt: First Chief Justice of Western Australia, 1861–1879*, J. M. Bennett, Annandale, 2002.

40   G. C. Bolton, 'The strange career of William Beresford', *Early Days*, vol. 9, no. 2, 1984, pp. 5–16.

41   G. C. Bolton, 'The price of protest: Press and judiciary in 1870', *SWAH*, vol. 15, 1994.

42   T. Austen, *A Cry in the Wind*, Darlington Publishing Group, Darlington, 1998, pp. 59–62.

43   F. F. B. Wittenoom, 'Some notes on his life', MS, Battye Library, c. 1925; R. F. B. Lefroy (ed.), *A Varied and Versatile Life*, Hesperian Press, Carlisle, 2003; C. Cameron, *F. F. B. Wittenoom: Pastoral Pioneer and Explorer*, Primary Industry Committee of the Western Australian 150th Anniversary Board, Perth, 1979; *VPLC*, 1882, paper 33, p. 7.

44   M. McCarthy, *Iron and Steamship Archaeology: Success and Failure on the SS Xantho*, Kluwer Academic/Plenum, New York, 2000.

45   *Inquirer*, 19 April 1876; P. F. Stevens, *The Voyage of the Catalpa*, Carroll & Graf, New York, 2002; M. Heseltine [Sir William Heseltine], 'The great escape: The escape of the military Fenians on the *Catalpa*, Easter Monday 1876', *Journal of Irish Heritage Association of Western Australia*, autumn 2002, pp. 10–39.

46   A. F. Ferguson Stewart, *Australia's Grace Darling*, Patersons, Perth, 1946; *Herald*, 27 January 1877; *Inquirer*, 31 January 1877, 14 February 1877, 23 May 1877, 5 September 1877. The account of an eyewitness, George Leake, differs in some respects from the accepted version, *History West*, vol. 45, no. 9, October 2006, pp. 4–5.

47   *VPLC*, 57/1877: Correspondence between his Excellency the Governor and the Secretary of State for the Colonies, on the subject of the claim advanced by Mr S. P. Lord in respect of the Lacepede Islands; *Victorian Express*, 28 April 1880, p. 2; B. Hillman (ed.), *The Hillman Diaries 1877–1884*, F. W. Bentley Hillman, Applecross, 1990, 28 October 1881, p. 587, 23 January 1882, p. 626.

48   J. Forrest, *Explorations in Australia*, Lowe & Co., London, 1875; facsimile edn New York, 1969; Crowley, *Big John Forrest*, ch. 2.

49   Edwards & Joyce, *Anthony Trollope in Australia*, p. 602.

50   ibid., p. 617.

51   Hillman, *Hillman Diaries*, 14 March 1879, p. 213.

Chapter 3: 'At last she moves', 1879–1894

1   Bolton, *Alexander Forrest*; 'Tommy Dower', *Aboriginal History*, no. 12, 1988, pp. 79–84; A. Hicks, 'First into the Kimberleys: The Forrest expedition of 1879', *Early Days*, vol. 3, pt 1, 1938, pp. 1–9.

2   M. Durack, *Kings in Grass Castles*, Constable & Company, London, 1960; G. Byrne, *Tom and Jack*, FACP, Fremantle, 2003; C. Clement, 'Australia's North West 1644–1844: A Study of Exploration, Land Policy and Land Acquisition', PhD thesis, Murdoch University, 1991.

3   G. C. Bolton, 'The Kimberley Pastoral Industry 1885 to 1953', MA thesis, The University of Western Australia, 1954.

4   Bolton, *Alexander Forrest*, ch. iv.

5   M. McCarthy, 'Failure and success: The Broadhursts and the Abrolhos islands guano industry', *SWAH*, vol. 12, 1992, pp. 10–23; Staples, *They Made Their Destiny*; R. Glover, *Plantagenet*, UWAP, Nedlands, 1979, p. 25; M. Bignell, *A Place to Meet: A History of the Shire of Katanning*, UWAP, Nedlands, 1981, p. 45.

6   T. Sten, 'Survey of Agricultural Development in the Hay River Area of Western Australia', MA thesis, The University of Western Australia, 1943; R. Erickson, 'Prue Arber, a legendary shepherdess', in L. Layman (ed.), *Rica's Stories*, RWAHS, Nedlands, 2001; E. Herbert, *Crediton to Cambellup*, E. Herbert, Birchgrove, 2001.

7   Sten, 'Survey of agricultural development'; M. Bignell, *The Fruit of the Country*, UWAP, Nedlands, 1977, p. 125, quoting *Albany Mail*, 14 July 1886.

8   R. Erickson, 'Jane Adams of Mangowine', *Early Days*, vol. 7, no. 5, 1974, pp. 7–25.

9   'Galatea', 'A lady's impression of Western Australia', *The West Australian*, 8 February 1895; *Victorian Express*, 22 September 1880; S. Stevens, 'Imaging colonial Greenough', *JAS*, vol. 72, 2002, pp. 139–50.

10   H. Edwards, *Port of Pearls—A History of Broome*, Rigby, Adelaide, 1983; V. Burton, *General History of Broome*, Broome Historical Society, Broome, 2000.

11   *WA Catholic Record*, 29 July 1880, p. 5; *WAPD*, 1880, vol. v, pp. 64–89, 167–8, 223–33.

12   Crowley, *Big John Forrest*, pp. 49–54, 69–73; W. F. P. Heseltine, 'The Movements for Self-government in Western Australia from 1882 to 1890', BA (Hons) thesis, The University of Western Australia, 1950; C. T. Stannage, 'Electoral Politics in Western Australia 1884–1897', BA (Hons) thesis, The University of Western Australia, 1967.

13   *WA Bulletin*, 17 May 1890, p. 3.

14   J. B. Gribble, *Dark Deeds in A Sunny Land, or Blacks and Whites in North-West Australia*, Daily News, Perth, 1905; UWAP, Nedlands/Institute of Applied Aboriginal Studies, Mount Lawley, 1987, with appendix by S-J. Hunt, 'The Gribble Affair'.

15   *WAPP*, 1891–92, no. 1: Final Report of the Commission on Agriculture.

16   Hillman, *Hillman Diaries*, p. 724, 8 September 1882; M. Hazzard, *Australia's Brilliant Daughter: Ellis Rowan, Artist, Naturalist, Explorer, 1848–1922*, Greenhouse Publications, Richmond, 1984, pp. 39, 54–5; F. K. Crowley, 'Western Australia's Lady Forrest 1844–1929: A memoir', *Melbourne Studies in Education 1960–61*, pp. 220–61.

17   *Diocese of Perth Quarterly Magazine*, London, July 1892, quoted by D. Gava, *Themes in Western Australian History*, Mount Lawley, n.d., p. 234.

18   P. M. Brown, *The Merchant Princes of Fremantle: The Rise and Decline of a Colonial Elite 1870–1900*, UWAP, Nedlands, 1997.

19   *West Australian*, 4 July 1887; G. Pow, *Barefoot Bandit: The Story of Tom Hughes, West Australian Bushranger*, G. Pow, Maylands, 2003.

20   Hetherington, *Settlers*, pp. 75–6.

21   *Eastern Districts Chronicle*, 27 February 1892; an example of 'a good death' as defined by P. Jalland, *Australian Ways of Death: A Social and Cultural History 1840–1918*, OUP, South Melbourne, 2002.

22   D. Garden, 'George Throssell', *ADB*, vol. 12, MUP, Carlton, 1990, p. 223.

23   M. Bignell, 'Frederick Henry Piesse', *ADB*, vol. 11, MUP, Carlton, 1988, pp. 229–30; *A Place to Meet*, passim; R. Anderson (ed.), *Katanning: A Century of Stories*, Katanning Shire Council, 1988, pp. 46–53.

24   F. Crowley, 'Master and servant in Western Australia, 1851–1901', *JPWAHS*, vol. 4, no. 6, 1953, pp. 15–32.

25   V. Courtney, *All I May Tell: A Journalist's Story*, Shakespeare Head Press, Sydney, 1956, pp. 160–1; unfortunately, there are no surviving copies of the York newspaper for that period.

26   I. van den Driesen, 'The evolution of the trade union movement in Western Australia', in Stannage, *A New History*, pp. 352–80.

27   G. Christian, *The Footballers*, St George Books, Perth, 1995; A. J. Barker, *Behind the Play: A History of Football in Western Australia from 1868*, West Australian Football Commission, Perth, 2004.

28   Stannage, *The People of Perth*, pp. 196–205.

29   Crowley, *Big John Forrest*, ch. 5.

30   M. Uren, *Glint of Gold*, Robertson & Mullens, Melbourne, 1948.

31   P. W. Johnston, 'The repeals of Section 70 of the Western Australian *Constitution Act* 1889, Aborigines and Governmental Breach of Trust', *University of Western Australia Law Review*, no. 19, 1989, pp. 318–51.

32   J. Hay, 'Literature and society', in Stannage, *A New History*, p. 608; *West Australian*, 22 October 1890.

33   J. Farrant, 'Playing in tune', in Bolton, Rossiter & Ryan, *Farewell Cinderella*, pp. 99–100.

34   C. T. Stannage, 'The composition of the Western Australian Parliament 1890–1911', *USH*, vol. 4, 1966, pp. 1–40; 'John Forrest and the formation of the first ministry under responsible government in Western Australia', *USH*, vol. 5, pt 2, 1968, pp. 23–33.

35   Crowley, *Big John Forrest*; M. Webb, 'John Forrest and West Australian goldrushes', *Early Days*, vol. 10, no. 5, 1993, pp. 473–88.

36   Throssell quotation in N. S. Coote, *Pioneers of the Collie District 1880–1930*, Literary Mouse Press, Gosnells, 1991, p. 63; K. Spillman, *Horizons: A History of the Rural and Industries Bank of Western Australia*, UWAP, Nedlands, 1989; E. Lang, *Grist to the Mill: A History of Flour Milling in Western Australia*, Goodman Fielder Mills Ltd, Perth, 1994.

37   M. Tauman, *The Chief: C. Y. O'Connor*, UWAP, Nedlands, 1978; A. G. Evans, *Charles Yelverton O'Connor: His Life and Legacy*, UWAP, Nedlands, 2001; V. H. LePage, *Building a State*, Water Authority of Western Australia, Leederville, 1986, ch. 4.

38   G. & K-J. Henderson, *Unfinished Voyages: Western Australian Shipwrecks 1851–1880*, UWAP, Nedlands, 1988.

39   *Albany Advertiser*, 24 July 1900, p. 3.

40   Quoted in P. Brown, 'Arthur James Diamond: A gentleman of scarce renown', *Early Days*, vol. 12, no. 3, 2003, p. 226.

41   L. Hunt (ed.), *Yilgarn: Good Country for Hardy People*, Southern Cross, 1988, p. 134; M. Webb & A. Webb, *Golden Destiny*, City of Kalgoorlie–Boulder, 1993, pp. 163–76.

42   J. W. McCarty, 'British investment in Western Australian goldmining, 1894–1914', in *University Studies*, 1961–62, pp. 7–23; Webb & Webb, *Golden Destiny*, pp. 275–85; G. Blainey, *The Rush That Never Ended*, MUP, Melbourne, 1963, pp. 202–5.

43   A. Porter, 'Richard Hamilton and the East Coolgardie mining industry', *SWAH*, vol. 16, 1982, pp. 1–21.

44   McCarty, 'British investment', pp. 7–23.

Chapter 4: The Golden West, 1895–1905

1   Conole, *Protect and Serve*, p. 110; J. L. Nicholls, *Family First: 100 Years of Halberts: A Family History, 1858–1958*, J. L. Nicholls, Scarborough, 2002, p. 47.

2   Conole, *Protect and Serve*, p. 117; V. Whittington, *Gold and Typhoid: The Two Fevers*, UWAP, Nedlands, 1988.

3   F. Alexander, J. D. Legge & F. K. Crowley, *The Origins of the Goldfields Water Scheme*, UWAP, Nedlands, 1953; 'Golden Pipeline', the story about Lady Forrest, is related by Mollie Skinner in an unpublished portion of her autobiography, *The Fifth Sparrow*.

4   *WAPD*, 1896, vol. 9, p. 145.

5   G. Blainey, *The Golden Mile*, Allen & Unwin, St Leonards, 1993, pp. 68–76; A. Gaynor & J. Davis, 'People, place and the pipeline: Visions and impacts of the Goldfields Water Supply Scheme', in M. Leybourne & A. Gaynor (eds), *Water: Histories, Cultures, Ecologies*, UWAP, Nedlands, 2006, pp. 15–26; also see *Kalgoorlie Miner*, 24 January 2003, p. 3.

6   Hetherington, *Settlers*, p. 46.

7   D. Mossenson, *State Education in Western Australia 1829–1960*, UWAP, Nedlands, 1972.

8   *WAPD*, 1893, vol. 5, p. 785; 1895, vol. 8, p. 853; P. Wellock, 'Religious education under attack: The challenge to general religious education in the Western Australian Parliament', *SWAH*, vol. 9, 1987, pp. 11–19.

9   Sister M. Cream, *Out of These Stones: The Mercedes Story: The School at the Square, 1846–1996*, Mercedes College, Perth, 1999; K. Massam, *On High Ground: Images of One Hundred Years at Aquinas College, Western Australia*, UWAP, Nedlands, 1998; A. Carnley, *Treading Lightly in their Steps: A Pictorial History of St Hilda's 1896–1996*, St Hilda's, Perth, 1996; J. Gregory, *Building a Tradition: A History of Scotch College 1897–1996*, UWAP, Nedlands, 1996; C. May, *Built on Faith: A History of Perth College*, UWAP, Nedlands, 2002.

10   G. Byrne, *Built on a Hilltop: A History of the Sisters of the Good Shepherd in Western Australia 1902–2002*, Sisters of the Good Shepherd, Leederville, 2002; E. Willis, 'Protestants and the dispossessed in Western Australia 1890–1910', *SWAH*, vol. 9, 1987, pp. 31–44.

11   B. Sewell, *The House of Northbourne: Parkers, Pioneers of Western Australia*, B. Sewell, Goomalling, 1983; P. J. Boyce, 'Charles Owen Leaver Riley', in F. Alexander (ed.), *Four Bishops and Their See*, UWAP, Nedlands, 1957, pp. 47–110; *ADB*, vol. 11, MUP, Carlton, 1988, pp. 393–9.

12   J. Gooding, 'An art gallery for all: The Art Gallery of Western Australia', *SWAH*, vol. 11, 1990, pp. 96–105.

13   C. Cunneen, *William John McKell: Boilermaker, Premier, Governor General*, UNSW Press, Sydney, 2000, pp. 12–13.

14   C. May, *Changes They've Seen: The City and People of Bayswater 1827–1997*, City of Bayswater, 1997; Bolton & Gregory, *Claremont*; J. Carter, *Bassendean: A Social History 1829–1979*, Town of Bassendean, Perth, 1986; C. Florey, *Peninsular City: A Social History of the City of South Perth*, City of South Perth, 1995.

15   Hunt & Bolton, 'Cleansing the dunghill'; Stannage, *The People of Perth*, pp. 271–8; George Meudell quoted in *Kalgoorlie Miner*, 30 September 1896.

16   B. F. Hambling, 'Maurice Coleman Davies', *Early Days*, vol. 6, no. 8, 1969, pp. 38–56; J. Mills, *The Timber People*, Wescolour Press, Perth, 1986.

17   B. Bunbury, *Timber for Gold: Life on the Goldfields Woodlines*, FACP, Fremantle, 1997; *WAPP*, 1901–02, vol. 4, paper A37; *WAPD*, 1902, vol. 23, pp. 28, 35–44.

18   L. W. Johnson, 'History of the Collie Coalmining Industry', MA thesis, The University of Western Australia, 1957.

19   R. O. Giles, 'William Gordon Brookman 1859–1910', *ADB*, vol. 7, p. 430.

20   G. C. Bolton, 'Alfred Edward Morgans 1850–1933', *ADB*, vol. 10, p. 586; R. Pascoe, 'Eugenio Vanzetti 1844?–1908?', *ADB*, vol. 12, p. 310.

21   Crowley, *Australia's Western Third*, p. 140.

22   *ADB*, vol. 7, pp. 30–1; *ADB*, vol. 9, pp. 183–4; *ADB*, vol. 12, p. 310; J. Ludbrook, *The Big Q: A History of Quairading and Its Surrounding Districts*, Shire of Quairading, 2003, pp. 82–7.

23   Hackett to Barton, 7 May 1891, Barton Papers, MS 51/71, NLA.

24   J. A. La Nauze, *The Making of the Australian Constitution*, MUP, Carlton, 1972, pp. 139–48.

25   ibid., pp. 202–13, 259–60.

26   D. Mossenson, 'Gold and Politics: Influence of the Eastern Goldfields on the Political Development of Western Australia 1894–1914', MA thesis, The University of Western Australia, 1952.

27   P. Biskup, 'The Westralian feminist movement', *USH*, vol. 3, 1959, pp. 71–84; P. Crawford & J. Skene (eds), *Women and Citizenship: Suffrage Centenary*, vol. 19, *SWAH*, 1999, pp. 1–126.

28   B. Oliver, *Union Is Strength: A History of the Australian Labor Party and the Trades and Labor Council in Western Australia*, API Network, Australian Research Institute, Curtin University, Perth, 2003, p. 107; van den Driesen, 'The evolution of the trade union movement', pp. 352–80.

29   B. de Garis, 'British Influence on the Federation of the Australian Colonies, 1880–1901', DPhil thesis, 1965, Oxford; W. E. Hill, 'The 1900 federal referendum in Western Australia', *SWAH*, vol. 2, 1977, pp. 51–65.

30   F. K. Crowley, 'A vice-regal defendant: Sidelights on Westralian Federation', *HS*, vol. 9, no. 34, 1960, pp. 117–30.

31   Bolton, *Alexander Forrest*, pp. 172–7.

32   H. Colebatch, *Steadfast Knight: A Life of Sir Hal Colebatch*, FACP, Fremantle, 2004, pp. 40–6.

33   D. Davidson, *Women on the Warpath: Feminists of the First Wave*, UWAP, Nedlands, 1997, pp. 2–16.

34   Oliver, pp. 1–23. In regard to the spelling of 'labour', I have adopted the precedent of Stannage in *A New History*, using 'labour' when referring to the labour movement and 'Labor' when referring to the political party (from 1901).

35   R. Virtue, 'Lunacy and social reform 1886–1903', *SWAH*, vol. 1, 1976, pp. 29–65.

36   M. Webb, 'Death of a hero: The strange suicide of C. Y. O'Connor', *Early Days*, vol. 11, no. 1, 1995, pp. 81–111.

37   W. F. de Mole to his wife, 24 January 1903, quoted in *Kalgoorlie Miner*, 24 January 2003.

38   J. P. Stokes, *Cunderdin–Meckering: A Wheatlands History*, Hyland House, Melbourne, 1986, p. 150.

39   *WAPD*, 1906, vol. 29, pp. 721–63; vol. 30, pp. 1871, 2826–9, 2948–53; D. I. Wright, 'The tyranny of distance: A note on Western Australia and Federation, the first decade', *USH*, vol. 5, pt 3, 1969, pp. 33–41.

40   *WAPD*, 1897, vol. 11, pp. 423–8; *Coolgardie Miner*, 16 June 1894, p. 2; A. Atkinson, 'Placing restrictions upon them', *SWAH*, vol. 16, 1995, pp. 60–88, *Asian Immigrants to Western Australia, 1829–1901*, UWAP, Nedlands, 1988; J. Ryan, *Ancestors: Chinese in Colonial Australia*, FACP, Fremantle, 1995; J. Ryan & A. Meerwald, 'Chinese in Western Australia: Language, identity and belonging', in R. Wilding & F. Tilbury (eds),

A Changing People: Diverse Contributions to the State of Western Australia, Office of Multicultural Interests, Perth, 2004, pp. 120–33.

41 J. Gentilli, C. Stransky & C. Iraci, *Italian Roots in Australian Soil: Italian Migration to Western Australia, 1829–1946*, Italo-Australian Welfare Centre, Marangaroo, 1983; L. Baldassar, 'Italians in Western Australia, from "dirty ding" to multicultural mate', in Wilding & Tilbury (eds), *A Changing People*, pp. 266–83.

42 A. Haebich, *For Their Own Good: Aborigines and Government in the South West of Western Australia, 1900–1940*, UWAP, Nedlands, 1988.

43 Aborigines Department File 278/05 quoted by G. C. Bolton, 'Black and white since 1897', in Stannage, *A New History*, p. 127. For the Pindan movement, see ch. 7.

44 H. Pedersen, '"Pigeon": An Australian Aboriginal rebel', *SWAH*, vol. 8, 1984, pp. 7–15; H. Pedersen & Woorunmurra, *Jandamarra and the Bunuba Resistance*, Magabala Books, Broome, 1995.

45 W. E. Roth, 'Report of the Royal Commission on the Condition of the Natives', *WAPP*, 1905, no. 5.

Chapter 5: Optimism dismayed, 1905–1918

1 S. Glynn, *Government Policy and Agricultural Development: A Study of the Role of Government in the Development of the Western Australian Wheatbelt 1900–1930*, UWAP, Nedlands, 1975; Cooper, Moore & White, *Adversity and Achievement*, chs 6–7; G. H. Burvill (ed.), *Agriculture in Western Australia 1829–1979*, ch. 3, UWAP, Nedlands, 1979.

2 Ludbrook, *The Big Q*, p. 19; M. N. Melic, 'The Zunini scheme—a plan for Italian Group Settlement in Western Australia, 1906–1908', *SWAH*, vol. 12, 1991, pp. 17–27.

3 Q. Beresford, H. Bekle, H. Phillips & K. Mulcock, *The Salinity Crisis: Landscapes, Communities and Politics*, UWAP, Nedlands, 2001, p. 45.

4 'The Pastoralists' Association of Western Australia: Its inauguration and development', *WA Pastoralist and Grazier*, 26 January 1925, p. 9; N. Maisey, *No Man Alone: The Pastoralists and Graziers Association of Western Australia 1907–1979 (Inc)*, Pastoralists and Graziers Association, Perth, 1979; G. McLaren & W. Cooper, *A Long Hard Road: A Centenary History of the Pastoralists and Graziers Association of Western Australia*, Pastoralists and Graziers Association, Perth, 2006.

5 G. Sherington & C. Jeffrey, *Fairbridge: Empire and Child Migration*, UWAP, Nedlands, 1998; anon., *ADB*, vol. 8, p. 460; J. Lane, *Fairbridge Kid*, FACP, Fremantle, 1990; M. Creelman, 'A surrogate parent approach to child emigration: The first Kingsley Fairbridge Farm School 1912–1924', in P. Hetherington (ed.), *Childhood and Society in Western Australia*, UWAP, Nedlands, 1988, pp. 127–43.

6 G. D. Snooks, 'Development in adversity 1913–1946', in Stannage, *A New History*, pp. 237–66.

7 R. Davis, *Eileen Joyce: A Portrait*, FACP, Fremantle, 2001.

8 A history of Boans by David Hough is in progress. See also G. Moor, 'Perth department stores', *The Little Battler*, vol. 28, no. 1, 2000, pp. 10–14; S. W. Davies, *Foy's Saga: An Account of the Genesis and Progress of the House of Foy & Gibson (WA) Limited*, Foy & Gibson, Perth, 1945.

9 R. Frances, 'Dealing with the social evil: Prostitution and the police in Perth and on the Eastern Goldfields 1895–1924', in K. Daniels (ed.), *So Much Hard Work*, Fontana/Collins, Sydney, 1984; *Sunday Times*, 3 March 1901, p. 5.

10   B. Moore, *A Superior Kind of Savings Bank: The Perth Building Society 1862–1987*,
      UWAP, Nedlands, 1987; R. M. C. Lourens, 'Building Societies in Western Australia
      1862–1966', PhD thesis, The University of Western Australia, 1969.

11   T. Stannage, 'William Ernest Bold', *ADB*, vol. 7, pp. 335–7; R. E. Robertson, 'W. E. Bold',
      MA thesis, The University of Western Australia, 1970; W. E. Bold, 'Looking backwards',
      Early Days, vol. 3, no. 8, 1946, pp. 18–25.

12   Stannage, *The People of Perth*, pp. 293–300.

13   B. de Garis, 'From amateur to professional and back again: The Swan Districts Football
      Club 1934–1997', *SWAH*, vol. 18, 1997, p. 64. Other histories of football clubs in the
      first decades of the twentieth century include D. Heinrichs, *The Jubilee Book of the East
      Fremantle Football Club*, Patersons, Perth, 1948; B. Atkinson, *West Perth Football Club
      1885–1955*, Action Press, Morley, 1985; A. East, B. Forrest & G. Stocke, *The Royals: 100
      Years of Football Tradition: A History of the East Perth Club*, East Perth Football Club,
      Leederville, 2006; Barker, *Behind the Play*, chs 1–4.

14   J. Christensen, 'The Life of J. G. Hay: An Early Western Australian Conservationist',
      paper read to the RWAHS, 16 April 2005.

15   C. Fitzgerald, 'Sanatoria in Western Australia: The institutional response to
      tuberculosis 1903–1940', *Early Days*, vol. 12, no. 3, 2003, pp. 297–314; *Kissing Can Be
      Dangerous: The Public Health Campaign to Prevent and Control Tuberculosis in Western
      Australia 1900–1960*, UWAP, Nedlands, 2006.

16   Connolly's career has not been given the attention it deserves. I give a brief account in
      ADB, vol. 8, p. 90. His papers are held at the Battye Library, MN6.

17   Davidson, *Women on the Warpath*, pt 2; article also by Davidson, 'A citizen of Australia
      and the world', *SWAH*, vol. 19, 1999, pp. 99–113.

18   Sphinx Foundation Inc., *Perth Modern School: The History and the Heritage*, B+G
      Resource Enterprises, Cottesloe, 2005; but see also J. Gregory, 'Education and upward
      mobility in inter war Western Australia: The case of Perth Modern School', *SWAH*,
      vol. 11, 1990, pp. 83–95.

19   T. Dolin, 'The Secret Reading Life of Us', paper read to the Australian Academy of the
      Humanities, Melbourne, November 2004.

20   *WAPD*, 1903–04, vol. 23, pp. 41–2, 1394–5; 1910–11, vol. 40, pp. 3308–24.

21   A. Reid, *Those Were the Days*, Hesperian Press, Carlisle, 1986 [1933], p. 71.

22   H. Hawke, *My Own Life: An Autobiography*, Text, Melbourne, 1996, pp. 26–7.

23   G. Blainey & R. Jamieson (eds), *Charles Court: The Early Years: An Autobiography*,
      FACP, Fremantle, 1995, pp. 97–107; Gregory, 'Education and upward mobility'.

24   'Koombana—account of the loss of the ship and passenger list', *Western Ancestor*, vol. 3,
      no. 7, September 1986, pp. 323–30.

25   J. R. Robertson, 'The practical socialist', in L. Hunt (ed.), *Westralian Portraits*, UWAP,
      Nedlands, 1979, pp. 139–45.

26   J. Mitchell, *The First Hundred Years: The Mitchell Family on Barnong Station*, J. Mitchell,
      Perth, 2000, p. 36; Collard quoted in A. Thomas, *Kalkarni: The Brookton Story*, Shire of
      Brookton, 1993, pp. 37–8.

27   B. K. Hyams, 'The Political Organisation of Farmers in Western Australia, 1914–1944',
      MA thesis, The University of Western Australia, 1964.

28   S. Welborn, *Lords of Death: A People, A Place, A Legend*, FACP, Fremantle, 1982, p. 43;
      W. Olson, *Gallipoli: The Western Australian Story*, UWAP, Nedlands, 2006.

29   From a forthcoming biography of Dr G. W. Barber by Jenny Mills.

30   *The West Australian*, 1 April 1916, p. 7.

31   Welborn, *Lords of Death*, pp. 157–61.

32   *Western Mail*, 4 January 1918, p. 26.

33   N. Segal, *Who and What Was Siebenhaar: A Note on the Life and Persecution of a Western Australian Anarchist*, Centre for Western Australian History, The University of Western Australia, Nedlands, 1988.

34   J. N Yiannakis, 'Kalgoorlie alchemy: Xenophobia, patriotism and the 1916 anti-Greek riots', *Early Days*, vol. 11, pt 2, 1996, pp. 199–211; B. Latter, 'The night of the stones: The anti-German riots in Fremantle 1915', *Early Days*, vol. 10, no. 4, 1992, pp. 387–406.

35   Bolton & Byrne, *May It Please Your Honour*, pp. 142–3.

36   D. Black, 'Party politics in turmoil 1911–1924', in Stannage, *A New History*, p. 392.

37   WAPP, 1917, no. 5: Royal Commission on Esperance Lands and Mallee Belt.

38   WAPP, 1917–18, vol. 2, no. 7: Progress Report of the Royal Commission on the Agricultural Industries of Western Australia.

Chapter 6: A fine country to starve in, 1919–1933

1   D. Hutchison, 'Bloody Sunday' (for publication in 2008); B. de Garis, 'An incident in Fremantle', *Labor History*, no. 10, 1966, pp. 32–7; J. Williams, *The First Furrow*, Lone Hand Print, Perth, 1976, pp. 71–7; H. Colebatch, *Steadfast Knight: A Life of Sir Hal Colebatch*, FACP, Fremantle, 2004, pp. 63–72; for events in Kalgoorlie, J. Murray, 'The Kalgoorlie woodline strikes 1919–1920: A study of conflict within the working class', *SWAH*, vol. 5, 1982, pp. 22–37; B. Oliver, 'Disputes, diggers and disillusionment: Social and industrial unrest in Perth and Kalgoorlie 1918–1920', *SWAH*, vol. 11, 1990, pp. 19–28.

2   Oliver, *Union Is Strength*, chs 3, 4; Conole, *Protect and Serve*, p. 202.

3   W. Brady, 'Serfs of the sodden scene: Women workers in the Western Australian hotel and catering industry 1900–1925', *SWAH*, vol. 7, 1983, pp. 33–45.

4   *West Australian*, 18 March 1919; *WA Record*, 22 March 1919, p. 8.

5   P. R. Heydon, *The Bishop's Men*, Order of the Knights of the Southern Cross, Perth, c. 1998.

6   D. H. Lawrence, 'Letters 1922–1923', ACC2385A, Battye Library, Perth; W. Roberts, J. T. Boulton & E. Mansfield (eds), *The Letters of D. H. Lawrence*, vol. iv, CUP, Cambridge, 1987, pp. 238–40.

7   ibid.

8   *WAPD*, 1919, vol. 60, p. 182.

9   Quoted in J. Mills, *The Timber People: A History of Bunnings Limited*, Wescolour Press, Perth, 1986, p. 65.

10   J. P. Gabbedy, *Group Settlement*, vols 1, 2, UWAP, Nedlands, 1988; I. L. Hunt, 'Group settlement in Western Australia: A criticism', *USH*, vol. 3, pt 2, 1958, pp. 5–42.

11   Hunt, 'Group settlement', p. 42.

12   'A vision splendid: The de Garis story, Kendenup', in B. Bunbury, *Caught in Time*, FACP, Fremantle, 2006, pp. 84–113; R. Glover, *Plantagenet: A History of the Shire of Plantagenet, Western Australia*, UWAP, Nedlands, 1979, pp. 125–41; C. J. de Garis, Kendenup papers 1893–1992, MN831, Battye Library, Perth.

13   Beresford, Bekle, Phillips & Mulcock, *The Salinity Crisis*, pp. 49–50.

14   P. Cowan, *A Unique Position: A Biography of Edith Dircksey Cowan, 1861–1932*, UWAP, Nedlands, 1978; M. Simms, 'Edith Cowan: Feminist or philanthropist?', *SWAH*, vol. 6, 1988, pp. 78–83.

15   Black, 'Party politics in turmoil', pp. 402 ff.

16   D. W. Black, 'The Collier government 1924–1930', *SWAH*, vol. 8, 1984, pp. 16–25. Between 1917 and 1945 the predecessor of today's Liberal Party was styled 'the National party'; it is not to be confused with the modern National Party, the successor of the Country Party.

17   *WAPP*, 1927, no. 3: Report of the Royal Commission; N. Green, *The Forrest River Massacres*, FACP, Fremantle, 1995; R. Moran, *Massacre Myth*, Access Press, Bassendean, 2001; C. Fitzgerald, 'Blood on the saddle: The Forrest River Massacres 1926', *SWAH*, vol. 8, 1984, pp. 16–25; K. Auty, 'Patrick Bernard O'Leary and the Forrest River massacres, Western Australia: Examining "Wodgil" and the significance of 8 June 1926', *Aboriginal History*, vol. 28, 2004, pp. 122–55. Each of these interpretations contains points to which objection might be raised, but I think Auty comes closest.

18   *West Australian*, 18 June 1932, p. 15.

19   A. Davis, 'Good times for all? Popular entertainment and class cultural issues in Western Australia between the wars', *SWAH*, vol. 11, 1987, pp. 68–82, esp. pp. 72–3.

20   R. Davidson, *High Jinks at the Hot Pool*, FACP, Fremantle, 1994, pp. 71–81.

21   G. C. Bolton, *A Fine Country to Starve In*, UWAP, Nedlands, 1972, pp. 139–40.

22   L. Edmonds, *The Vital Link: A History of Main Roads in Western Australia*, UWAP, Nedlands, 1997.

23   A. Murray Gordon, 'Pioneering days in the Eastern Wheatbelt', *JPWAHS*, vol. 4, pt 4, 1952, pp. 76–88.

24   A. G. Evans, 'John Cyril Hawes', *ADB*, vol. 9, MUP, Carlton, 1983, p. 331; *The Conscious Stone: A Biography of John C. Hawes*, Polding Press, Melbourne, 1984; J. Taylor, *Between Devotion and Design: The Architecture of John Cyril Hawes*, UWAP, Nedlands, 2000.

25   Ludbrook, *The Big Q*, p. 128.

26   K. P. Smith, *A Bunch of Pirates: The Story of a Farmer Co-operative: Wesfarmers*, Wesfarmers, Perth, 1984; J. Sanford, *Walter Harper and the Farmers*, Wesfarmers, Perth, 1955. A history completed by Professor Tom Stannage was due for publication in 2007.

27   There is no good history of the RSL in Western Australia. Files of the RSL publication *The Green Letter*, 1942–55, and several oral histories are held by the Battye Library, Perth.

28   Tom Adams, quoted in W. E. Greble, *A Bold Yeomanry: Social Change in a Wheat Belt District: Kulin, 1848–1970*, Creative Research in Association with Kulin Shire Council, Perth, 1979.

29   R. Erickson, B. Gibbings & L. Higgins, *Her Name Is Woman*, Country Women's Association of Western Australia, Perth, 1974; R. Erickson & R. Heywood, *She's No Milkmaid: A Biography of Dame Raigh Roe* DBE, Hesperian Press, Carlisle, 1991.

30   Lady Hackett (ed.), *The Australian Household Guide*, E. S. Wigg, Perth, 1916; P. Joske, 'Lady Hackett's Household Guide', *Early Days*, vol. 8, pt 2, 1978, pp. 68–83.

31   A. K. B. Barnes et al., *The CWA Cookery Book and Household Hints*, E. S. Wigg & Sons, Perth, 1936.

32   B. Bennett, 'Wartime culture: The Westralia Gift Book, 1916', *SWAH*, vol. 10, 1986, pp. 37–48; R. Nile, 'Eroticism, sex and the politics of the imagination', *SWAH*, vol. 11, 1987, pp. 119–28.

33   E. Shann, *Economic History of Australia*, CUP, Cambridge, 1930.

34   A. Hasluck, *Unwilling Emigrants*, pp. xi–xiii.

35   A. O. Neville, *Australia's Coloured Minority: Aborigines' Place in the Community*, Currawong Publishers, Sydney, 1948; P. Jacobs, *Mister Neville*, FACP, Fremantle, 1990; S. Maushart, *Sort of a Place Like Home: Remembering the Moore River Settlement*, FACP, Fremantle, 1993.

36   R. S. Schenk, *The Educability of the Native*, Service Print, Perth, 1937; M. R. Morgan, *A Drop in a Bucket: The Mount Margaret Story*, United Aborigines Mission, Box Hill, 1986.

37   G. T. Snooks, *Depression and Recovery in Western Australia, 1928–1929 to 1938–1939: A Study in Cyclical and Structural Change*, UWAP, Nedlands, 1974.

38   R. Jamieson, 'Country Storekeeping: A Case Study of the Daw Family Businesses in Ravensthorpe and Other Country Areas of Western and South Australia 1838–1957', PhD thesis, Murdoch University, 2001; 'The Daw family: Storekeepers of Esperance and Ravensthorpe', *Early Days*, vol. 12, no. 2, 2002, pp. 95–104.

39   Bolton, *A Fine Country to Starve In*, chs 6–9; C. J. Fox, 'The unemployed and the labour movement: The Western Australian Relief and Sustenance Workers Union 1933–1934', *SWAH*, vol. 5, 1982, pp. 48–61.

40   C. Fox, 'Bookies, punters and parasites: Off-course betting, conflict and consensus in Western Australia between the wars', *SWAH*, vol. 11, 1987, pp. 57–67.

41   Heinrichs, *The Jubilee Book*, p. 191.

42   E. D. Watt, 'Secession in Western Australia', *USH*, vol. 3, pt 2, 1958, pp. 43–86; Bolton, *A Fine Country to Starve In*, pp. 115–20, 247–57.

43   P. J. Ayres, *Owen Dixon*, Miegunyah Press, Carlton, 2003.

44   Snooks, 'Development in adversity', pp. 237–47.

Chapter 7: Recovery and war, 1935–1951

1   J. H. Lawrence, 'Claude Albo de Bernales', *ADB*, vol. 8, 1981, p. 264; R. T. Appleyard & M. Davies, 'Financiers of Western Australian goldfields', in R. T. Appleyard & C. B. Schedvin, *Australian Financiers: Biographical Essays*, Macmillan, Melbourne, 1988, pp. 175–89; H. Colebatch, *Claude de Bernales: The Magnificent Miner*, Hesperian Press, Carlisle, 1996.

2   D. Brooks, 'Glimpses into the depression years in Western Australia 1931–1935', PR 4405, Battye Library, Perth, quoted in Bolton, *A Fine Country to Starve In*, pp. 259–60.

3   R. Gerritsen, 'The 1934 Kalgoorlie riots: A Western Australian crowd', *USH*, vol. 5, pt 3, 1969, pp. 56–66; L. Dick, 'Kalgoorlie: A frontier town 1934', *Early Days*, vol. 6, pt 8, 1969, pp. 26–37; H. Schmitt, 'A time of terror relived', *West Australian*, 18 October 1984; B. Bunbury, 'A bad blue: The Australia Day riots of 1934', in *Reading Labels on Jam Tins*, FACP, Fremantle, 1993.

4   F. J. Wise, 'A few "butts" and faith began banana industry', *Sunday Times*, 4 September 1966, p. 35.

5   L. Layman, 'Sir Russell Dumas', *ADB*, vol. 14, 1996, pp. 46–7. His papers are held in the Battye Library, Perth, MN156.

6   C. Ayris, *A Heritage Ingrained: A History of Co-operative Bulk Handling Ltd, 1933–2000*, CBH, Perth, 1999.

7   Nicholls, *Family First*, p. 74.

8   Williams, *The First Furrow*, pp. 112–14; P. Crawford & I. Crawford, *Contested Country*, UWAP, Nedlands, 2003, pp. 118–24.

9   Burvill, *Agriculture in Western Australia*, UWAP, Nedlands, pp. 47–57.

10   B. Chapman & D. Richards, *Marshall Clifton: Architect and Artist*, FACP, Fremantle, 1989, p. 13.

11   L. Fisher, 'Dancing queen: A story of dance', in Bolton, Rossiter & Ryan, pp. 56–90.

12   See introduction by Richard Nile to the facsimile edition of J. M. Harcourt, *Upsurge: A Novel*, UWAP, Nedlands, 1986 [1934].

13   The Fellowship of Australian Writers is the subject of a PhD thesis (The University of Western Australia) in progress by Tricia Kotai-Ewers. See also P. Cowan, 'The novel in the nineteen-thirties: A Western Australian view', *Westerly*, vol. 31, no. 4, 1986, pp. 22–9; J. Croft, 'Poetry in the 1930s', ibid., pp. 84–94; C. Ellers, 'Social realism in the Australian literary context: With specific reference to the writing of Katharine Susannah Prichard', *JAS*, vol. 55, pt 55, 1997, pp. 38–46; R. Throssell, *My Father's Son*, Heinemann, Richmond, 1989.

14   C. Crouch, 'Spaces and places: Architecture', in Bolton, Rossiter & Ryan, *Farewell Cinderella*, pp. 262–6; also N. Weston, 'Visual sites: Art', in ibid., pp. 186–93.

15   *West Australian*, 1 August 1937, p. 46; 20 October 1987, p. 32.

16   Hough, 'The playmakers', pp. 31–2.

17   T. Craig, 'Radical and conservative theatre in Perth in the 1930s', *SWAH*, vol. 11, 1990, pp. 106–18; for Harald Vike, J. Goddard, 'Harald Vike', *Art in Australia*, vol. 25, pt 3, 1988, p. 246.

18   P. Hasluck, *Mucking About: An Autobiography*, UWAP, Nedlands, 1994, pp. 244–8.

19   Bolton & Gregory, *Claremont*, p. 183.

20   G. Farwell, *Rejoice in Freedom*, Nelson Publishers, Melbourne, 1976; B. Hooper, 'The unpromised land: A Jewish settlement in the Kimberley?', in R. Bosworth & M. Melia, *Aspects of Ethnicity*, UWAP, Nedlands, 1991; L. Gettler, *An Unpromised Land*, FACP, Fremantle, 1993.

21   B. Bunbury, *Rabbits and Spaghetti: Captives and Comrades, Australians, Italians and the War 1938–1945*, FACP, Fremantle, 1995; M. Bosworth, 'Fremantle interned: The Italian experience', in R. Bosworth & R. Ugolini (eds), *War, Internment and Mass Migration: The Italo-Australian Experience*, Gruppo Editoriale Internazionale, Rome, 1992.

22   J. Yiannakis & R. Appleyard, *Greek Pioneers in Western Australia*, UWAP, Nedlands, 2002.

23   J. Gregory (ed.), *On the Homefront: Western Australia and World War II*, UWAP, Nedlands, 1996.

24   The discovery of the *Sydney* and the *Kormoran* in 2008 ended a long controversy. Publications include K. Kirsner & M. McCarthy (eds), *Papers from the HMAS Sydney Forum*, Fremantle, 21–23 November 1991, published by the WA Maritime Museum, Fremantle, 1992; W. J. Olson, *With All Hands*, WA Maritime Museum, Fremantle, 1996; T. Frame, *HMAS Sydney: Loss and Controversy*, Hodder, Sydney, 1998; Joint Standing Committee on Foreign Affairs, Defence and Trade, *Report on the Loss of HMAS Sydney*, Australian Government, Canberra, 1999; J. A. Montagu, *The Lost Souls and Ghosts of HMAS Sydney II*, J. A. Montagu, Perth, 2006.

25   M. McCarthy, 'War on the doorstep', in Gregory, *On the Homefront*, pp. 109–18. The refugee experience is described in A. Wood (ed.), *If This Should Be Farewell: A Family Separated by War*, FACP, Fremantle, 2003.

26   P. Pendal & D. Black, *House to House: The Story of Western Australia's Government and Parliament Houses*, WA Parliament, Perth, 2004, pp. 133–40.

27   P. Burns, *The Brisbane Line: Political Opportunism versus National Security, 1942–1945*,
      Allen & Unwin, St Leonards, 1998.

28   A. J. Barker & L. Jackson, *Fleeting Attraction: A Social History of American Servicemen
      in Western Australia during the Second World War*, UWAP, Nedlands, 1996; A. J. Barker,
      'Yanks in Western Australia: The impact of United States servicemen', in Gregory, *On
      the Homefront*; R. G. Lloyd Thomas, 'American impact', *West Australian*, 15 August 1945,
      p. 4.

29   S. Graham-Taylor, 'The war for health', in Gregory, *On the Homefront*, pp. 216–23.

30   The subject requires further research. *WAPD*, 1942, vol. 109, p. 213 (and pp. 212–16).

31   B. Oliver & W. S. Latter, 'Spooks, spies and subversives: The wartime security service', in
      Gregory, *On the Homefront*, pp. 183–5; B. Muirden, *The Puzzled Patriots: The Story of the
      Australia First Movement*, MUP, Carlton, 1968.

32   D. Black, 'The era of Labor ascendancy', in Stannage, *A New History*, pp. 422–40;
      R. F. Pervan, 'Cabinet and caucus: Labor in Western Australia, 1933–1947', *USH*, vol. 5,
      pt 1, 1967, pp. 1–38.

33   A. C. Frost, *Green Gold*, Donnybrook–Balingup Shire Council, Donnybrook, 1976,
      pp. 157–9; J. Purse, *A Flax Mill by the River*, Boyup Brook Shire Council, 1990;
      H. D. Evans, *Southern Sketches*, Department of Agriculture, Perth, 1993, pp. 47–54.

34   G. Sleight, 'Wundowie Charcoal and Iron', typescript, Battye Library, Perth.

35   G. Reekie, 'Shunted back to the kitchen? Women's responses to war work and
      demobilization', in Gregory, *On the Homefront*, pp. 75–81; S. Butterworth, 'Women
      colonising the wartime landscape', in ibid., pp. 56–70.

36   *West Australian*, 16 August, 17 August 1945.

37   J. Farrant, 'Playing in tune', in Bolton, Rossiter & Ryan, *Farewell Cinderella*, p. 122;
      P. M. Crawford, 'Early childhood in Perth 1940–45', in P. Hetherington (ed.), *Childhood
      and Society in Western Australia*, UWAP, Nedlands, 1998, pp. 187–207.

38   K. Murray, *Voice for Peace*, Kaye Murray Productions, Bayswater, 2005.

39   J. Gregory, *City of Light: A History of Perth since the 1950s*, City of Perth, 2005,
      pp. 63–7.

40   P. Æ. Hutchings & J. Lewis, *Kathleen O'Connor: Artist in Exile*, FACP, Fremantle, 1987.

41   Thomas, *Kalkarni*, p. 37; P. J. Biskup, 'The Royal Commission that never was: A
      chapter in government–mission relations in Western Australia', *USH*, vol. 5, pt 1, 1967,
      pp. 89–113.

42   T. Hunter, 'The myth of equality', *SWAH*, vol. 22, 2001, pp. 69–82.

43   Still the most authoritative account is J. Wilson, 'Authority and Leadership in a "New
      Style" Aboriginal Community: Pindan, Western Australia', MA thesis, The University
      of Western Australia, 1961. See also M. Brown, *Black Eureka*, Australasian Book Society,
      Sydney, 1976; and D. W. McLeod, *How the West Was Lost*, D. W. McLeod, Port
      Hedland, 1984; J. Armstrong, 'On the freedom track to Narawunda', *SWAH*, vol. 22,
      2001, pp. 23–40.

44   K. Spillman, *Horizons: A History of the Rural and Industries Bank of Western Australia*,
      UWAP, Nedlands, 1981.

45   Pers. comm., Mrs Jenny Mills; for the York air disaster, *West Australian*, 27 June 1950.

46   Oliver, *Union Is Strength*, ch. 8.

47   D. Black, 'Liberals triumphant 1947–1980', in Stannage, *A New History*, pp. 441–57.

48   K. Evans 'Peace returns: Western Australia in the early postwar years', in Gregory, *On
      the Homefront*, pp. 241–4.

49   C. Turnbull, 'Widening the field', in A. G. Lowndes (ed.), *South Pacific Enterprise*, Angus
       & Robertson, Sydney, 1956, pp. 213–18; but see also L. Layman, 'Work and workers'
       responses at Wittenoom, 1943–1966'; B. Hills, *Blue Murder*, Sun Books, Melbourne,
       1989; F. Dunn, 'Lethal legacy', *Sunday Times*, 27 December 1998.

50   N. Olive, *Enough Is Enough*, FACP, Fremantle, 2007.

51   A. Woolfe, 'A cruel business: Whaling and the Albany community 1946–1988', in
       A. Gaynor, M. Trinca & A. Haebich, *Country: Visions of Land and People in Western
       Australia*, WA Museum, Perth, 2002, pp. 83–103; D. Saunders, 'The Cheynes Beach
       whaling station 1952–1978', *Historicus*, May/June 1990, pp. 8–20.

52   J. Gladstones, 'Sir Eric Fleming Smart', *ADB*, vol. 16, 2002, pp. 265–6; E. Smart, *The
       West Australian Wasteland Transformed*, E. Smart, Geraldton, 1960.

53   L. C. Webb, *Communism and Democracy in Australia*, Cheshire, Melbourne, 1954.

54   N. Peters, *Milk and Honey—but No Gold: Postwar Migration to Western Australia
       1945–1964*, UWAP, Nedlands, 2001; K. Evans, 'Dreams and disappointments: The
       Displaced Persons Scheme in Western Australia', in Gregory, *On the Homefront*,
       pp. 265–71.

Chapter 8: The coming of the iron age, 1951–1971

1   Gregory, *City of Light*, pp. 21–38; *West Australian*, 26 March 1954, p. 2.

2   *West Australian*, 15–17 May, 20–21 June 1956; R. Cross, *Fallout: Hedley Marston and the
       British Bomb Test in Australia*, Wakefield Press, Kent Town, 2003.

3   W. L. Grayden, *Adam and Atoms*, Frank Daniels, Perth, 1957; *A Nomad Was Our
       Guide*, N. H. Holdings, South Perth, 2002.

4   For one account of developments at that time, K. Chesson, *Jack Davis: A Life Story*,
       Dent, Melbourne, 1988.

5   G. Stephenson & J. A. Hepburn, *Plan for the Metropolitan Region, Perth and Fremantle,
       Western Australia*, WA Government, 1955; G. Stephenson, *The Design of Central Perth:
       Some Problems and Possible Solutions*, UWAP, Nedlands, 1975.

6   Gregory, *City of Light*, pp. 106–9.

7   *West Australian*, 6 March 2003, p. 44; *Sunday Times*, 2 March 2003, p. 61.

8   J. Mills, *I Buried My Dolls in the Garden: The Life and Works of Elizabeth Blair Barber*,
       UWAP, Nedlands, 2000; C. Sharkey, 'Rose Skinner, modern art and the Skinner
       Galleries', *Early Days*, vol. 12, pt 4, 2004, pp. 373–84.

9   A. J. Hasssell, *Strange Country: A Study of Randolph Stow*, University of Queensland
       Press, St Lucia, 1986; D. Hewett, 'Silence, exile and coming: The poetry of Randolph
       Stow', *Westerly*, vol. 33, pt 2, 1988, pp. 59–66.

10   B. Bennett (ed.), *The Literature of Western Australia*, UWAP, Nedlands, 1979, pp. 87–101,
       124–44, 156–83.

11   J. Rintoul, *History of Esperance: The Port of the Goldfields*, J. Rintoul, Esperance, 1946;
       also *Esperance—Yesterday and Today*, Esperance Shire Council, 1964; B. Senior, 'The
       Coming of the Americans, 1956–1988', in R. Moran (ed.), *Faith, Hope and Reality,
       Esperance, 1895–1995*, Esperance Shire Council, 1995; Rintoul, *History of Esperance*;
       Esperance Express, 6 June 2002, p. 13; *WAPD*, 1958, vol. 177, pp. 1477–502, 1901, 1922.

12   L. Layman, 'Changing resource development policy in Western Australia, 1960–1980', in
       E. J. Harman & B. W. Head (eds), *State, Capital and Resources in the North and West
       of Australia*, UWAP, Nedlands, 1982, pp. 149–66; E. J. Harman, 'Ideology and mineral
       development in Western Australia', in ibid., pp. 167–96.

13   K. Spillman, *A Rich Endowment: Government and Mining in Western Australia 1829–1994*, UWAP, Nedlands, 1993, chs 8–9.

14   From here on, the political material is drawn from the ongoing series 'Political chronicles: Western Australia', published twice yearly since 1955 in the *Australian Journal of Politics and History*.

15   B. Eakins, 'History of the TAB in Western Australia—new turf', *West Magazine* (*West Australian*), 17 March 2001, pp. 15–16.

16   B. Oliver, 'Stephen Frederick Schnaars', *ADB*, vol. 16, MUP, Carlton, 2002, p. 190.

17   G. Smith, 'Energy policy and the State Electricity Commission', in Harman & Head, *State, Capital and Resources*, pp. 257–75.

18   The New Coolbaroo League was the subject of an ABC documentary in 2006, and features in L. Marsh & A. Haebich, 'Living the dream', in A. Haebich (ed.), *Imagining Assimilation: A Cultural History*, FACP, Fremantle, in press.

19   B. Bunbury, *It's Not the Money, It's the Land: Aboriginal Stockmen and the Equal Wages Case*, FACP, Fremantle, 2002.

20   'Sir Kenneth Townsing', *Leader*, University of Western Australia, vol. 16, no. 14, 8 September 1997, p. 9.

21   F. K. Crowley, *State Election: The Fall of the Hawke Government*, Paterson Brokensha, Perth, 1959.

22   For an account of the politics of this period by a prominent player, F. E. Chamberlain, *My Life and Times*, Harold Chamberlain, North Beach, 1998. The modern Trades and Labour Council is not to be confused with the goldfields and metropolitan Trades and Labour Councils founded in the 1890s, which were merged early in the twentieth century with their respective district councils.

23   A. Kerr, 'The economic and social significance of Western Australia's mining developments', in R. T. Prider (ed.), *Mining in Western Australia*, UWAP, Nedlands, 1979, pp. 293–302.

24   G. Blainey, *White Gold: The Story of Alcoa of Australia*, Allen & Unwin, St Leonards, 1997, p. 127.

25   J. Brown, 'Infrastructure policies in the Pilbara', in Harman & Head, *State, Capital and Resources*, pp. 237–56.

26   N. Phillipson, *Man of Iron*, Wren Publishers, Melbourne, 1974.

27   R. Duffield, *Rogue Bull*, Collins, Sydney, 1979, ch. 7.

28   B. R. Davidson, *The Northern Myth*, MUP, Carlton, 1965; B. R. Davidson & S. Graham-Taylor, *Lessons from the Ord*, Centre for Independent Studies, Perth, 1982; S. Graham-Taylor, 'A History of the Ord River Scheme', PhD thesis, Murdoch University, 1981.

29   Blainey, *White Gold*, pts 1, 2.

30   G. Adamson, *Miners and Millionaires: The First One Hundred Years of the Stock Exchange in Perth, 1889–1989*, Australian Stock Exchange, Perth, pp. 140–53.

31   R. Stow, 'The utopia of Lord Mayor Howard', in *A Counterfeit Silence: Selected Poems*, Angus & Robertson, Sydney, 1969, p. 31.

32   Gregory, *City of Light*, pp. 77–93.

33   ibid., pp. 71–3.

34   T. Winton, *Cloudstreet*, Viking, Ringwood, 1996; R. Drewe, *The Shark Net*, Viking, Ringwood, 2000; R. Stow, *The Girl Green As Elderflower*, Secker & Warburg, London, 1980.

35   R. Harding, *Police Killings in Australia*, Penguin, Ringwood, 1970, p. 158.

36   Gregory, *City of Light*, pp. 252, 312.

37   C. T. Stannage, 'Sir Thomas Wardle, the grocer', in Hunt, *Westralian Portraits*, pp. 287–95; *West Australian*, 13 February 1997, p. 7.

38   Gregory, *City of Light*, p. 268.

39   G. S. Reid, 'Perth's Arc de Triomphe', *Westerly*, 1967, pp. 53–61.

40   Minutes of the meetings of the Australian Netherlands Committee on Old Dutch Shipwrecks since its inception in 1973 are held at the WA Maritime Museum, Fremantle.

41   D. Sanders, 'From Colonial Outpost to Popular Tourist Destination: A Historical Geography of the Leeuwin–Naturaliste Region 1829–2005', PhD thesis, Murdoch University, 2005.

42   B. Kearns, *Stepping Out for Peace*, People for Nuclear Disarmament, Maylands, 2004.

43   P. M. Crawford & M. Tonkinson (eds), *The Missing Chapters: Women Staff at The University of Western Australia 1963–1987*, UWAP, Nedlands, 1988.

Chapter 9: The gilded age, 1971–1992

1   M. Russell, 'Fighting time again in Western Australia', *Sunday Times*, 29 October 1989, p. 28.

2   *WAPD*, 1970, vol. 188, p. 1666; 1971, vol. 191, p. 1213; *Daily News*, 25 August 1971, p. 1.

3   Environmental Protection Authority, *Report on Alumina Refinery: Upper Swan Project*, EPA, Perth, 1971.

4   L. C. Furnell (commissioner), *Report of the Royal Commission into Aboriginal Affairs: Western Australia*, Perth, 1974.

5   T. Stephens, 'The gong show: Bitter rivalries for rewards', *Sydney Morning Herald*, 4–5 June 2005, p. 6.

6   B. Hayden, *An Autobiography*, Angus & Robertson, Sydney, 1996, pp. 209–11.

7   A. Horin, 'Sir Charles stays on as his heirs cool their heels', *National Times*, 23–29 August 1981, p. 10.

8   H. M. Thompson, 'The devil's pebbles: Diamonds in the Kimberley', in Head & Harman, *State, Capital and Resources*, pp. 277–98.

9   Blainey, *White Gold*, ch. 13.

10   *West Australian*, 20 July 1976, p. 1; 23 December 1976, p. 1; Crawford & Crawford, *Contested Country*, pp. 154–61.

11   S. Cockburn, *Playford: Benevolent Despot*, Axion, Kent Town, 1991, p. v.

12   Q. Beresford, *Rob Riley: An Aboriginal Leader's Quest for Justice*, Aboriginal Studies Press, Canberra, 2006, pp. 88–90.

13   S. Hawke & M. Gallagher, *Noonkanbah: Whose Land, Whose Law?*, FACP, Fremantle, 1989; Beresford, *Rob Riley*, pp. 104–17.

14   For an illustration of Court's style as patron of the arts, D. Hough, *A Dream of Passion*, His Majesty's Theatre Foundation, Perth, 2004, pp. 14–24.

15   G. C. Bolton, 'WAY 1979: Whose celebration?', *SWAH*, vol. 10, 1989, pp. 20–4.

16   J. Hamilton, *Burkie: A Biography of Brian Burke*, St George Books, Perth, 1988.

17   Oliver, *Union Is Strength*, p. 304.

18   B. Purdue, *Legal Executions in Western Australia*, Foundation Press, Victoria Park, 1993.

19   See the essays in C. Choo & S. Hollbach (eds), *SWAH*, vol. 23, *History and Native Title*, pp. 1–212.

20 Hamilton, *Burkie*, p. 201.
21 Gregory, *City of Light*, pp. 232–7.
22 The material for this paragraph and the next is drawn from M. J. McCusker, *Report of Inspector on a Special Investigation into Rothwells Ltd, Pursuant to Companies Code Part VII*, Government Printer, Wembley, 1990; and [G. Kennedy, R. Wilson & P. Brinsden], *Report of Royal Commission on the Commercial Activities of Government*, 2 vols, Government Printer, Perth, 1992.
23 Critics include P. O'Brien, *The Burke Ambush: Corporation and Society in Western Australia*, Apollo Press, Dianella, 1986; A. McAdam & P. O'Brien, *Burke's Shambles: Parliamentary Contempt in the Wild West*, Burke Press, Melbourne, 1987; and P. O'Brien & J. Norrish (eds), *The Great Collapse of 1989*, Australian Institute of Public Policy, Perth, 1990.
24 A. Bond with B. Murdle, *Bond*, HarperCollins, Pymble, 2003.
25 P. Barry, *The Rise and Fall of Alan Bond*, rev. paperback edn, Bantam, Milsons Point, 1991, chs 16–18.
26 *West Australian*, 18 November 1985, p. 3.
27 O'Brien, *Burke's Ambush*; forthcoming biography of Ric New by John McIlwraith.
28 *Australian*, 18 March 2006, p. 2.
29 T. Sykes, *The Bold Riders*, Allen & Unwin, St Leonards, 1994, pp. 56–140, 186–238.
30 McCusker, *Report of Inspector*.
31 J. Grill, 'The quality of mercy…', in A. Peachment (ed.), *The Years of Scandal: Commissions of Inquiry in Western Australia, 1991–2004*, UWAP, Nedlands, 2006, pp. 266–77.
32 Gregory, *City of Light*, pp. 269–80.
33 *West Australian*, 15 September 1992, p. 1.
34 *Report of Royal Commission on the Commercial Activities of Government*.
35 A. Peachment, 'The Marks Royal Commission into the use of executive power: A tale of three leaders', in Peachment, *The Years of Scandal*, pp. 113–26.
36 P. Hasluck, 'An inexact comparison', in *Crude Impieties*, Rainy Creek Press, Flemington, 1991.

Chapter 10: Happily ever after? 1993–

1 Commission on Government, Western Australia (J. Gregor, chair), *Reports*, 4 vols, Commission on Government, Perth, 1995–96; F. Harman, 'The recommendations of the Commission on Government: Did anyone take any notice?', in Peachment, *The Years of Scandal*, pp. 67–91.
2 *WAPD*, 1993–94, vol. 311, pp. 11677–82.
3 Gregory, *City of Light*, pp. 330–2.
4 Professor Tom Stannage's forthcoming history of Wesfarmers ably covers this period.
5 V. Tanti, 'Project had potential', *Geraldton Guardian*, 18 March 2001, p. 4.
6 J. Miller, 'Can't see the trees for wood? Visions and re-visions of old growth forests in Western Australia', in Gaynor, Trinca & Haebich, *Country*, pp. 57–81; J. Ajani, *The Forest Wars*, MUP, Carlton, 2007, pp. 267–79.
7 A short biographical sketch, 'Geoffrey Gallop: Rhodes Scholar and politician', can be found in Geraldton Regional Library, *Geraldton: 150 Years 150 Lives*, Geraldton, 2001. Dr Gallop's papers have been donated to the John Curtin Library, Curtin University of Technology.

8   N. Rothwell, 'Lives in the sand', *Australian*, 25–26 January 2003, 'Review' section, pp. 4–6; S. Bertola, 'Burrup Peninsula', *Trust News*, January 2004, p. 14.

9   Department of Premier and Cabinet, *Options for Bringing Water to Perth from the Kimberley*, Government of Western Australia, Perth, 2006.

10   Beresford, Bekle, Phillips & Mulcock, *The Salinity Crisis*, pts III, IV.

11   *North-West Telegraph*, 22 August 2001, p. 3.

12   *Age* (Melbourne), 27 January 1973, quoted in Gregory, *City of Light*, p. 178.

13   Select Committee on Road Safety (R. Ainsworth, chair), 'Road Crash Causes and the Extent to the Problem in Western Australia', paper presented to the Legislative Assembly, 17 November 1994; Insurance Commission of Western Australia, *2001: A Road Safety Odyssey*, Perth, 1997.

14   The Nyungar patrol is briefly described in 'Taking people out of harm's way', *Intersector*, 15 February 2006, pp. 22–3.

15   P. Toohey, 'Perth: Another coast, another country', *Australian*, 13–14 September 2003, colour supplement, p. 26.

16   J. Kelly, 'Mad Jack', *Sunday Times*, 1 August 2004, pp. 1, 3; J. van Tongeren, *The ANM Story*, True Blue Aussie Underground, [Perth, 2004?].

17   T. Brabazon, *Liverpool of the South Seas: Perth and Its Popular Music*, UWAP, Nedlands, 2005, p. 3.

18   V. Laurie, 'Black Swan Theatre Company', *Fremantle Arts Review*, September 1991, p. 13; 'Black Swan heading for a showdown', *Australian*, 13 December 2002, p. 15.

19   Brabazon, *Liverpool of the South Seas*, p. 212.

20   Weston, 'Visual sites', p. 200.

21   *Australian*, 28 February 2005, p. 10; J. McNamara, 'History shows the "Yes" vote had no chance', *Business News*, 10 March 2005, pp. 6–7.

22   A history of Lotterywest and its predecessor, the Lotteries Commission, is in preparation under the editorship of Richard Nile.

23   Law Society of Western Australia, 'Work choices or worst of choices? The new world of workplace relations', *Lexis Nexis*, Perth, 2006.

24   *Sunday Times*, 11 June 2006, p. 1.

25   V. Laurie, 'Visitors to Limbo', *Australian*, 17–18 February 2001, colour supplement, pp. 14–19.

26   D. Worth, 'Reconciliation in the Forest' (PhD thesis, Murdoch University 2004).

27   P. Millett, *The Sanctified Verses*, St George Books, Perth, 1991.

28   'The Bali bombings', *Sunday Times*, 20 October 2002; J. A. Froude, *Oceana*, London, 1905, pp. 165–6.

29   J. Sanderson, 'Alienation in the Australian federation', *The Order*, no. 21, Winter 2007, p. 8.

Select bibliography

Journals and newspapers

Albany Advertiser
Australian, The
Daily News
Early Days
Herald (Fremantle)
Historical Studies
Inquirer
International Journal of Music Education
Journal and Proceedings of the Western Australian Historical Society
Journal of Australian Studies
Journal of the Historical Society of Western Australia
Leader
Little Battler, The
Musicological Society of Australia Newsletter
Perth Gazette
Revelation Magazine
Studies in Western Australian History
University Studies in History
UWA Law Review
Victorian Express
WA Catholic Record
West Australian, The
Westerly
Western Ancestor
Western Mail

Books

Adamson, G., *Miners and Millionaires: The First One Hundred Years of the Stock Exchange in Perth, 1889–1989*, Australian Stock Exchange, Perth, 1989.

Alexander, F. (ed.), *Four Bishops and Their See: Perth Western Australia, 1857–1957*, UWAP, Nedlands, 1957.

—— *Campus at Crawley*, UWAP, Nedlands, 1963.

Alexander, F., Crowley, F. K. & Legge, J. D., *The Origins of the Eastern Goldfields Water Scheme in Western Australia: An Exercise in the Interpretation of Historical Evidence*, UWAP, Nedlands, 1954.

Appleyard, R. & Manford, T., *The Beginning: European Discovery and Early Settlement of Swan River Western Australia*, UWAP, Nedlands, 1980.

Appleyard, R. & Yiannakis, N., *Greek Pioneers in Western Australia*, UWAP, Nedlands, 2002.

Atkinson, B., *West Perth Football Club, 1885–1955*, Action Press, Morley, 1985.

Austen, T., *A Cry in the Wind: Conflict in Western Australia 1892–1929*, Darlington Publishing Group, Darlington, 1998.

Auty, K., *Black Glass: West Australian Courts of Native Affairs 1939–1954*, FACP, Fremantle, 2005.

Aveling, M. (ed.), *Westralian Voices: Documents in Western Australian Social History*, UWAP, Nedlands, 1979.

Bain, M. A., *Ancient Landmarks: A Social and Economic History of the Victoria District of Western Australia, 1839–1894*, UWAP, Nedlands, 1975.

Barker, A. J., *Behind the Play: A History of Football in Western Australia from 1868*, West Australian Football Commission, Perth, 2004.

Barker, A. J. & Laurie, M., *Excellent Connections: A History of Bunbury, Western Australia, 1836–1901*, City of Bunbury, 1991.

Bassett, M., *The Hentys: An Australian Colonial Tapestry*, OUP, London, 1954.

Battye, J. S., *Western Australia: A History from Its Discovery to the Inauguration of the Commonwealth*, Clarendon Press, Oxford, 1924.

Bennett, B. (ed.), *The Literature of Western Australia*, UWAP, Nedlands, 1979.

Beresford, Q., *Rob Riley: An Aboriginal Leader's Quest for Justice*, Aboriginal Studies Press, Canberra, 2006.

Beresford, Q., Bekle, H., Phillips, H. & Mulcock, J., *The Salinity Crisis: Landscape, Communities and Politics*, UWAP, Nedlands, 2004.

Bignell, M., *The Fruit of the Country: A History of the Shire of Gnowangerup, Western Australia*, UWAP, Nedlands, 1977.

—— *A Place to Meet: A History of the Shire of Katanning, Western Australia*, UWAP for the Shire of Katanning, Nedlands, 1981.

Biskup, P., *Not Slave Not Citizens: The Aboriginal Problem in Western Australia 1898–1954*, University of Queensland Press, St Lucia, 1973.

Black, D. (ed.), *The House on the Hill: A History of the Parliament of Western Australia, 1832–1990*, Western Australian Parliamentary History Project, Perth, 1991.

Black, D. & Bolton, G., *Biographical Register of Members of the Parliament of Western Australia*, vol. 1, *1879–1930*, Offices of the Clerk of the Legislative Assembly, Perth, 1990.

Blainey, G., *The Golden Mile*, Allen & Unwin, St Leonards, 1993.

—— *White Gold: The Story of Alcoa of Australia*, Allen & Unwin, St Leonards, 1997.

Blainey, G. & Jamieson, P. (eds), *Charles Court: The Early Years: An Autobiography*, FACP, Fremantle, 1995.

Bolger, P., *Hobart Town*, Australian National University Press, Canberra, 1973.

Bolton, G. & Byrne, G., *The Campus That Never Stood Still: Edith Cowan University 1902–2002*, Edith Cowan University, Churchlands, 2001.

—— *May It Please Your Honour: A History of the Supreme Court of Western Australia from 1861–2005*, Supreme Court of Western Australia, Perth, 2005.

Bolton, G., Rossiter, R. & Ryan, J., *Farewell Cinderella: Creating Arts and Identity in Western Australia*, UWAP, Nedlands, 2003.

Bolton, G. C., *Alexander Forrest: His Life and Times*, MUP, Carlton, 1958.

—— *A Fine Country to Starve In*, UWAP, Nedlands, 1972.

—— *Daphne Street*, FACP, Fremantle, 1996.

Brabazon, T., *Liverpool of the South Seas: Perth and Its Popular Music*, UWAP, Nedlands, 2005.

Bourke, D. F., *The History of the Catholic Church in Western Australia 1829–1979*, Archdiocese of Perth, Perth, 1979.

Braid, E. & Forbes, E., *From Afar a People Drifted: The Story of Koorda, a Wheatbelt Settlement*, Elizabeth Forbes, Peppermint Grove, 1997.

Brown, P. M., *The Merchant Princes of Fremantle: The Rise and Decline of a Colonial Elite 1870–1900*, UWAP, Nedlands, 1996.

Buddee, P., *Fate of the Artful Dodger: Parkhurst Boys Transported to Australia and New Zealand 1842–1852*, St George Books, Perth, 1984.

Bunbury, B., *It's Not the Money, It's the Land: Aboriginal Stockmen and the Equal Wages Case*, FACP, Fremantle, 2002.

—— *Rabbits and Spaghetti: Captives and Comrades: Australians, Italians and the War, 1939–1945*, FACP, Fremantle, 2006.

—— *Caught in Time*, FACP, Fremantle, 2006.

Burton, V., *General History of Broome*, Broome Historical Society, Broome, 2000.

Byrne, G., *Valiant Women: Letters from the Foundation Sisters of Mercy in Western Australia, 1845–1849*, Polding Press, Melbourne, 1981.

—— *Built on a Hilltop: A History of the Sisters of the Good Shepherd in Western Australia 1902–2002*, Sisters of the Good Shepherd, Leederville, 2002.

—— *Tom and Jack*, FACP, Fremantle, 2003.

Cameron, J. M. R., *Ambition's Fire: The Agricultural Colonisation of Pre-convict Western Australia*, UWAP, Nedlands, 1981.

—— (ed.), *The Millendon Memoirs: George Fletcher Moore's Diaries and Letters 1830–1841*, Hesperian Press, Carlisle, 2007.

Carnley, A., *Treading Lightly in their Steps: A Pictorial History of St Hilda's 1896–1996*, St Hilda's Anglican School for Girls, Perth, 1996.

Carter, J., *Bassendean: A Social History, 1829–1979*, Town of Bassendean, 1986.

Chapman, B. & Richards, D., *Marshall Clifton, Architect and Artist*, FACP, Fremantle, 1989.

Choo, C., *Mission Girls: Aboriginal Women on Catholic Missions in the Kimberley, Western Australia, 1900–1950*, UWAP, Nedlands, 2001.

Colebatch, Sir H., *The Story of One Hundred Years*, Government Printer, Perth, 1929.

Colebatch, H., *Claude de Bernales: The Magnificent Miner*, Hesperian Press, Carlisle, 1996.

—— *Steadfast Knight: A Life of Sir Hal Colebatch*, FACP, Fremantle, 2004.

Conole, P., *Protect and Serve: A History of Policing in Western Australia*, Western Australian Police Service, Perth, 2002.

Cooper, W. S. & McDonald G., *A City for All Seasons: The Story of Melville*, City of Melville, Ardross, 1989.

Courtney, V., *All I May Tell: A Journalist's Story*, Shakespeare Head Press, Sydney, 1956.

Cowan, P. (ed.), *A Faithful Picture: The Letters of Eliza and Thomas Brown in the Swan River Colony 1841–1852*, FACP, Fremantle, 1977.

—— *A Unique Position: A Biography of Edith Dircksey Cowan, 1861–1932*, UWAP, Nedlands, 1978.

Crawford, P. & Crawford, I., *Contested Country*, UWAP, Nedlands, 2003.

Crawford, P. & Tonkinson, M., *The Missing Chapters: Women Staff at The University of Western Australia 1963–1987*, UWAP, Nedlands, 1988.

Cream, Sister M., *Out of These Stones: The Mercedes Story: The School at the Square 1846–1996*, Mercedes College, Perth, 1999.

Crowley, F. K., *State Election: The Fall of the Hawke Government*, Paterson Brokensha, Perth, 1959.

—— *Australia's Western Third: A History of Western Australia from the First Settlement to Modern Times*, Heinemann Press, Melbourne, 1960.

—— *Big John Forrest 1847–1918: A Founding Father of the Commonwealth of Australia*, UWAP, Nedlands, 2000.

Cullity, M., *A History of Dairying in Western Australia*, UWAP, Nedlands, 1979.

Cunneen, C., *William John McKell: Boilermaker, Premier, Governor General*, UNSW Press, Sydney, 2000.

Daniels, K. (ed.), *So Much Hard Work*, Fontana/Collins, Sydney, 1984.

Davidson, B. R., *The Northern Myth: A Study of the Physical and Economic Limits to Agricultural and Pastoral Development in Tropical Australia*, MUP, Carlton, 1972.

Davidson, D., *Women on the Warpath: Feminists of the First Wave*, UWAP, Nedlands, 1997.

Davidson, R., *High Jinks at the Hot Pool: Mirror Reflects the Life of a City*, FACP, Fremantle, 1994.

Davis, J., *A Boy's Life*, Magabala Books, Broome, 1991.

Davis, R., *Eileen Joyce: A Portrait*, FACP, Fremantle, 2001.

Davis, S. W., *Foys Saga: An Account of the Genesis and Progress of Foy and Gibson, (WA) Limited*, Service Print, Perth, 1945.

De La Rue, K., *Pearl Shell and Pastures: The Story of Cossack and Roebourne, and their Place in the History of the North West, from the Earliest Exploration to 1910*, Cossack Project Committees, Cossack, 1979.

Duffield, R., *Rogue Bull*, Collins, Sydney, 1979.

Dunstan, K., *Ratbags*, Cassell Australia, Sydney, 1979.

Durack, M., *Kings in Grass Castles*, Constable & Company, London, 1960.

—— *To Be Heirs Forever*, Constable & Company, London, 1976.

Dyson, M. R., *Flying Foam Massacre: A Grey Era in the History of the Burrup Peninsula*, Karratha CAD Centre, Karratha, 2002.

East, A., Forrest, B., & Stocke, G., *The Royals: 100 Years of Football Tradition: A History of the East Perth Club*, East Perth Football Club, Leederville, 2006.

Edmonds, L., *The Vital Link: A History of Main Roads, Western Australia, 1926–1996*, UWAP, Nedlands, 1997.

Edwards, H., *Port of Pearls: A History of Broome*, Rigby Ltd, Adelaide, 1983.

Erickson, R., *The Victoria Plains*, Lamb Paterson Press, Osborne Park, 1971.

—— *Old Toodyay and Newcastle*, Toodyay Shire Council, 1974.

—— *The Dempsters*, UWAP, Nedlands, 1978.

—— (ed.), *The Brand on His Coat: Biographies of Some Western Australian Convicts*, UWAP, Nedlands, 1983.

—— *The Bride Ships: Experience of Immigrants Arriving in Western Australia 1848–1889*, Hesperian Press, Victoria Park, 1992.

Erickson, R., & Heywood, R., *She's No Milkmaid: A Biography of Dame Raigh Roe* DBE, Hesperian Press, Carlisle, 1991.

Erickson, R., Gibbings, B. & Higgins, L., *Her Name Is Woman*, CWA, Perth, 1974.

Evans, A. G., *A Fanatic Heart: Life of John Boyle O'Reilly, 1844–1890*, UWAP, Nedlands, 1997.

—— *C. Y. O'Connor: His Life and Legacy*, UWAP, Nedlands, 2001.

Fairbridge, K., *The Autobiography of Kingsley Fairbridge*, OUP, London, 1928.

Field, T. P. (ed.), *Swanland 1829–1956: The Agricultural Districts of Western Australia*, Lexington, USA, 1957.

Firkins, P. (ed.), *A History of Commerce and Industry in Western Australia*, UWAP, Nedlands, 1979.

Florey, C., *Peninsular City: A Social History of the City of South Perth*, City of South Perth, 1995.

Forrest, K., *The Challenge and the Change: The Colonization and Settlement of the North-West 1861–1914*, Hesperian Press, Victoria Park, 1996.

Frost, A. C., *Green Gold*, Donnybrook/Balingup Shire Council, Donnybrook, 1976.

Fyfe, C., *The Bale Fillers: Australian Wool 1826–1916*, UWAP, Nedlands, 1983.

Gabbedy, J. P., *Yours in the Earth: Life and Times of Charles Mitchell*, UWAP, Nedlands, 1972.

—— *Group Settlement*, vol. 1, Its Origins: Politics and Administration, UWAP, Nedlands, 1988.

—— *Group Settlement*, vol. 2, Its People: Their Life and Times—An Inside View, UWAP, Nedlands, 1988.

Garden, D. S., *Albany: A Panorama of the Sound from 1827*, Thomas Nelson, West Melbourne, 1977.

Garrick, P. & Jeffrey, C., *Fremantle Hospital: A Social History to 1987*, Fremantle Hospital, 1987.

Gaynor, A., *Harvest of the Suburbs*, UWAP, Nedlands, 2006.

Gaynor, A., Trinca, M. & Haebich, A., *Country: Visions of Land and People in Western Australia*, WA Museum, Perth, 2002.

Gettler, L., *An Unpromised Land*, FACP, Fremantle, 2003.

Gill, A., *Forced Labour for the West: Parkhurst Convicts 'Apprenticed' in Western Australia 1842–1851*, A. Gill, Maylands, 1997.

Glover, R., *Plantagenet: A History of the Shire of Plantagenet, Western Australia*, UWAP, Nedlands, 1979.

Grayden, W. L., *Adam and Atoms*, Frank Daniels, Perth, 1957.

—— *A Nomad Was Our Guide: The Story through the Land of Wonji, the Central Desert of Australia*, NH Holdings, South Perth, 2002.

Greble, W. E., *A Bold Yeomanry: Social Change in a Wheat Belt District: Kulin, 1848–1970*, Creative Research, Perth, in association with Kulin Shire Council, 1979.

Green, N., *Broken Spears: Aborigines and Europeans in the South West of Western Australia*, Focus Education Services, Perth, 1984.

—— *The Forrest River Massacre*, FACP, Fremantle, 1995.

Gregory, J., *Building a Tradition: A History of Scotch College, Perth, 1897–1996*, UWAP, Nedlands, 1996.

—— (ed.), *On the Homefront: Western Australia and World War II*, UWAP, Nedlands, 2000.

—— *City of Light: A History of Perth since the 1950s*, City of Perth, 2003.

Gribble, J. B., *Dark Deeds in a Sunny Land, or Blacks and Whites in North West Australia*, Daily News, Perth 1905; UWAP, Nedlands/Institute of Applied Aboriginal Studies, Mount Lawley, 1987.

Hackett, Lady (ed.), *The Australian Household Guide*, E. S. Wigg, Perth, 1916.

Hallam, S., *Fire and Hearth: A Study of Aboriginal Usage and European Usurpation in South Western Australia*, Australian Institute of Aboriginal Studies, Canberra, 1975.

Halse, B., *The Salvation Army in Western Australia, Its Early Years: Ours is a Fast Express Train*, Brad Halse, Nedlands, 1990.

Hamilton, J., *Burkie: A Biography of Brian Burke*, St George Books, Perth, 1988.

Hansford-Miller, F. A., *A History of Medicine in Western Australia 1829–1870*, vol II, *Hospital Services in Early Colonial Western Australia*, Abcado, Willetton, 1997.

Harding, R., *Police Killings in Australia*, Penguin Books, Ringwood, 1970.

Harman, E. & Head, B. W. (eds), *State Capital and Resources in the North and West of Australia*, UWAP, Nedlands, 1981.

Hasluck, A., *Portrait with Background: A Life of Georgiana Molloy*, OUP, Melbourne, 1955.

—— *Unwilling Emigrants*, OUP, Melbourne, 1959; FACP, Fremantle, 1990.

—— *Thomas Peel of the Swan River*, OUP, Melbourne, 1965.

—— *Royal Engineer: A Life of Sir Edmund DuCane*, Angus & Robertson, Sydney, 1973.

Hasluck, P., *Black Australians: A Survey of Native Policy in Western Australia, 1829–1897*, MUP, Melbourne, 1942.

—— *Mucking About: An Autobiography*, MUP, Carlton, 1977.

Hawke, H., *My Own Life: An Autobiography*, Text, Melbourne, 1996.

Hawke, S. & Gallagher, M., *Noonkanbah: Whose Land, Whose Law*, FACP, Fremantle, 1989.

Hazzard, M., *Australia's Brilliant Daughter: Ellis Rowan, Artist, Naturalist, Explorer 1848–1922*, Greenhouse Publications, Richmond, 1984.

Heinrichs, D., *The Jubilee Book of the East Fremantle Football Club*, Patersons, Perth, 1948.

Hetherington, P., *Childhood and Society in Western Australia*, UWAP, Nedlands, 1988.

—— *Settlers, Servants and Slaves: Aboriginal and European Children in Nineteenth-century Western Australia*, UWAP, Nedlands, 2002.

Heydon, P. R., *The Bishop's Men*, Order of the Knights of the Southern Cross, Perth, c. 1998.

Hillman, B. (ed.), *The Hillman Diaries 1877–1884*, F. W. Bentley Hillman, Applecross 1990.

Hough, D., *A Dream of Passion*, His Majesty's Theatre Foundation, Perth, 2004.

Hunt, L. (ed.), *Westralian Portraits*, UWAP, Nedlands, 1979.

Hutchison, D., *A Town Like No Other: The Living Tradition of New Norcia*, FACP, Fremantle, 1995.

Jack, J. & Robertson, R. (eds), *Cape of Contrasts: Stories of Cape Naturaliste, Western Australia*, Dunsborough Writers Group Press, Dunsborough, 2001.

Jacobs, P., *Mister Neville*, FACP, Fremantle, 1990.

James, R. M., *Heritage of Pines: History of the Town of Cottesloe, Western Australia*, Town of Cottesloe Council, Cottesloe, 1977.

Jebb, M. A., *Blood, Sweat and Welfare: A History of White Bosses and Aboriginal Pastoral Workers*, UWAP, Nedlands, 2002.

Kearns, B., *Stepping Out for Peace*, People for Nuclear Disarmament, Maylands, 2004.

Kerr, A., *North Western Australia*, Department of Economics, The University of Western Australia, Nedlands, 1962.

Kimberly, W. B., *History of West Australia: A Narrative of Her Past, Together with Biographies of Her Leading Men*, F. W. Niven, Melbourne, 1897.

La Nauze, J. A., *The Making of the Australian Constitution*, MUP, Melbourne, 1972.

Lane, J., *Fairbridge Kid*, FACP, Fremantle, 1990.

Lang, E., *Grist to the Mill: A History of Flour Milling in Western Australia*, Goodman Fielder Mills Ltd, Perth, 1994.

Law, F. A., *The History of the Merredin District*, Merredin Shire Council, Merredin, 1961.

Layman, L. (ed.), *Rica's Stories*, RWAHS, Nedlands, 2001.

Love, M., *The Sherwood Papers: A Swan River Story*, M. J. Love, Dalkeith, 1996.

Ludbrook, J., *The Big Q: A History of Quairading and Its Surrounding Districts*, Shire of Quairading, 2003.

McAdam, A. & O'Brien, P., *Burke's Shambles: Parliamentary Contempt in the Wild West*, Burke Press, Melbourne, 1987.

Macknight, C., *The Voyage to Marege: Macassan Trepangers in Northern Australia*, MUP, Melbourne, 1976.

McLaren, G. & Cooper, W., *A Long Hard Road: The Pastoralists and Graziers Association 1906–2006*, Pastoralists and Graziers Association, Perth, 2006.

Marchant, L. R., *Aboriginal Administration in Western Australia, 1886–1905*, Australian Institute of Aboriginal Studies, Canberra, 1981.

Markey, D. S., *More a Symbol Than a Success: The Foundation Years of the Swan River Colony*, Westbooks, Bayswater, 1977.

Massam, K., *On High Ground: Images of One Hundred Years at Aquinas College, Western Australia*, UWAP, Nedlands, 1998.

Maushart, S., *Sort of a Place Like Home: Remembering the Moore River Settlement*, FACP, Fremantle, 1993.

May, C., *Changes They've Seen: The City and People of Bayswater 1827–1997*, City of Bayswater, Perth, 1997.

—— *Built on Faith: A History of Perth College*, UWAP, Nedlands, 2002.

Millett, Mrs E., *An Australian Parsonage, or, The Settler and the Savage in Western Australia*, E. Stanford, London, 1872.

Mills, J., *The Timber People: A History of Bunnings Limited*, Wescolour Press, Perth, 1986.

Ministry for Culture and the Arts, *State Living Treasures*, Government of Western Australia, Perth, 1999.

Mitchell, J., *The First Hundred Years: The Mitchell Family on Barnong Station*, J. Mitchell, Perth, 2000.

Moore, B., *From the Ground Up: Bristile, Whittakers and Metro Brick in Western Australian History*, UWAP, Nedlands, 1987.

—— *A Superior Kind of Savings Bank: The Perth Building Society, 1862–1987*, Challenge Bank in association with the Centre for Western Australian History, UWAP, Nedlands, 1989.

Moore, G. F., *Diary of Ten Years Eventful Life of an Early Settler in Western Australia and also a Descriptive Vocabulary of the Language of the Aborigines*, M. Walbrook, London, 1884; facsimile edn with introduction by C. T. Stannage, UWAP, Nedlands, 1978.

Moran, R., *Massacre Myth*, Access Press, Bassendean, 2001.

Morgan, M. R., *A Drop in a Bucket: The Mount Margaret Story*, United Aborigines Mission, Box Hill, 1986.

Mossenson, D., *State Education in Western Australia 1829–1960*, UWAP, Nedlands, 1972.

Murray, K., *Voice for Peace*, Kaye Murray Publications, Bayswater, 2005.

Nairn, J., *Walter Padbury: His Life and Times*, North Stirling Press, Padbury, 1985.

Nannup, A., Marsh, L. & Kinnane, S., *When the Pelican Laughed*, FACP, Fremantle, 1992.

Neville, A. O., *Australia's Coloured Minority: Aborigines' Place in the Community*, Currawong Publishers, Sydney, 1948.

O'Brien, P. (ed.), *The Burke Ambush: Corporation and Society in Western Australia*, Apollo Press, Dianella, 1986.

O'Brien, P. & Norrish, J. (eds), *The Great Collapse of 1989*, Australian Institute of Public Policy, Perth, 1990.

Ogle, N., *The Colony of Western Australia: A Manual for Emigrants*, J. Arrowsmith, London, 1839.

Oldham, R., *Western Heritage: A Study of the Colonial Architecture of Perth, Western Australia*, Paterson Brokensha, Perth, 1961.

Olive, N., *Enough Is Enough*, FACP, Fremantle, 2007.

Oliver, B., *Unity Is Strength: A History of the Australian Labor Party and the Trades and Labor Council in Western Australia 1899–1999*, API Network, Australian Research Institute, Curtin University, Bentley, 2003.

Oliver, B. and Bertola, P., *The Workshops: a History of the Midland Government Railway Workshops*, UWAP, Nedlands, 2006.

Peachment, A. (ed.), *The Business of Government, Western Australia, 1983–1990*, Federation Press, Sydney, 1991.

—— *The Years of Scandal: Commissions of Inquiry in Western Australia, 1991–2004*, UWAP, Nedlands, 2006.

Pendal, P. & Black, D., *House to House: The Story of Western Australia's Government and Parliament Houses*, Western Australian Parliament, Perth, 2004.

Peters, N., *Milk and Honey—but No Gold: Postwar Migration to Western Australia, 1945–1965*, UWAP, Nedlands, 2001.

Pow, G., *Barefoot Bandit: The Story of Tom Hughes, West Australian Bushranger*, G. Pow, Maylands, 2003.

Purse, J., *A Flax Mill by the River*, Boyup Brook Shire Council, Boyup Brook, 1990.

Reid, A., *Those Were the Days*, Hesperian Press, Carlisle, 1986.

Reid, A., *The Grand Experiment*, Hachette, Sydney, 2007.

Roberts, W., Boulton, J. T. & Mansfield, E. (eds), *The Letters of D. H. Lawrence*, vol. iv, CUP, Cambridge, 1987.

Robin, A. de Q., *Matthew Blagden Hale: The Life of an Australian Pioneer Bishop*, Hawthorn Press, Melbourne, 1976.

Russell, E., *A History of the Law in Western Australia and Its Development from 1829 to 1979*, UWAP, Nedlands, 1980.

Russo, G., *Lord Abbot of the Wilderness: The Life and Times of Bishop Salvado*, Polding Press, Melbourne, 1980.

Schenk, R. S., *The Educability of the Native*, Service Print, Perth, 1937.

Seddon, G., *Swan River Landscape: A Response to an Environment, The Swan Coastal Plain in Western Australia*, UWAP, Nedlands, 1978.

Seddon, G. & Ravine, D., *A City and Its Setting: Images of Perth, Western Australia*, FACP, Fremantle, 1986.

Segal, N., *Who and What Was Siebenhaar: A Note on the Life and Persecution of a Western Australian Anarchist*, Centre for Western Australian History, The University of Western Australia, Nedlands, 1988.

Shann, E. O. G., *Cattle Chosen: The Story of the First Group Settlement in Western Australia 1829–1841*, OUP, London, 1926.

Shann, E., *Economic History of Australia*, CUP, Cambridge, UK, 1930.

Sherrington, G. & Jeffrey, C., *Fairbridge: Empire and Child Migration*, UWAP, Nedlands, 1998.

Snooks, G. T., *Depression and Recovery in Western Australia, 1928–1929 to 1938–1939: A Study in Cyclical and Structural Change*, UWAP, Nedlands, 1974.

Spillman, K., *Horizons: A History of the Rural and Industries Bank of Western Australia*, UWAP, Nedlands, 1981.

—— *Identity Prized: A History of Subiaco*, UWAP, Nedlands, 1985.

—— *A Rich Endowment: Government and Mining in Western Australia 1829–1994*, UWAP, Nedlands, 1993.

Stannage, C. T., *The People of Perth: A Social History of Western Australia's Capital City*, Perth City Council, Perth, 1979.

—— (ed.), *A New History of Western Australia*, UWAP, Nedlands, 1981.

—— *Lakeside City: The Dreaming of Joondalup*, UWAP, Nedlands, 1996.

Staples, A. C., *They Made Their Destiny: A History of Settlement of the Shire of Harvey 1829–1929*, Shire of Harvey, Harvey, 1979.

Statham, P. (ed.), *The Tanner Letters: A Pioneer Saga of Swan River and Tasmania, 1831 to 1845*, UWAP, Nedlands, 1981.

Statham-Drew, P., *James Stirling: Admiral and Foundation Governor of Western Australia*, UWAP, Nedlands, 2003.

Stephenson, G., *The Design of Central Perth: Some Problems and Possible Solutions and a Study Made for the Perth Central Area Design and Co-ordinating Committee*, UWAP, Nedlands, 1975.

Stormon, E. J. (ed.), *The Salvado Memoirs*, UWAP, Nedlands, 1977.

Tauman, M., *The Chief: C. Y. O'Connor*, UWAP, Nedlands, 1978.

Taylor, J., *Between Devotion and Design: The Architecture of John Cyril Hawes, 1876–1956*, UWAP, Nedlands, 2000.

Taylor, N. W., *Yeera-muk-a-doo: A Social History of the Settlement of North Western Australia*, FACP, Fremantle, 1980.

Thomas, A., *Kalkarni: The Brookton Story*, Shire of Brookton, Brookton, 1993.

Tonkin, J., *Cathedral and Community: A History of St George's Cathedral, Perth*, UWAP, Nedlands, 2001.

van den Driesen, I., *Essays on Immigration Policy and Population in Western Australia 1856–1901*, UWAP, Nedlands, 1986.

Vivienne, M., *Travels in Western Australia: Being a Description of the Various Cities and Towns, Goldfields and Agricultural Districts of That State*, William Heinemann, London, 1901.

Webb, A., *Kondinin, Karlgarin, Hyden: Community, Time and Place*, UWAP, Nedlands, 1988.

Webb, M. & Webb, A., *Golden Destiny*, City of Kalgoorlie–Boulder, Kalgoorlie–Boulder, 1993.

—— *Edge of Empire*, Artlook Books, Perth, 1983.

Welborn, S., *Lords of Death: A People, A Place, A Legend*, FACP, Fremantle, 1982.

Whittington, V., *Sister Kate: A Life Dedicated to Children in Need of Care*, UWAP, Nedlands, 1999.

Williams, J., *The First Furrow*, Lone Hand, Perth, 1976.

Theses

Dalton, P., 'Broome: A Multiracial Community: A Study of Social and Cultural Relationships in a Town in the West Kimberleys, Western Australia', MA thesis, The University of Western Australia, 1964.

de Garis, B. K., 'British Influence on the Federation of Australian Colonies, 1880–1901', DPhil thesis, Oxford, 1965.

Gertzel, C., 'The Convict System in Western Australia 1850–1870', BA (Hons) thesis, The University of Western Australia, 1949.

Hyams, B. K., 'The Political Organisation of Farmers in Western Australia, 1914–1944', MA thesis, The University of Western Australia, 1964.

Lourens, R. M. C., 'Building Societies in Western Australia 1862–1966', MCom thesis, The University of Western Australia, 1969.

Robertson, J., 'A History of the Timber Industry of Western Australia', BA (Hons) thesis, The University of Western Australia, 1956.

Index

INDEX